THE RISE
OF THE BJP

THE RISE OF THE BJP

The Making *of* the World's Largest Political Party

Bhupender Yadav *and* Ila Patnaik

PENGUIN
VIKING
An imprint of Penguin Random House

VIKING

USA | Canada | UK | Ireland | Australia
New Zealand | India | South Africa | China

Viking is part of the Penguin Random House group of companies
whose addresses can be found at global.penguinrandomhouse.com

Published by Penguin Random House India Pvt. Ltd
4th Floor, Capital Tower 1, MG Road,
Gurugram 122 002, Haryana, India

Penguin
Random House
India

First published in Viking by Penguin Random House India 2022

ISBN 9780670095254

Typeset in Minion Pro by Manipal Technologies Limited, Manipal
Printed at Thomson Press India Ltd, New Delhi

www.penguin.co.in

Contents

Preface

In elections after Independence, the Congress dominated the political landscape of India. The RSS, the Jana Sangh and the BJP emerged from this background facing enormous challenges. The Jana Sangh and the BJP faced a difficult situation where their chances of winning were small, and therefore they got little support. In the Lok Sabha elections of 1984, the BJP got 8 per cent vote share and two seats in Parliament.

A long journey started from there and has changed India's political landscape. With decisive wins in the Lok Sabha elections of 2014 and 2019, when the party came to win 37.7 per cent votes polled, and showed numerous remarkable outcomes in state elections, the BJP is now the dominant force of Indian politics.

How did this happen? What was the history of this party? What were the stories along the way? What were the forces at work, who were the people who helped bring this momentous transformation? What makes the BJP successful? What are the political strategies and the organizational design which drove this transformation? How have the two tracks—of fighting elections and of making policy—interacted and fed off each other? These are some of the most interesting and important questions in India today.

The present authors have been fascinated with this journey, despite coming from very different perspectives. One has dedicated his life to organizational work, politics and Parliament, and the other, an economist, has spent a life in academic social science. We felt that we could bring together unique knowledge and perspectives in telling this remarkable story. We have written it primarily for a reader who is interested in understanding politics in India.

We have tried to reconstruct an interesting and insightful story. We have sifted through a vast amount of factual material, letters, resolutions and stories and have focused on a narrative that gives the gist of what happened. There are endnotes linking the facts to sources, so that the curious reader can find out more.

Our attempt in the book is to sketch the essence of a long journey within a compact book, and to offer some insights along the way about what was going on and why certain things happened. Our hope is that this book will bring about a greater understanding about what the BJP stands for, how it works and the nature of modern Indian politics.

—Bhupender Yadav and Ila Patnaik

1

The Jana Sangh

India's democratic journey started along with the movement for Independence. The freedom movement was not just a political fight; the journey had an overlay of cultural, spiritual and social movements. The BJP and its ideology were formed during this journey.

By the early 20th century, a nationalistic awakening was igniting the political movement which sought to end British rule in India. Alongside this, India was also going through a social churning, where questions about many social evils were springing up. This process was assisted by the turmoil experienced by the Indian intelligentsia who started understanding the West. But this process was not unique to that time period. There were poets and social reformers, going all the way back to the Middle Ages, who had created a body of stories, songs and poems, broaching questions on human values and dignity, gender equality and untouchability in society. These messages were particularly influential as they were penned in the lingua franca of the people. Alongside this, there was thinking about spirituality and high philosophy. These strands of thought came together in India's response to British rule.

This backdrop laid the social, cultural and intellectual foundations for the remarkable achievements of the freedom movement after Mahatma Gandhi returned to India from South

Africa. Gandhi was able to bring diverse groups together around a coherent ethos. He steered the Independence movement paying great attention to not just the proximate goal of freedom, but the moral and political foundations of the future Republic. He thus emerged as the focal point of both political and philosophical leadership. He gave India the concept of Hind Swaraj and wanted the country to work under the framework of Swaraj or 'self-rule' in its journey as an independent nation. In many ways, mainstream Indian culture of the 20th century was shaped by the synthesis of Indian and Western cultures.

Gandhi's call for Swaraj was an attempt to regain not just freedom but also control of the self—our self-respect, self-responsibility and capacities for self-realization—from institutions of dehumanization. In his vision, politics was not a means to power but an act of service. For this reason, he wanted the Congress to be disbanded after Independence, believing that the party, as it existed then, had outlived its use.[1] India's Independence brought great pain for Gandhi when the country was divided along religious lines. Gandhi did not want India to be partitioned, least of all based on religion.[2] Gandhi, however, had to give in after the Congress relented before the Muslim League's demand for Partition.[3]

After Independence, the Congress, having led the freedom movement, enjoyed public popularity. Political parties require large-scale institutional infrastructure, and in 1947, the only party with significant institutional capability in the country was the Congress. However, the Congress back then was not monolithic, it was not dominated by any one person or ideology. The Congress housed many different voices such as the Congress Socialist Party, the Swaraj Party, and the Nationalist Party. In spite of differences amongst them and with the Congress, they continued to function under the umbrella of the All India Congress Committee.[4] On the other hand, under the leadership of C.N. Annadurai, regional parties in the south were inspired by Dravidian ideologies. Although, for twenty years after Independence, the Congress was the ruling party in Tamil Nadu. The Congress's hegemony ended when the Dravida Munnetra Kazhagam (DMK) won the state elections.

One such political party that emerged during this period was the Bharatiya Jana Sangh.[5] It was formed in October 1951, in Delhi. The Jana Sangh was formed by people who felt deeply about India as a cultural and spiritual entity. The events that led to the formation of the Jana Sangh began much earlier with the formation of the *Rashtriya Swayamsevak Sangh* (RSS).

Rashtriya Swayamsevak Sangh (RSS)

The RSS was established on 27 September 1925, on the day of Vijayadashami,[6] by Keshav Baliram Hedgewar.[7]

Hedgewar was born in Nagpur, the city where the foundation of the RSS was laid and which continues to be its headquarters. Hedgewar was enrolled in a British school in Nagpur but was expelled from it for participating in anti-British demonstrations. He obtained a medical degree from the University of Calcutta. Upon his return to Nagpur, after establishing his medical practice, he began giving shape to the RSS. He did not marry, nor did he take the ritualistic *sanyas* but dedicated his life to building an organization with nationalism as its bedrock. Hedgewar did not start the RSS with any customary speech. He believed real change could not be ushered in with speeches but only through actions and dedication. Hedgewar was pragmatic about the goals of the RSS. So he gathered the youth in Nagpur city and started a *shakha* where young men exercised, played sports and learnt discipline. He then sent these inspired and motivated youths to different parts of the country. Like Hedgewar, these men too dedicated their lives to RSS's mission. These men created a nationalistic awakening and helped solidify the foundations of RSS and lay the ground work for its sister organizations like Bharatiya Kisan Sangh, Bharatiya Mazdoor Sangh and Swadeshi Jagaran Manch among several others later.

Political polarization had not set in during that kinder age; while Hedgewar was the founder and leader of the RSS, he continued to be a member of the Congress and attended sessions of the Congress Seva Dal. The Congress Seva Dal had been established in 1923. The Hindu Mahasabha, set up to protect the rights of the Hindus in 1915, was transformed into a political party in 1933. Hedgewar's friends, Narayan Subbarao Hardikar, the founder of the Congress Seva Dal, and Vinayak Damodar Savarkar, leader of the Hindu Mahasabha, urged him to launch RSS as a political party. But Hedgewar was pursuing a different objective; he wanted the RSS to be a socio-cultural organization.

Several other organizations such as the Hindu Mahasabha, the Arya Samaj and many caste-based outfits existed then. What distinguished the RSS from the rest was its nationalistic outlook.

Till 1940, when he fell ill, Hedgewar remained focused on building and expanding the RSS as a cultural nationalistic organization. In 1940, Hedgewar, in the presence of the RSS leadership, decided that Madhavrao Sadashivrao Golwalkar would be his successor. Like Hedgewar, Golwalkar too hailed from Nagpur. Golwalkar had a Master of Science degree from Banaras Hindu University (BHU) and was deeply influenced by the nationalistic ideas of BHU founder Madan Mohan Malaviya. He came to be popularly and respectfully known as Guruji, when he taught Zoology at BHU. The traditions of Ramakrishna Paramhansa and Swami Akhandanand had shaped Guruji. He became the RSS chief (*Sarsanghchalak*) in 1940.[89] Under Golwalkar's leadership, the RSS expanded its activities and reach considerably. Golwalkar was highly educated and spiritual but also not a *sanyasi*. He believed in living a value-based life. Golwalkar always donned a simple dhoti-kurta and his face revealed the grace of a sage. Despite his gentle demeanour, Guruji commanded authority. He extensively travelled across India all his life the youth were drawn to him naturally. By now, the RSS had a rich base of *swayamsevaks* or volunteers. When India was partitioned in 1947, the swayamsevaks helped refugees who came from the newly carved out Pakistan. Like his predecessor Hedgewar, Golwalkar too did not envision the RSS as a political party but only as a cultural, nationalistic organization.[10]

Tragically, on 30 January 1948, Gandhi was assassinated by Nathuram Godse. Along with Godse, eight other persons, all associated with the Hindu Mahasabha, were charged with conspiring to kill Gandhi. The Jawaharlal Nehru government decided that the RSS should also be banned immediately.

Golwalkar distanced himself and the RSS from the murder. He closed down all the operating shakhas of the RSS for thirteen days in mourning over Gandhi's demise.[11] But the Uttar Pradesh government, amongst others, threatened to withdraw recognition and forfeit grants-in-aid to schools associated with the RSS. Teachers associated with the RSS were dismissed.[12] On 1 February 1948, two days before his arrest, Golwalkar issued a press statement asking swayamsevaks to practise the doctrine of love and service. He said, 'In the presence of this appalling tragedy I hope people will learn the lesson and practise the doctrine of love and service. Believing in this doctrine, I direct all my brothers of swayamsevaks to maintain a loving attitude towards all, even if there be any sort of provocation born out of misunderstanding and to remember that even this misplaced frenzy is an expression of unbounded love and reverence, in which the whole country held the great Mahatma, the man who made the name of our motherland great in the world. Our salutations to the revered departed one.'[13]

However, on 3 February 1948, Golwalkar was arrested. The murder trial opened in May 1948 at the Red Fort in Delhi. Golwalkar and others denied their involvement in the conspiracy. The prosecution failed to prove a link between the RSS and the assassination.[14] On 5 August 1948, Golwalkar was set free, and by the end of the same month, most other RSS members who had been jailed were also set free.[15] However, the ban on the RSS was not lifted till July 1949.[16]

During the intervening period there were prolonged discussions between the Congress leader and India's Home Minister Sardar

Vallabhbhai Patel and Golwalkar, regarding the future of the RSS. On 11 September 1948, in a letter to Golwalkar, Patel wrote, 'You are very well aware of my views about RSS. I have expressed those thoughts at Jaipur in December [1947] last and at Lucknow in January [1948] . . . I once again ask you to give your thoughts to my Jaipur and Lucknow speeches . . . I am thoroughly convinced that the RSS men can carry on their patriotic endeavour only by joining the Congress and not by keeping separate or by opposing.'[17]

The RSS had by then established an English weekly, *Organiser*, to obtain greater reach for its ideas. While launching it, Golwalkar said, 'For clear, straightforward, impartial views on subjects of national and international importance and for imbibing unadulterated patriotism, it is useful to read *Organiser*. It will fulfil the expectations for correct guidance in all current affairs.'[18]

The Birth of Jana Sangh

The ban helped the RSS realize that even if it was not to convert itself into a political party, it must have a political voice, in order to contest state actions such as a ban. At the time, the RSS spoke for itself, but lacked political representation. Golwalkar knew that the RSS needed a political organization that could give shape to the nationalistic vision for India. He, however, still remained clear that the RSS was not going to be a political organization.

Golwalkar left the question of the formation of a political party to the RSS members.[19] In a statement dated 2 November 1948, he said, 'At the outset, let me make it clear that the RSS is not a political party with any ambition for political power in the country. All these years of its existence it has steered clear of politics. It left its members free to choose and to subscribe to whatever political outlook they prefer and to join and work in the party of their choice'.[20]

Writing in the *Organiser* in 1949, chief editor K.R. Malkani said, 'Sangh must take part in politics not only to protect itself against the greedy designs of politicians but to stop the un-Bharatiya and anti-

Bharatiya politics of the Government and to advance and expedite the cause of Bharatiyata through state machinery side-by-side with official effort in the same direction. Sangh must continue as it is, an "ashram" for the national cultural education of the entire citizenry, but it must develop a political wing for the more effective and early achievement of its ideals.'[21]

Similarly, RSS worker Balraj Madhok wrote, 'So far the Sangh has confined its activities to the social and cultural fields with the object of creating much needed unity and national character in the country on the basis of Bharatiya culture and ideals. But there are other problems whose proper handling and solution is as vital to national health as unity and character. They are mainly political and economic which the Sangh has decided not to touch . . . It is necessary that the Sangh must give the lead to the country in regard to the political and economic problems of the country as well. It is essential for the very existence of Sangh itself. Any institution or organization of the people which fails to guide its component parts about the vital question influencing their lives is bound to lose the driving force which keeps any organization alive.'[22]

One of the non-Congress members of the cabinet was Dr Syama Prasad Mookerjee, formerly the president of the Hindu Mahasabha. Mookerjee had a Barrister's degree from the United Kingdom and had been Calcutta University's youngest vice chancellor. A member of the Congress till 1930, Mookerjee was a proponent of Hindu rights in the partition of Bengal from the time before Independence.[23]

After Independence in 1947 but before the first Parliamentary election of independent India in 1951, an interim government was formed under Nehru. The leadership of the time felt that until the first election results were in, fairness demanded giving significant representation to a diverse canvas of political parties.[24][25][26] Mookerjee became the minister of industry and supply in the government.

This Congress-led interim government faced significant disagreements within the Cabinet. In 1950, India and Pakistan were discussing a treaty on the protection of religious minorities in the two countries. Mookerjee strongly felt for the Hindus being persecuted in Pakistan. He opposed the terms of the treaty on the grounds that Pakistan was not protecting the rights of its Hindu minority adequately. Mookerjee felt that India should adopt a hard-line attitude towards Pakistan over its treatment of minorities. On the other hand, Nehru hoped for a negotiated settlement, which ultimately led to the signing of the Nehru-Liaquat Pact on 8 April 1950. To express his strong disagreement with the government's stance, Mookerjee resigned from the interim government cabinet on 1 April 1950, just before the pact was signed.[27] In his resignation letter, Mookerjee wrote, 'Apart from the fact that it will bring little solace to the sufferers it has certain features which are bound to give rise to fresh communal and political problems in India, the consequences of which we cannot foresee today. In my humble opinion the policy you are following, will fail. Time alone can prove this.'[28]

In addition to the disagreement on the issue of Nehru-Liaquat pact, Mookerjee also opposed the Nehru government on its Kashmir stance. He believed that by involving the United Nations in the Kashmir issue, Nehru had committed a blunder. Mookerjee warned that the country would one day come to regret Nehru's follies on the Kashmir front. He said, 'I agree with the Prime Minister that the matter of Kashmir is a highly complicated one and each one of us, whatever may be his point of view, must approach this problem from a constructive standpoint. I cannot share the view that we are creating a new heaven and a new earth by accepting the scheme which has been placed before the House on the motion of the Prime Minister.'[29]

In the meanwhile, there was a power struggle within the Congress. Before 1948, the path of the Congress was shaped by the triumvirate of Gandhi, Nehru and Patel. Mookerjee and the RSS were interested in cooperating with the Congress as long as it was not spearheaded by Nehru.[30][31] However, these hopes were dashed when Patel died on 15 December 1950, followed by the resignation of Congress president

Purushottam Das Tandon who had opposed Partition. Nehru was elected as the Congress President on 8 September 1951.[32]

The departure of Gandhi and the end of the freedom movement led to a gradual unravelling of the erstwhile Congress as a 'big tent'. Many parties cropped up on India's electoral map right after Independence, and most of them were formed by Congressmen who left their parent party due to disagreements with Nehru's policies. These included the Congress Socialist Party, the Kisan Mazdoor Praja Party, the Swaraj Party and the Nationalist Party.[33]

At this time, Mookerjee developed important differences with the Hindu Mahasabha. He was uncomfortable with its pro-British stance, the weak organization, and its unwillingness to accept members who were not Hindu.[34][35]

Internal debates within the RSS about whether it should transform itself into a political party, or support one of the existing parties, continued. While it had decided not to become a party, it had also decided not to support either of the two bigger Hindu political parties, i.e. the Hindu Mahasabha or the Ram Rajya Parishad.[36] These two parties were seen as having a few key weaknesses: their emphasis on high caste Hindus, on Hindi, and their support for orthodox religious beliefs.[37] In the context of the forthcoming first national elections in independent India, Mookerjee felt a new party was required.

Mookerjee met RSS functionaries and Golwalkar. He suggested that the RSS convert itself into a party, but Golwalkar disagreed. However, Golwalkar went on to say that RSS workers were free to collaborate with Mookerjee for the formation of a new party. In one such meeting, Mookerjee and Golwalkar agreed that the Bharatiya Jana Sangh would be formed.[38]

Golwalkar later recounted his discussions with Mookerjee, '. . . Naturally I had to warn him [Mookerjee] that the RSS could not be drawn into politics, that it could not play second fiddle to any political or any other party since no organization devoted to wholesale regeneration of the real, i.e., cultural life of the nation could ever function successfully if it was tried to be used as a handmaid of political parties.'"[39]

Buoyed by the support of RSS workers, Mookerjee on 5 May 1951, laid the foundation of the new party in Calcutta.[40] Mookerjee was chosen as the leader of the party, which adopted an eight-point programme that spelt out the party's objectives. Mookerjee knew that a pan-India party was not possible then and so it began building upwards at the state level. It first registered state units separately. The Punjab-Delhi unit was the first unit to be set up with people like Balraj Madhok, Balraj Bhalla, Mauli Chandra Sharma and Bhai Mahavira as its members. Vaidya Guru Datta was chosen as the President of the Delhi unit. Subsequently, a separate Punjab unit was formed.[41][42]

The Uttar Pradesh unit was set up on 2 September 1951 with Rao Krishna Pal Singh as its president and Pandit Deen Dayal Upadhyaya, who was later to lead the Bharatiya Jana Sangh, as secretary. The Madhya Bharat unit also came into existence the same day. The Rajasthan, Bihar and Assam units then came up in quick succession.

The Punjab unit then formally called an all-India convention of the state units along with like-minded organizations such as the Jammu-based Praja Parishad and Orissa-based Swadheen Jana Sangh. This convention was organized on 21 October 1951 at Raghumal Arya Kanya Higher Secondary School in Delhi.[43] It was here that all the state units merged together giving birth to the Bharatiya Jana Sangh. Mookerjee was chosen as its president. Bhai Mahavir and Mauli Chandra Sharma were made its general secretaries.

Mookerjee had always maintained the need for a strong Opposition party in the country. He considered it necessary for the survival of a democracy lest it degenerate into one-party rule. Speaking at the convention, he said, 'I rise to welcome you all to this historic [Delhi] convention which meets at a momentous period in the history of India. I am well aware of the fact that the task ahead of us is a difficult one . . . I am confident that if we all proceed unitedly with undaunted courage and vigour, not deviating from the right path, keeping to service of the people and the advancement of the honour and dignity of our beloved motherland as the principal aim before us, we are bound ultimately to attain success . . . One of the chief reasons for the manifestation of dictatorship in Congress rule is the absence of well organised opposition parties which alone can act as a healthy check on the majority party and can hold out before the country the prospect of an alternative Government . . . The Bharatiya Jana Sangh, therefore emerges today as an All India Political Party which will function as the principal party in opposition . . . Opposition does not mean a senseless or destructive approach to all problems that confront a responsible government . . . our aim will be to approach all problems in a constructive spirit.'[44]

The First General Elections

India established itself as a Republic on 26 January 1950. The first national elections in independent India were announced in December 1951, just two months after the Jana Sangh was formed.

Mookerjee began efforts to form an alliance among the non-Congress parties when elections were announced. While efforts were on to form a broader coalition, the Jana Sangh wrote its first manifesto. This document promised to put the 'Nation First'. The Jana Sangh manifesto said that India is demographically, culturally and historically a cohesive and unified nation and they envisioned this India as 'Bharat Mata'.

The Jana Sangh manifesto read, 'Unity in diversity has been the characteristic feature of Bharatiya culture which is a synthesis of different regional, local and tribal growths, natural in such a vast country. It has never been tied to the strings of any particular dogma or creed. All the creeds that form the commonwealth of Bharatiya Rashtra have their share in the stream of Bharatiya culture which has flown down from the Vedas in an unbroken continuity absorbing and assimilating contributions made by different peoples, creeds

and cultures that came in touch with it in the course of history . . .
Bharatiya culture is, thus, one and indivisible.'[45]

The focal point of the Jana Sangh's political agenda was
preserving, protecting and propagating India's culture and
traditions. The manifesto spoke about a state based upon equality for
all and boosting India's agricultural and industrial economy.[46] It laid
emphasis on strengthening the rural economy in sync with Gandhi's
vision for Swadeshi.[47] The manifesto also promised a strong army to
fight external threats and enemies.[48]

By this time, pronounced differences on secularism had emerged
between the Congress and the Jana Sangh. While Nehru saw the Hindu
Code Bills as advancing the idea of secularism, the Jana Sangh saw it
as Muslim appeasement. Mookerjee challenged Nehru in Parliament.
He said, 'If he [Nehru] was a true secularist, he should work towards
achieving the final goal given in Article 44 of the Directive Principles.
This Article says, "The state shall endeavour to secure for the citizens
a uniform civil code throughout the territory of India."'[49]

The Jana Sangh's nationalistic views contradicted those of
Nehru. Just like Gandhi, Jana Sangh too was opposed to the
partition of India. Nehru opposed the Jana Sangh and called it a
communal party to discredit the organization. He said, 'If there is a
communal organisation in India today, it is the Jana Sangh, which
is not only communal, but is utterly reactionary in every way. I am
saying this from my personal knowledge.'[50]In 1951, the Lok Sabha,
the lower house of the Parliament of India, had 489 seats spread
across 26 states. The Jana Sangh fielded candidates on ninety-three
of these 489 seats. It was not able to put up any candidates in at
least 11 states—Bombay, Madras, Orissa, Hyderabad, Saurashtra,
Travancore-Cochin, Bhopal, Bilaspur, Coorg, Kutch and Manipur.
The party managed to win three seats out of the ninety-three that it
contested.[51] Two of these three seats were in West Bengal, and one
was in Rajasthan.

Despite being a barely two-month-old party, the Jana Sangh
won 3 per cent of the total votes polled, thus emerging as a political

force in national politics.[52] Given that the Congress was a much older party and the Socialist Party consisted of old Congress warhorses, the Jana Sangh's performance was significant. The party had contested elections without celebrity endorsements or adequate funds.

Table 1: Lok Sabha Elections of 1951[53]

Political Party	LS 1951	
	Vote Share	Seats Won
Bharatiya Jana Sangh	3.06%	3
Indian National Congress	45%	364
Socialist Party	10.60%	12

In the Assembly elections in 1951-52, held simultaneously on 3,283 seats, the Jana Sangh contested 725 seats.[54] It won thirty-five seats. While the party won few seats in these elections, it achieved the status of a national party.[55]

Personally, for Mookerjee, the election results were more significant because he was the only party president, apart from Congress's Nehru and the Jharkhand Party's Jaipal Singh, who was elected to the Lok Sabha.

After the elections, Mookerjee began playing the role of an active opposition member of Parliament. He brought together members of other parties in a coalition and formed the National Democratic Party, a group of thirty MPs, who agreed to work under his leadership.[56] [57] This marked the beginning of a collaborative approach, which laid the foundations for the success in organizing a coalition government in 1999.

Kanpur Session

When the Bharatiya Jana Sangh's first session was held in Kanpur from 29 December to 31 December 1952, it was also the beginning of Jana Sangh's organizational journey as a national party. The party opened itself to deliberations on a range of issues that it had so far not spoken about. For example, it spoke about the need for electoral reforms in the country. A resolution was passed saying, 'There are numerous allegations received from different parts of the country of serious malpractices and irregularities in the conduct of elections especially those indicating the tampering of ballot boxes. It has been demonstrated that the ballot boxes are capable of being opened without breaking the seals . . . These allegations are bound to shake the faith of people in Democracy, which would have a very unfortunate effect on the future of the country.' The Jana Sangh further demanded reforms that would ensure no tampering with ballot boxes to restore people's faith in electoral processes.

The Kanpur session was critical for the party not just from the organizational standpoint but also in terms of how a new leadership arose in the party. The newly formed party set about building its organization. The main responsibility of strengthening the party was placed upon the UP Organization General Secretary Deen Dayal Upadhyaya. Upadhyaya was a full-time *pracharak* of the RSS and one of the important functionaries of the Jana Sangh who was sent by Golwalkar to the Jana Sangh to work with Mookerjee. He was well liked by Mookerjee.[58] The Kanpur session was organized largely by Nanaji Deshmukh, but is remembered for the contributions made by Upadhyaya who drafted seven of the fifteen resolutions passed in Kanpur.[59]

Article 370 and Accession of Jammu and Kashmir

At the Kanpur annual meeting of the Jana Sangh, the party decided to launch a nationwide agitation on Jammu and Kashmir. A day before this, a meeting was held in Delhi and it was decided that 5 March 1953 would be observed as 'Jammu and Kashmir Day' throughout the country in support of the agitation by the Praja Parishad in the erstwhile state.

Jammu and Kashmir had acceded to India after Independence, but Article 370 of the Indian Constitution gave it a special status. The state had its own flag, constitution and Prime Minister. The arrangement between Nehru and Sheikh Abdullah that came to be known as the Delhi Agreement of July 1952 allowed Kashmir to join India for the limited purposes of defence, foreign policy and communications. This was not acceptable to many at the time. There was an agitation against the pact led by the Praja Parishad.[60]

On 10 February 1952, the Jana Sangh passed a resolution stating, 'The Central Working Committee is of the view that the policy followed by the Government of India concerning Jammu-Kashmir state has failed to achieve the objective it had in view. The accession of Kashmir to India was full and it was wrong to offer a plebiscite. It was likewise wrong to take the matter to UNO [United Nations Organization] where it is not the justice that governs votes but power-politics and Cold War tactics. The result has been the passing of one third of the State under the aggressive occupation of Pakistan and there is a suspense about the future of the rest. Further, the way the Government of Kashmir is being run indicates as if it is not a full-fledged integration with India that it has in view. The Committee, therefore, feels that time has come when the Government should take a realistic view of the situation and alter this policy of soft-pedalling and dependence on the UNO. It must take a stand on its rights and on the justness of its Cause, withdraw this question from the UNO and complete the integration of the Jammu-Kashmir state with India in the same manner as of other acceding states.'[61]

The Kanpur session discussed the issue of Kashmir at length and argued in favour of its full integration with the Union. It said, 'Recent decision of the State's Constituent Assembly, however, regarding an elected President and a separate flag, coupled with the recommendation of the Basic Principle Committee that Kashmir will be Autonomous Republic within the Indian Republic, are in violation of India's sovereignty and the spirit of India's Constitution.'[62]

Immediately after the Kanpur session, Mookerjee focused his attention on Kashmir. The Kanpur resolution on Kashmir promised the Jana Sangh's support to the Kashmir Satyagraha. The Praja Parishad opposed the special status granted to Jammu and Kashmir and launched the Satyagraha, with the slogan, *Ek desh mein do Vidhan, do Pradhan aur do Nishan nahi chalenge*, which meant that one country cannot have two constitutions, two prime ministers and two national emblems.[63]

Prem Nath Dogra, the leader of the Praja Parishad, met Mookerjee in Jullundur, during the Punjab Jana Sangh session on 8 November 1952, and the two leaders discussed the Kashmir Satyagrah plan.[64] Dogra requested Mookerjee to visit Kashmir. Both leaders and people in Jammu and Kashmir were angered over the fact that Nehru had taken the issue of Kashmir to the United Nations. Dogra apprised Mookerjee of the issue of Inner Line permit and how this came in the way of J&K's full integration with India.[65]

By February 1953, the movement had gained momentum with various other parties also joining forces with Mookerjee. A number of Jana Sangh leaders were arrested in Punjab.[66]

Amid all this, by-elections were held in three Delhi Assembly seats (Deputy Ganj, Ajmeri Gate and Roshanara).[67] The Jana Sangh's main campaign issue was Kashmir. The Jana Sangh emerged victorious in these three seats.

The party leaders of the Kashmir agitation were already in prison in Punjab. Mookerjee decided to enter Kashmir at this point. Two more leaders of the Jana Sangh, Atal Bihari Vajpayee and Balraj Madhok, accompanied Mookerjee to J&K. All of them were denied entry permits that were required to enter the state. Madhok was back then working in J&K as a pracharak of the Sangh and was also associated with the Praja Parishad. In 1948, Sheikh Abdullah directed him to leave the region. Vajpayee had entered the Jana Sangh from the RSS and had been appointed national secretary of the Jana Sangh.

Mookerjee's intention to enter J&K without a permit was to raise the question of non-applicability of the Indian Constitution and the right to appeal to the Supreme Court, if arrested. Mookerjee entered the region on 11 May 1953. He was immediately arrested. The Kashmir police lodged him in a cottage near Srinagar. He sent Balraj Madhok and Atal Bihari Vajpayee back to Delhi and asked Vajpayee to take the fight into the Indian mainstream discourse. In prison, Mookerjee developed pain in the right leg, fever and chest pain.[68] Mookerjee was moved to a state hospital ten miles away. What took place in the hospital is still unclear.[69] It is alleged that on 22 June, he was given an injection that he was allergic to. On 23 June 1953, Mookerjee passed away.[70]

When Nehru wrote to Jogmaya Devi, Mookerjee's mother, conveying his condolences on 30 June 1953, she responded by saying: 'My son died in detention—a detention without trial . . . You say, you had visited Kashmir during my son's detention. You speak of the affection you had for him. But what prevented you, I wonder, from meeting him there personally and satisfying yourself about his health and arrangements? . . . Ever since his detention there, the first information that I, his mother, received from the Government of Jammu and Kashmir was that my son was no more . . . And in what cruel cryptic way the message was conveyed.'[71] Nehru did not respond and no inquiry was conducted into the circumstances that led to Mookerjee's death.[72]

In Mookerjee, the Jana Sangh lost the person who envisioned and laid the foundation of the party.

2

The Jana Sangh after Mookerjee

The death of Jana Sangh's president was a serious jolt to the young party. The party already suffered from not having many known faces. There were many young enthusiastic members, but Mookerjee's demise left a leadership vacuum in the party.

Also, with Mookerjee's death, the party's strength in Parliament came down to two.[1] A by-election held to find a successor for Mookerjee's Parliamentary erstwhile constituency Calcutta South East, saw the Jana Sangh get trounced and Communist leader Sadhan Gupta emerge victorious.[2] A search for Mookerjee's successor within the party began and Mauli Chandra Sharma was named the acting president.[3] But now after Mookerjee, the organization was reduced to a handful of youths. Many began to write political obituaries for the Jana Sangh.

It was clear to party workers that while Mookerjee was irreplaceable, the party had to be rebuilt; it had to continue with its political agenda, and not just contest elections. Deen Dayal Upadhyaya, the general secretary of the party at that time, spoke about this, saying, 'Bharatiya Jana Sangh is a party with a difference. It is not a set of people interested in coming to power anyhow ... Jana Sangh is not a party but a movement. It springs from the craving of the nation to assert and accomplish what it has been destined to do.'[4]

After Mookerjee's death, many leaders began to think that they would take over the reins of the party.[5] It also seemed plausible that the Jana Sangh would get someone from Hindu Mahasabha to take over as its leader. But as the party's focus was not on winning elections but on the organization and its agenda, the Jana Sangh was not searching for well-known faces to lead the party.

By then Mauli Chandra Sharma had developed many differences with the members of the organization.[6] He did not attend the Indore session of the party held in August 1954, and his address had to be read out.[7] His primary differences with fellow partymen revolved around the appointment of members of the party's working committee, where he wanted his chosen men. After Mookerjee there was a strong chance that Mauli Chandra Sharma would become the full-time president of the party. However, Sharma quit the Jana Sangh and went back to the Congress when Nehru offered him a plum position.[8]

The Indore session was significant for another reason as well. It was here that the Jana Sangh first spelt out its economic policy. One of the resolutions emphasized that the economic development of the country could be achieved only on the strength of small and cottage industries, and small industries should be saved from competition with big ones. It welcomed foreign capital on the condition that no political strings be attached.[9]

During this time, the party also continued to put pressure on the government to act against Pakistan over the ill treatment of religious minorities in Pakistan both on the eastern and western borders of the country.[10]

Amid all this, the party was organizing agitations for the liberation of Goa which was under Portuguese rule.[11] The Portuguese police firing in Goa led to the death of over twenty people in July 1955, six years before the Indian government sent the Army to Goa.[12]

Mookerjee's death was not just a shock to the newly formed Jana Sangh, but also to all the opposition parties who had recently come together under his leadership. He was the only nationally known leader that the Mahasabha, the Jana Sangh or the Parishad had. He had been a member of the cabinet and one of the six non-Congress ministers.[13] He was able to hold the RSS and non-RSS activists together.[14] After his death, the Opposition was unable to come to a consensus on Mookerjee's successor.

In this period there was a debate about whether these opposition parties—whose political leaders had come together as the National Democratic Party and become politically close during the Kashmir agitation—should be merged. The leader of the Hindu Mahasabha, N.C. Chatterjee (father of Somnath Chatterjee, the well-known CPI(M) leader) was in favour of merging into the Jana Sangh.[15] Another party of this front, the Ram Rajya Parishad, was also considering merging into the Jana Sangh.

However, this merger did not materialize as Deen Dayal Upadhyaya and Mauli Chandra Sharma objected to it. During a press conference in Bombay, Sharma said, '. . . there were no possibilities of unison between the Hindu Mahasabha and the Jana Sangh . . . The Hindu Mahasabha is a communal body and welcomes princes, zamindars and other vested interests in its midst . . .'[16] In the meeting held on *Shraddha* day of Dr Syama Prasad Mookerjee, Chatterjee expressed the departed leader's desire that the two parties become one.[17] This, however, was not possible as long as the Hindu Mahasabha stuck to its communal politics.[18]

These differences were similar to the issues that had emerged when Mookerjee had left the Mahasabha and was considering forming a new party. He had proposed inclusion of non-Hindus into the Mahasabha, but the other leaders of the party had disagreed. Instead, they were looking to include non-Hindus as non-members contributing to the electoral work of the party.[19][20]

There were also merger talks with Ram Rajya Parishad. However, the leadership of the Jana Sangh felt that the party followed a path of nationalism that was too conservative. Jana Sangh felt that Praja Parishad's conservatism went to the extent that it completely opposed anything that sounded even remotely foreign. The party was insistent upon the caste system. Its aims and objectives virtually made it impossible for a party like the Bharatiya Jana Sangh to go too far with it. This was not acceptable to the Jana Sangh and the merger talks failed.[21]

The journey from 1952 to 1957 was rather tumultuous for the Jana Sangh. While the party lost one of its presidents in a tragic death, another lost interest and joined the Congress.

1957 and 1962 elections

Despite the many hiccups that it went through, by the time of the 1957 elections, the Jana Sangh had gained ground across India barring some states like Assam, Orissa, Kerala and Madras.[22] The party's manifesto this time was a continuation of the 1952 manifesto and the many resolutions it had passed since it came into being.

The party emerged with 5.97 per cent votes in the elections, winning four Lok Sabha seats.[23] Upadhyaya declared, 'After the death of Dr Syama Prasad Mookerjee, it was presumed in the political circles that Jana Sangh would now be finished. We have fought against this presumption for the last five years. Now, the results of the second General Elections have proved that Jana Sangh is not only alive but also progressing. This would never have happened had we not been true to our principles and our leader.'

Table 1: Lok Sabha Elections of 1957[24]

Political Party	LS 1951		LS 1957	
	Vote Share	Seats Won	Vote Share	Seats Won
Bharatiya Jana Sangh	3.06%	3	5.97%	4
Indian National Congress	45%	364	47.80%	371
Communist Party of India	3.30%	16	8.90%	27

Atal Bihari Vajpayee was elected to the Lok Sabha from Uttar Pradesh's Balrampur constituency.[25] Vajpayee, who was a member of the RSS became active in politics by the time he turned sixteen. He was active in India's freedom movement and had gone to jail for participating in the Quit India Movement in 1942. He was studying law in Kanpur in 1946 when the RSS asked him to leave his education and set up a Hindi newspaper for the United Provinces. Vajpayee's wit and gift of oratory helped him become a much-respected person in no time. His amiable personality helped him win over people easily.

Vajpayee was elected leader of the four-member Jana Sangh group in Lok Sabha and rapidly made his mark in parliamentary debates. His persistent interventions led the Nehru government to issue a white paper on the Kashmir issue.[26]

In October 1957, municipal elections were held in many parts of Uttar Pradesh giving the Jana Sangh a chance to strengthen its hold.[27] Of 2,222 seats for which elections were held, the Congress won 856 and the Jana Sangh 187.[28] In the Delhi Municipal Corporation[29] elections held on 21 March 1958, of the eighty seats the Congress won thirty-one and the Jana Sangh twenty-five. The Congress failed to get a full majority. The Congress, communists and a few independents came together and elected a former communist, Aruna Asaf Ali, as the mayor of Delhi.[30] Even though the Jana Sangh did not win Delhi, it created a support base there. In the 1962 Lok Sabha elections, the Jana Sangh increased its tally to fourteen.[31]

Table 2: Lok Sabha Elections of 1962[32]

Political Party	LS 1957		LS 1962	
	Vote Share	Seats Won	Vote Share	Seats Won
Bharatiya Jana Sangh	5.976%	4	6.44%	14
Indian National Congress	47.80%	371	44.70%	361
Communist Party of India	8.90%	27	9.90%	29
Swatantra Party	-	-	7.89%	18

1962 War with China

The Jana Sangh was critical of China's annexation of Tibet. The party also tried to draw the government's attention to Chinese adventurism across the shared Indo-China borders and areas in Ladakh being occupied by China.[33][34]

The first attack by China came on 8 September 1962.[35] On 20 October there was a massive attack in the North-East Frontier Agency and Ladakh.[36] Finding India unprepared to guard its borders, the Chinese entered and captured significant Indian territory. Deen Dayal Upadhyaya asked the Jana Sangh members to support the Nehru government. 'Our fight today is not with the Congress, but with the Chinese,' he said.[37] The RSS workers served the Indian Army personnel on the borders and subsequently the organization was invited to participate in the Republic Day parade of 1963.[38]

In 1963, the Jana Sangh suffered another blow when its president Dr Raghu Vira, a known scholar of Sanskrit and Buddhism, died in a car accident. Raghu Vira had been a Congress member of the Upper House of Parliament but had joined the Jana Sangh in 1959 after developing differences with the party over its China policy.[39] Acharya Deva Prasad Ghosh, who had been the party chief from 1956–59, took over as interim president.[40]

All this while, Upadhyaya had been taking up the issue of cow slaughter vociferously. At the Nagpur Central Working Committee meeting of the Jana Sangh in 1966, the party resolved to work towards attaining a ban on the practice in accordance with the Directive Principles of State Policy under Article 48 of the constitution.[41][42] The party began a concerted movement for cow protection. On 7 November 1966, thousands of gau-rakshaks, with sadhus and other religious leaders, marched towards Parliament demanding a law banning cow slaughter across the country.[43] Eight people, including a constable, were killed in these protests.[44]

1967 Elections

Meanwhile, another important development was unfolding as
Ram Manohar Lohia, a member of the Samyukta Socialist Party,
was drawing closer to the Jana Sangh. Both believed that sustained
Congress rule could harm the country. Lohia had made anti-
Congressism his main plank.[45]

Lohia came to understand the Jana Sangh when the 1963 by-
polls came knocking. In the run-up to the elections, the Jana Sangh
members campaigned for the Opposition, and this impressed
Lohia. He credited the Jana Sangh for his win in the Farrukhabad
parliamentary constituency. The constituency had been represented
till 1963 by Mool Chand Dube of the Congress. His death early in
1963 caused the by-election. Lohia defeated Congress candidate B.V.
Keskar by more than 50,000 votes.[46]

After his parliamentary victory, Lohia began holding discussions
with Upadhyaya on issues where the two parties could work
together. On 12 April 1964, they issued a joint statement: 'Large-
scale riots in Pakistan have compelled some over two lakh Hindus
and other minorities to come over to India. Indians naturally feel
incensed by the happenings in East Bengal. To bring the situation
under control and to prescribe the right remedy for the situation
it is essential that the malady be properly diagnosed. And even in
this state of mental agony, the basic values of our national life must
never be forgotten.'[47]

When the 1967 elections came close, the Jana Sangh forged
alliances with the Swatantra Party in major states like Gujarat,
Haryana, Punjab and Himachal Pradesh.[48] In Madhya Pradesh, the
party struck an electoral alliance with Rajmata Vijayaraje Scindia,
who was earlier in the Congress.

Table 3: Lok Sabha Elections of 1967[49]

Political Party	LS 1962		LS 1967	
	Vote Share	Seats Won	Vote Share	Seats Won
Bharatiya Jana Sangh	6.44%	14	9.31%	35
Indian National Congress	44.70%	361	40.80%	283
Swatantra Party	7.90%	18	8.67%	44

Born in Madhya Pradesh's Sagar in 1919, Rajmata, wife of Jiwajirao Scindia of the princely state of Gwalior, was initiated into electoral politics in 1957 when she contested and won the Guna Lok Sabha seat in Madhya Pradesh on a Congress ticket. By 1967 she had realized that she wasn't aligned with the Congress ideologically. She decided to contest on both the Jana Sangh and the Swatantra Party tickets. She contested from Karera as a Jana Sangh candidate in the Assembly elections and from Guna Lok Sabha seat as a Swatantra Party candidate.[50] Rajmata won both seats but eventually decided to accept the assembly seat that she had won on a Jana Sangh ticket and became the Leader of Opposition in Madhya Pradesh assembly.

Following this, Rajmata gained a significant role in the Jana Sangh. She helped in strengthening the roots of Jana Sangh in central India. Rajmata's growing influence and her nationalistic ideals were seen as a threat to the Indira Gandhi government, which arrested and jailed her during the Emergency. Despite the Congress government's oppressive tactics, Rajmata did not succumb and continued to work for nation building. She promoted and mentored many women leaders from the Jana Sangh and later the BJP, including Uma Bharti, Mridula Sinha, Sushma Swaraj and Jayawantiben Mehta. Later in the 1980s, Rajmata also played an instrumental role in the Ram Janmabhoomi movement.

In Rajasthan, for the assembly elections in 1967 it was decided that the Jana Sangh would contest sixty-three seats, and the Swatantra Party 107.[51] For Lok Sabha, a decision was taken that the Jana Sangh would contest seven seats, while the Swatantra Party would fight on fourteen seats.[52] The Samyukta Socialist Party led by Lohia chose to opt out of the group.[53]

In Gujarat, the Jana Sangh was the junior partner of the Swatantra Party as the former was weak in the state. In accordance with the agreement, the Jana Sangh did not contest any seat. For the assembly polls, the Jana Sangh fought on sixteen seats, while the Swatantra Party on 168 seats.[54]

When the results of the 1967 elections came, the Jana Sangh improved its Lok Sabha tally from fourteen to thirty-five and its vote share rose from 6.44 per cent to 9.31 per cent.[55] The best results for the party came in Delhi where it won six of the seven seats.[56] In the Assembly elections, the Jana Sangh had managed to do very well, opening the opportunity for it to form coalition governments in eight states and Delhi. But voices within the party differed on the issue.[57] Balraj Madhok, who was president of the Jana Sangh then, was against any tie-up with the Communists. Upadhyaya, however, saw no harm in forming governments with Communist support even though he was sceptical of them. A Central Working Committee (CWC) resolution of the party read thus: 'The Central Working Committee favours the inclusion of the Jana Sangh MLAs in non-Congress Ministries. These members will remain in the Ministry so long as they can effectively serve the people on the basis of the principles and programmes of the Jana Sangh. Even while participating in non-Congress Ministries, the Jana Sangh Legislative Party should maintain its organization and working according to its Constitution.'[58]

This led to the formation of Samyukta Vidhayak Dal (SVD) governments in many states. The SVD governments aimed at ending the Congress' hegemony in politics.[59] [60] The foundation of such coalition politics was laid by Mookerjee when he had formed the National Democratic Party.[61]

The Jana Sangh at this time was caught in its own internal debates. Madhok wanted a united front against the Congress. He wanted to move closer to the Swatantra Party and avoid the Communists and Socialists. Any closeness with the Swatantra Party could, however, have been read as the Jana Sangh being in favour of the erstwhile royals. Hence, Vajpayee opposed this. Upadhyaya, on his part, was against using anti-Congressism as a rallying plank. He wanted the party to build up its own base. He felt the party had been weakened due to its participation in the SVD governments. He wanted the Jana Sangh to walk out of the SVD governments but his views were rejected.[62]

In 1967, Upadhyaya took over as the Jana Sangh president at the party's fourteenth annual session in Calicut.[63] A brief account of the personal background of Deen Dayal Upadhyaya is provided in his book *Political Diary*.[64] He was born on 25 September 1916 in the village of Dhankia in Jaipur, Rajasthan. He went on to do his graduation in mathematics from S.D. College, Kanpur. While in Kanpur, he joined the RSS in 1937. After completing his studies, he decided to dedicate his life to the RSS. He began as district pracharak in Lakhimpur, Uttar Pradesh in 1942, and rose to become a joint provincial pracharak within five years. He served in this position till 1951. When the Jana Sangh was established, the RSS gave some active, highly efficient and dedicated swayamsevaks to the political outfit. Among those who joined the Jana Sangh from the RSS were the likes of Jagannathrao Joshi and Nanaji Deshmukh. Deen Dayal Upadhyaya, too, was among those who joined the Jana Sangh from RSS. In 1951, in the Kanpur session, he became the Uttar Pradesh State Bharatiya Jana Sangh secretary. He played a pivotal role by blending the party's political philosophy with a practical work culture. In 1952, Dr Syama Prasad Mookerjee appointed him as the general secretary of the Bharatiya Jana Sangh, a position he held till 1967, when he became the party's president.[65]

Deen Dayal Upadhyaya was short and frail but highly determined. Upadhyaya entered politics to serve a mission and not for the lure of power. The Jana Sangh was looking at nationwide expansion and needed a fine balance between Indian ethos and a modernistic approach. Upadhyaya had a modernistic and accommodative outlook which brought him to the centre stage of the Jana Sangh's strategy. He had lost his father early in life but ensured he got a good education. Upadhyaya was able to manage individual ambitions, multiple egos and umpteen organizational issues.

The philosophy of *Ekatma Manavvad* or Integral Humanism propounded by Upadhyaya through a series of speeches in Mumbai between 22 and 25 April 1965, was imbued in India's cultural ethos, and went on to become the Jana Sangh's official doctrine. He said that every country had its own peculiar historical, social and economic situation, and hence it was illogical to think that the solutions which the leaders of one country decided to adopt would be effective for all other people. While western nations had accepted nationalism, democracy, socialism and equality as their ideals, the attention of Indians should be claimed by the *Bharatiya* culture, he said.[66] He laid stress on sarvodaya (progress of all), swadeshi (go indigenous), and gram swaraj (village self-rule). His ideas ran counter to the idea that the individual is supreme; he emphasised that the individual was subservient to the nation and cultural-national values.[67]

Upadhyaya also proposed the concept of *antyodaya*, the rise of the last person, as a measure of true economic and social development in a society. He believed that unless economic prosperity reached the last person in the social hierarchy, real progress did not happen.

In his time in the Jana Sangh, Deen Dayal Upadhyaya focused on building organizational capability. He drew attention to the fact that the democratic set-up in India was copied from the British Parliamentary System and implored that India must shape its own system in keeping with its rich and unique tradition. Forty-three days after Upadhyaya became the president of the Jana Sangh, he died under mysterious circumstances. His body was found on 11 February 1968, along railway tracks, while he was on his way to Patna from Lucknow. His death remains an unsolved mystery.[68]

Summarising his role in the strengthening of the Jana Sangh, Vajpayee said, 'Panditji never became a member of Parliament, but all of us who are in Parliament today are there because of him.'[69]

Soon after Upadhyaya's death, Vajpayee took over as the party president.

As intra-party differences began to weaken the SVD governments, the Indira Gandhi government left no stone unturned to ensure their fall. By 1968, many governments in regions such as Haryana, Punjab, Nagaland, Pondicherry, West Bengal, Bihar and Uttar Pradesh were pulled down and mid-term elections were scheduled.[70] The mid-term polls held in 1969 were catastrophic for Jana Sangh. Its tally in Uttar Pradesh, Bihar, Haryana, Punjab and West Bengal went down in comparison to the parliamentary elections of 1967. In UP, of the 425 seats, the Jana Sangh contested 397 and won forty-nine. In Bihar, the party contested 303 seats and won thirty-four. In Haryana, the party won seven seats of the forty-four it contested, out of the total of 81 seats. In West Bengal, the party won no seat despite contesting fifty. Of the 104 seats in Punjab, Jana Sangh fought on thirty and won eight.[71][72]

As president, Vajpayee had a tough time dealing with internal problems. Balraj Madhok had differences with the party over leadership issues.[73] Upadhyaya had suggested making him the president to buy peace.[74] But after Upadhayay's death, Madhok became more intransigent.[75] Vajpayee continued in the position till 1972. He wanted the Jana Sangh to be seen as a party of the common man. While Vajpayee was struggling to keep the discord at bay, L.K. Advani became a Rajya Sabha member. Born in Karachi, Advani came from a well-to-do and educated family. He received his early education in Karachi, but Partition forced his family to migrate to Bombay.

While Advani's grandfather was a Sanskrit scholar, his father Kisinchand was a trader in his family business. Advani himself took an early liking for books and turned into an avid reader. This helped him understand a range of issues and develop an analytical mind along with the ability to articulate his thoughts well.

1971 Elections

The 1971 elections were fought by the Jana Sangh in alliance with the Swatantra Party, the Samyukta Socialist Party and the Congress (Organisation).[76] This was the first election covered by radio. The results, however, were disappointing for the Jana Sangh. The Congress (I) won 352 seats in a house of 518. The Jana Sangh was limited to twenty-two seats.[77] The defeat left the cadre demoralized. Vajpayee owned up to the defeat and requested senior vice-president Bhai Mahavir to preside over the party meeting in Bhagalpur so that an open discussion could take place on the reasons for the party's performance.[78]

Table 4: Lok Sabha Elections of 1971[79]

Political Party	LS 1967		LS 1971	
	Vote Share	Seats Won	Vote Share	Seats Won
Bharatiya Jana Sangh	9.31%	35	7.35%	22
Indian National Congress	40.80%	283	43.68%	352
Indian National Congress (Organization)	-	-	10.43%	16

Vajpayee then requested that he be allowed to step down as the Jana Sangh president. As a consequence, Lal Krishna Advani stepped in to fill the position on 11 January 1973. In one of his first decisions as the Jana Sangh president, Advani expelled Madhok from the party.[80]

Success in the 1971 Bangladesh liberation war changed domestic politics in India. It burnished the nationalist credentials of the Congress, which was able to claim victory in the freedom movement and in the 1971 war. As power was concentrated in the hands of Indira Gandhi, the abuse of power began, and economic performance collapsed. This led to widespread unrest in the country as unemployment increased and prices rose. The anger was channelled by Jaiprakash Narayan, or JP, as he was popularly known, who had quit the Congress to form the Socialist Party. JP had exited active politics right after the first general elections, but Indira Gandhi's authoritarianism and widespread corruption made him return to active politics and take centre stage once again.[81]

The first major protest against the Indira Gandhi Congress government started from Bihar on 16 March 1974.[82] As the police began assaults on unarmed students, they approached JP for guidance. JP urged the students to engage in peaceful demonstrations. The students protested non-violently, but the state responded with violence. On 12 April 1974, according to official figures, eight students were killed in police firing.[83] Vajpayee raised the issue in Parliament. From a student movement, the agitation turned into a people's movement and spread from Delhi across the country.

During a protest march in Delhi, both JP and Nanaji Deshmukh were beaten by the police. Vajpayee continued to take on the government on the issue of violence that was being meted out to people protesting peacefully. JP had so far maintained that the protests remain free of political parties, but as the government continued to use force, he opened the doors for parties.[84]

As the opposition to the government grew, Indira Gandhi declared internal Emergency on 25 June 1975, under Article 352. An external Emergency had already been underway since the 1971 War. The two kinds of Emergency induced extreme power in the hands of the executive.

Overnight some 400 warrants were signed for arrests.[85] Within hours, after the declaration of internal Emergency, the government put almost the entire Opposition behind bars.

The RSS too was banned once again by the Congress government. Balasaheb Deoras, the RSS *sarsanghchalak* (RSS chief) at that time was arrested and wrote letters to Indira Gandhi from prison, in which he clarified the organization's stance stating that although the organization was concerned with the Hindu community it did not teach anything against any non-Hindu.[86] The RSS leaders went into hiding soon after Deoras' arrest. The swayamsevaks were directed to continue showing up at the shakhas, but not in their uniforms.

Advani wrote a letter to the Jana Sangh Executive members from inside jail. It read: 'With the declaration of Emergency in June 1975, a new chapter has commenced. Democracy has come under eclipse. Those who believe in democracy have had to undergo many kinds of suffering and have had to make many sacrifices. As a result of this, the cordiality, closeness and mutual trust generated during this last one year among parties and persons committed to democracy could not have been ordinarily created even in one decade. The emergence of a strong, unified Opposition party with democracy as its main plank should be regarded as a natural culmination of this chain of events.'[87]

By March 1977, most leaders were released. Following this, Jaiprakash Narayan convened a meeting of opposition leaders. Among those who attended were Acharya Kriplani, Charan Singh, Shanti Bhushan, Om Prakash Tyagi and P.G. Mawalankar. On 26 September 1976, the Jana Sangh in a resolution expressed support to the unity movement and urged all party members to 'unconditionally' merge their separate entities into a single political party.

JP announced the formation of a new national party. It was an amalgamation of the Jana Sangh, the Congress (O), the Socialist Party and the Bharatiya Lok Dal. This was not a coalition but a single party into which the Jana Sangh merged, giving shape to the Janata Party. Meanwhile, Jagjivan Ram quit the Congress on 2 February 1977, after Indira Gandhi refused to lift the Emergency. He formed the Congress For Democracy (CFD).

In the 1977 elections, for the first time since Independence, the Congress lost. Neither Indira Gandhi nor her son Sanjay Gandhi won their seats. The newly formed Janata Party won 271 seats.

CFD won twenty-eight. With the support of three Independents, the Janata Party formed the government and Morarji Desai became India's first non-Congress Prime Minister.[88]

Table 5: Lok Sabha Elections of 1977[89]

Political Party	LS 1971		LS 1977	
	Vote Share	Seats Won	Vote Share	Seats Won
Janata Party-plus	7.35%	22	41.32%	295
Indian National Congress	43.68%	352	34.52%	154
Communist Party of India (Marxist)	5.12%	25	4.29%	22

* * *

In the early 20th century, the Indian National Congress was the dominant political and nationalist force in the country. It was a big tent, where a diverse array of anti-colonial voices came together. After Independence, many politicians left the Congress and floated their own parties. Many parties were also floated by individuals driven by various ideas and ideologies. C. Rajgopalachari established the Swatantra party with Minoo Masani and Piloo Modi. Jaiprakash Narayan and Ram Manohar Lohia established the Socialist Party. Ambedkar founded the Republican Party. Syama Prasad Mookerjee founded the Jana Sangh. As diversity inside the Congress declined, inner party democracy also suffered, particularly as political power was concentrated into one person, Indira Gandhi. Party elections were called off in 1967. In the period of the Emergency, there was an atrophying of the foundations of the Congress, the district and block committees, and internal democracy in the Congress ended. This left the Congress more vulnerable to the criticism of being a mere instrument of one family and marked the beginning of the sustained decline of the party.

On the other hand, the Jana Sangh began its journey in 1951 with nationalism as the core of its ideological and structural being. It was a coming together of people who shared the same ideological beliefs, understanding and cultural ethos.

The RSS, which began way before in 1925, and the Jana Sangh had independent journeys even though they worked very closely with each other and believed and practised the same ideals, yet the fine line was discernible. The RSS was more of a moral force for the Jana Sangh.

Like any organization, the Jana Sangh too had its share of individual ambitions that sometimes ran in contradiction to the party's principles and goals. But when it came to enforcing discipline, the party did not show partisan behaviour. The party was always bigger than the individual. When Vasantrao Oak showed an objectionable degree of over-ambition, Golwalkar who was then sarsanghchalak remarked, 'One of my colleagues developed a liking for political work to a degree uncommon and undesirable for a swayamsevak.'[90]

Oak had been actively involved in the setting up of the Jana Sangh and yet the party dealt with his indiscipline strictly, expelling him and fourteen other prominent members from the Delhi unit of the Jana Sangh because the whole unit had become undisciplined.

Ideology was important for the Jana Sangh. As an example, the party was opposed to *zamindari* in Rajasthan, a system through which *zamindars* or landowners earned revenue from their agricultural land by renting it out to peasants in return for a share of the produce. Many of the Jana Sangh's legislators left the party in support of the zamindari system, but the party chose to remain committed to its stance against the system. The parties came together as the Samyukta Dal to take on the Congress on the floor of the house. But the Samyukta Dal was opposed to land reforms. Instead of compromising on the issue, the Jana Sangh decided to walk out of the group.

The decision to join the Janata Party was also a decision based on principles. Despite winning ninety-three of the 271 seats that Janata

Party won together, the Jana Sangh constituents did not stake claim to the PM's chair.[91] The party wanted stability for the country and so wholeheartedly supported Morarji Desai as Prime Minister. Only a few members of the Jana Sangh took ministerial positions in the new government. Atal Bihari Vajapyee became external affairs minister, LK Advani became minister of information and broadcasting, and Satish Chandra Agarwal became minister of state for finance.[92]

The Jana Sangh had struggled to find its feet in the early days since it had no known face. It lost its founding leader, Syama Prasad Mookerjee, within less than two years of the party's establishment, and Deen Dayal Upadhyaya's untimely death a few months after becoming president left the Jana Sangh rudderless and in a shambles. What sustained the Jana Sangh through those years was a dedicated young cadre, most of them below the age of forty.

The principles of party discipline, commitment to ideology and a dedicated cadre are the same tenets that would help the BJP rise in the years to come.

3

A Party Is Born

Through the 1960s and 1970s, the years culminating in the Emergency, the Indian state amassed arbitrary power and crushed citizenry. The Janata Party-led government reversed many Emergency-era decrees and opened official investigations into abuses of that period. The Janata period was an important one in which political freedom was restored, fear of the government in the eyes of the citizens went down and a new path for economic policy began. At a political level, however, continuous infighting and ideological differences hampered the effectiveness of the new coalition government. The Janata Party was a political experiment born out of the Emergency, and one that died an early death owing to its inability to learn how to collaborate and share power.

There was a serious challenge in choosing India's new Prime Minister. Rival leaders from the original parties that made up the Janata Party desired this position, and their power struggles weakened the party. Morarji Desai (who was the party chairman), Charan Singh and Jagjivan Ram each enjoyed the support of a significant number of political workers and MPs in the newly formed Janata Party. To avoid a potentially divisive contest, Janata leaders asked Jaiprakash Narayan to select the party's leader, pledging to abide by his choice.[1] Some believed that if Morarji Desai wasn't made the prime minister, the likely choice would be Jagjivan Ram.[23]

The outcome of this leadership contest was that the Janata Party leaders voted to elect Morarji Desai as the head of the parliamentary party on the invitation of Jaiprakash Narayan.[4] However, the rivalry between the elements of the Janata Party did not end there. The coalition was riven with personal and policy frictions. Jaiprakash Narayan's failing health ruled out the possibility of his playing a role in building an amicable arrangement. The Congress, on its part, did its bit to bolster the centrifugal forces within the Janata Party. It pushed messages to the people about the fractious nature of the Janata Party, claiming that this interfered with the working of the government. Congress stalwart Y.B. Chavan nurtured Charan Singh's personal ambitions.

The Janata Party tried to investigate and prosecute some of the Congress figures, including Indira Gandhi, on the question of the abuses during the Emergency. This, however, gave the appearance in the public eye that the party used investigative agencies for narrow political ends, and reduced public support for the administration.

On the social policy front, the Janata Party achieved a milestone in 1978 when it fulfilled its election promise of not keeping right to property as a fundamental right by repealing Article 19(1)(f) and Article 31. Mentioned in its election manifesto for the 1977 parliamentary elections was the promise to 'delete property from the list of Fundamental Rights and, instead, affirm right to work.'[5]

In his autobiography *Courting Destiny*[6], former law minister Shanti Bhushan wrote that by 1978, a rumour gained ground that Charan Singh (who was the home minister) was set to initiate a major political manoeuvre. A controversy over instituting an inquiry into the alleged wrongdoings of Morarji Desai's son began to gain traction around March 1978. In the ensuing conflict, Desai removed Charan Singh from the Cabinet in June 1978.[7][8][9] On 24 January 1979, Charan Singh managed to return to the government, a step that reinforced the environment of mistrust.[10][11]

In 1979, Raj Narain and Charan Singh pulled out of the Janata Party, forcing Desai to resign from office and retire from politics.[12]

Upon his resignation, while the Lok Sabha was debating a no-confidence motion against his government, it was felt within the Janata Party that it was Jagjivan Ram's turn to be Prime Minister. But Desai refused to quit the leadership of his party in Parliament. He gave up this position only after President N. Sanjiva Reddy asked Charan Singh to form the government on 26 July 1979.[13] This late-stage acrimony widened the rift within the party.[14] Charan Singh had been testing support for himself among the Janata Party legislators, gearing up for such a moment. Once he got the support of over eighty MPs, he resigned from the Janata Party and formed a government with Congress support on 26 July 1979.[15][16]

The Charan Singh government lasted less than a month. The Congress withdrew its support so quickly that Charan Singh could not even visit his constituency after taking over as prime minister.[17] This sequence of events led to demoralization of the coalition partners. By this point, the Janata Party's majority was considerably weaker, and many Janata MPs refused to support Charan Singh. MPs loyal to Jagjivan Ram withdrew from the Janata Party. Former allies such as the DMK, the Shiromani Akali Dal, the CPI(M) got more concerned about their own political future and started distancing themselves from the Janata Party.

With no other political party in a position to establish a majority government, President Reddy dissolved Parliament and called for fresh elections in January 1980.[18] Jagjivan Ram had staked his claim to power as soon as Charan Singh announced his resignation on 21 August 1979.[19] But the President decided that Charan Singh would be the 'caretaker PM' until January 1980 and did not give Jagjivan Ram a chance to form even a caretaker government. Ram believed that this decision of the President reflected a continuation of their long-standing political conflict, which included Ram's active opposition to Reddy's candidature for the presidency a decade ago.[20]

While the Janata Party period, 1977–1980, was a successful one in terms of economic policy, it also demonstrated the inability of the non-Congress elements of the Indian political landscape to achieve amicable power sharing, the ground rules and culture which Vajpayee (many years later) termed as 'coalition dharma'. It created fresh confidence in the Congress about the sustained relevance of Congress as the Grand Old Party, the sense that 1977-1980 was an isolated blip in long-term Congress domination.

In the 1980 Lok Sabha elections, the Jana Sangh participated as part of the Janata Party. The Janata Party lost the elections and the Congress returned to power. Voters resoundingly went back to the Congress, taking them from 154 seats in 1977 to 374 seats (with allies) in 1980.[21] The Congress that badly lost the 1977 elections was re-elected with a clear majority.[22][23]

Table 1: Lok Sabha Elections of 1980[24]

Political Party	LS 1977		LS 1980	
	Vote Share	Seats Won	Vote Share	Seats Won
Janata Party	41.32%	295	18.97%	31
Indian National Congress(I)	34.52%	154	42.69%	353
Janata Party (Secular)	-	-	9.39%	41

This defeat led to a great deal of soul searching in the non-Congress elements of Indian politics, and in the strategic thinking of the Jana Sangh. The Janata Party had four constituents—the Jana Sangh, the Congress (O), the Samyukta Socialist Party and the Bharatiya Lok Dal.[25] The Jana Sangh and RSS's support and participation in Jaiprakash Narayan's movement against the Emergency had contributed to its popularity. But this did not prevent differences from emerging within the Janata Party.

Questions about the Jana Sangh and its relations with the RSS had begun to be raised within the Janata Party in March 1978. Politicians like Madhu Limaye had objected to the fact that leaders of the Jana Sangh in the Janata Party were also members of the RSS.

There were concerns about their divided loyalties. These issues were raised again after the defeat. The Jana Sangh members believed that they were neither instrumental in affecting Morarji's resignation, nor had they left the Janata Party. They maintained that the issue of their dual membership was resolved when the Jana Sangh joined the Janata Party.[26]

The Jana Sangh members had often felt they had been treated poorly in Indian politics over many decades. While the Sangh Parivar was treated as untouchable, it had made efforts to align forces in 1952 with the formation of a People's Democratic Front (PDF). With the death of Syama Prasad Mookerjee, other parties had distanced themselves from the Jana Sangh, and the PDF had disintegrated. Conventional political parties across the ideological spectrum in India began to feel insecure about the rise of the Jana Sangh and branded the party communal, treating it as a veritable untouchable (achoot).[27] Treating the Jana Sangh as untouchable was part of the oft-repeated strategy of the Congress and others to isolate the party. In a bid to isolate the Jana Sangh, the party was ironically branded communal right after its formation. As times changed, many non-Congress political parties formed alliances with the Jana Sangh on various occasions, but also distanced themselves from the party on other occasions using the pretext that the Jana Sangh was 'communal'. Jana Sangh and later, BJP leaders, pointed to this irony on several occasions and contested the communal tag. Later, when the BJP emerged at the centre stage of politics, the tendency to isolate the party proved wrong for its detractors.

In December 1967, at the Plenary Session of the Jana Sangh in Calicut, Deen Dayal Upadhyaya said that while enlightened minds regard untouchability as a sin in social life, in political life the same enlightened people feel proud about untouchability.[28] Political scientist Imtiaz Ahmad has argued that the mainstreaming of the right wing began with Jaiprakash Narayan's Bihar movement: 'Until that time the RSS was seen as untouchable in Indian politics. During that movement they came close to the Opposition parties because they had interacted in jail during the Emergency.'[29][30]

This issue of dual membership in the Janata Party was also raised at the earlier discussions about the establishment of the Janata Party, in 1976, while the Emergency was in force. Constructing the Janata Party required that all other parties accept the Jana Sangh into their fold. At that time, Charan Singh had said that Sangh members should not be part of the Janata Party.[31] O.P. Tyagi, who participated in that meeting from the Jana Sangh, expressed his disagreement with the issue by stating that the Janata Party was free to lay down whatever conditions it saw fit, as at the time the RSS was banned and stood dissolved.[32][33] However, in September 1976, when the Janata Party was still being discussed as a concept, the Jana Sangh was opposed to being a part of any political coalition which restricted its members from being a part of any social or cultural organization. Vajpayee firmly held on to the position that he would not join any party that prohibited RSS members from joining it.[34] Jana Sangh members unhappy with Janata Party leaders said, 'In March 1977, when the elections were held, not a single leader of the Janata Party said anything about RSS except to pay rich encomiums to it for the wonderful work it had done during the Emergency.'[35] They felt slighted at being cold-shouldered after 1977.

Despite these internal squabbles, the Jana Sangh remained focused on being part of the political alignment that could take on the Congress, towards the overall objective of reducing the influence of the Congress in India. It remained in the Janata Party even when it began to disintegrate. The Jana Sangh's influence in Indian politics was growing. As an example, a series of state governments were now being led by Jana Sangh leaders: In 1977, Bhairon Singh Shekhawat, Virendra Kumar Sakhlecha and Shanta Kumar—all from the Jana Sangh—were chief ministers of Rajasthan, Madhya Pradesh and Himachal Pradesh respectively.[36]

Bhairon Singh Shekhawat, who served as the three-time chief minister of Rajasthan, was a farmer's son. Before joining politics and entering Vidhan Sabha in 1952, Shekhawat worked as a sub inspector. During the Emergency, Shekhawat was a Rajya Sabha member and was incarcerated at the Rohtak Jail. In 1977, Shekhawat won from Chhabra as a Janata Party candidate and took over as the first non-Congress CM of Rajasthan.

Virendra Sakhlecha had joined the RSS at the age of fifteen. In 1962, when the Jana Sangh won forty-one seats in the 288-seat MP assembly, Sakhlecha was made the leader of Opposition.[37] He was the deputy CM from 1967 to 1969. After coming out of jail when the Emergency ended, he was number two in the Jana Sangh government led by Kailash Joshi. Sakhlecha became CM in January 1978.

Shanta Kumar had begun his political career in 1963 after getting elected as *panch* in gram panchayat elections and entered the Legislative Assembly in 1972. Kumar was jailed for his role in the Kashmir agitation under Syama Prasad Mookerjee and then again during the Emergency.

This was a new level of involvement in actual administration for the Jana Sangh, which created feedback loops of knowledge and capability in the party. There were thus strong incentives for the Jana Sangh to protect the status quo of the Janata Party arrangement.

Matters came to a head on the question of 'divided loyalties'. The Jana Sangh felt that there were fears in some camps of the Janata Party that the erstwhile Jana Sangh would *de facto* dominate the Janata Party and come to control the organizational capabilities of the Janata Party.[38] The conditions that Madhu Limaye and Chandrashekhar, who was then the president of the Janata Party Parliamentary Board, tried to impose on the Jana Sangh were a way to strengthen loyalty to the party. Consequently, the Janata Party Parliamentary Board passed a resolution barring member of the RSS from being members of the party. On 4 April 1980 the national executive of the Janata Party passed a resolution to that effect.

The Jana Sangh component of the Janata Party, led by Atal Bihari Vajpayee, had to choose between their commitment to the

RSS philosophy and their political career in the Janata Party. They decided to prioritize their ideology and leave the Janata Party.

A New Party

On 6 April 1980, the Jana Sangh leaders who had exited the Janata Party announced the creation of a new party, the Bharatiya Janata Party (BJP). While this was a start-up, it had significant assets. BJP leaders Atal Bihari Vajpayee and L.K. Advani had built a mass base. They had been arrested during the Emergency, along with Jayaprakash Narayan and Morarji Desai, which gave them enhanced moral stature.[39] Some key persons who were founding members of the BJP were Nanaji Deshmukh, Dr Murli Manohar Joshi, Sundar Singh Bhandari, K.R. Malkani, V.K. Malhotra, Kushabhau Thakre, Jana Krishnamurthy, Kidar Nath Sahani, J.P. Mathur, Sunder Lal Patwa, Bhairon Singh Shekhawat, Shanta Kumar, Rajmata Vijayaraje Scindia, Kailashpati Mishra, Jagannathrao Joshi and others. Some eminent persons who did not have an RSS background such as Ram Jethmalani and Sikander Bakht also joined the party.[40] Some of these persons now had the experience of being members of the cabinet at the union or state government levels. The party had a strong network of party workers in the west and the north. Ten months into the life of the Congress(I) government, the BJP ran its first national executive meeting between 28 and 30 December in 1980 in Mumbai at the Samta Nagar Maidan. This founding event is remembered as the 'Samta Nagar session'.[41]

Atal Bihari Vajpayee took charge as party president and L.K. Advani as general secretary. The party committed itself to *Panch Nishtha* (five commitments) as its roadmap. These were (a) nationalism and national integration, (b) commitment to democracy and fundamental rights, (c) *Sarva Dharma Sama Bhava*, the idea of positive secularism, (d) Gandhian socialism and (e) value-based politics.[42] Vajpayee delivered a memorable speech at the session in which he said, 'The BJP is resolved to devote itself to politics rooted in the soil. Only by that course can we restore the confidence of the people in politics, political parties and political leaders . . . With the Constitution of India in one hand and the banner of equality in the other, let us get set for the struggle.' Adopting the new symbol for the party, the lotus, Vajpayee is famously known to have predicted the rise of the BJP in Indian politics, saying, *Andhera Chatega, Sooraj Niklega, Kamal Khilega* (The darkness will be dispelled, the sun will rise and the lotus will bloom). Vajpayee said, among other things, that the BJP should fight against the dangers hovering over judicial independence, the government's bid to curtail the autonomy of democratic institutions, political violence in Kerala, misuse of government machinery for the pursuit of political ends, and the state of refugees in Assam.[43]

The young party invited the former chief justice of the Bombay High Court, Mohammadali Carim Chagla, a well-known opponent of the Emergency to the Samta Nagar session.[44] Chagla said the BJP was 'a glimmer of hope' in an otherwise very depressing situation. He went on to write in the *Times of India*, 'There is just a glimmer of hope which is beginning to show itself and that is the extraordinary strength which this new party, the Bharatiya Janata Party, has shown[45] . . . And if this party goes on from strength to strength and receives the support of people from all over the country, we might at last have a democratic alternative to Indira's Government.'[46]

Words like secularism and socialism meant different things to different people. The idea of positive secularism as understood by the BJP differed from the secularism that they believed was practised by Nehru and Indira Gandhi. The Congress approach, to allow special rights for minorities, was seen by the BJP as appeasement of the minorities in an attempt to obtain a reliable block of voters. When Indira Gandhi introduced an amendment to the Preamble to the Constitution to add the terms 'secular' and 'socialist' to it, the BJP opposed this. In the 42nd amendment of the Constitution, the Preamble to the Constitution was amended to 'India is a sovereign socialist secular democratic republic'. This 42nd amendment to the Constitution was done during the Emergency, when the rhythms of a parliamentary democracy were not in place, when opposition MPs were jailed. Therefore, to many independent thinkers, this amendment of the Constitution lacks legitimacy. The BJP had long held that Articles 25 and 26 of the Constitution already treated all religions as equal and that Indian ethos had always treated all faiths in equal regard, which sufficed for the objective of attaining positive secularism.

Secularism, in the BJP's ideology, meant tolerance among different religious communities. The BJP's concept of 'positive secularism' was grounded in the Gandhian idea of secularism as a distillation of common moral values derived from different religions and different historical and civilizational experiences. The party felt that the Constitution already gave special rights to minorities. For example, special status for minority education institutions already existed even before the 42nd amendment. In other words, the Constitution which gave these special rights and which treated all religions as equal was already secular and there was no need for this amendment.

In the BJP's vision, secularism was about respecting all sects, *panth nirpekshta*, and no dominance of one over the other. Prior to British rule, the state in India had not coerced its population to follow the religion of the king. So, the party felt that the 42nd amendment was redundant and motivated. It, therefore, opposed this amendment.

A similar difference existed around the word 'socialism' as used by the BJP. Gandhian socialism aims to ultimately do away with both capitalism (private ownership) and socialism (state ownership, state control) and bring in their place a system of cooperation and trusteeship in all economic fields. The objective was a nationalist version of socialism described by Gandhi as *Hind Swaraj*.[47] The Gandhinagar National Executive on 9 October 1985, described the objective of the party thus: 'The Bharatiya Janata

Party aims at establishing a democratic state which guarantees to all its citizens irrespective of caste, creed or sex, political, social and economic justice, equality of opportunity and liberty of faith and expression.'[48]

The young party contemplated these lofty debates while it had to also engage in gritty practical politics. In 1980, the BJP contested assembly elections and fared poorly. It won twenty-one seats out of 324 in Bihar, nine out of 182 in Gujarat, eleven out of 425 in Uttar Pradesh, fourteen out of 288 in Maharashtra, thirty-two out of 200 in Rajasthan and sixty out of 320 in Madhya Pradesh.[49]

This kicked off a phase of organization building in one state after another, starting from the inherited Jana Sangh organization and party workers. These capabilities were put to test in the assembly elections in four states in 1982—in Himachal Pradesh, Haryana, Kerala and West Bengal—and an improvement of performance was discernible. In Haryana, the BJP won six of the 90 seats and in Himachal Pradesh, it won twenty-nine of the sixty-eight constituencies.[50] Apart from this, the BJP also won the by-elections held for the Thane and Jabalpur seats.[51] A year later, Vajpayee tried to re-initiate the Janata Party playbook, urging parties opposed to the Congress to come together in the form of a National Democratic Front. This move, however, did not gain much traction. The same untouchability that had once existed towards the Jana Sangh continued to plague the BJP.

Indira Gandhi's Assassination

The year 1984 was a watershed moment in Indian politics. The violence in Punjab had escalated for many years and had increasingly become an issue of national importance. Politics in Punjab consisted of competition between the Congress and the Akali Dal. While the green revolution of the 1960s had kicked off great prosperity, it had also initiated socio-economic changes which led to discontent among some Sikhs.[52] By the 1980s, the Khalistan movement came to challenge the Indian state through an insurgency. Pakistan fomented trouble for India by supporting the insurgency.[53]

It has been argued that Indira Gandhi saw the rise of Sikh radicalism as a useful tool, to turn Hindu voters in Punjab away from the Akali Dal and to the Congress.[54] She may have felt that going beyond Punjab, there could be a reaction in favour of the Congress all over North India in response to Sikh radicalism. However, the terrorism organized from the Golden Temple against Hindus went out of hand, and the union government chose to use military power to restore peace in the Golden Temple.[55]

Subsequent intelligence reports suggested that there was a threat to the PM's life. Unfortunately, these reports were ignored. In a tragic turn of events, four months after Operation Blue Star, on 31 October 1984, Indira Gandhi was assassinated by her bodyguards Satwant Singh and Beant Singh. This assassination shocked the nation. At the National Executive on 14 November 1984, Vajpayee said, 'Prime Minister Indira Gandhi is not amid us now. The callous hands of the killers have taken her away. As prime minister and leader of her party, she had to tour the entire country. She went to see the Golden Temple when tension in Punjab was at its peak. But this sad incident happened in her own house at the hands of those entrusted with her security. The incident makes it clear that despite the claims of impregnable security there are loopholes in the system. What can be a bigger embarrassment for the government than the fact that it could not even protect its own prime minister.'[56]

Indira's assassination was followed by riots in Delhi and other parts of India. Many Sikhs were killed in Delhi, about a million people were displaced and 3,000 lost their lives.[57] Congress leaders were suspected to be complicit in instigating the riots.[58] On 18 November 1984, Prime Minister Rajiv Gandhi said, 'When Indiraji was assassinated, some riots took place in our country. We know the hearts of Indians were filled with anger, and for some days, people felt that India was shaking. But when a big tree falls, then the earth does shake a little.'[59]

Rajiv Gandhi took office after the 1984 assassination of his
mother, to become the youngest Indian Prime Minister at the age
of forty. Elections were announced as soon as the mourning period
ended. A sympathy wave had emerged in favour of the Congress.
For many voters, to vote against the Congress at a time like this was
tantamount to supporting Indira Gandhi's murderers. This led to
a remarkable victory with 49.1 per cent vote share, and 415 seats,
for the Congress in the 1984 Lok Sabha elections. After the freedom
movement and Nehru's period as prime minister, the Congress had
experienced one peak in 1971 with 352 seats in the Lok Sabha.[60]
From that point onwards, Indira Gandhi's achievements and power
had declined. The 1984 elections represented the next peak for the
Congress as a viable political formation looking beyond Mahatma
Gandhi, Jawaharlal Nehru and Indira Gandhi. Few observers in
1984 could have envisioned that in coming years, the INC would fall
from grace, and that no single party in the Lok Sabha would ever get
back to such numbers.

For the young party, the BJP, the 1984 elections were a catastrophe,
as they won only two seats. The Jana Sangh had first tasted power as
part of the Janata Party. Of the 295 seats that the Janata Party had won
in 1977, ninety-three were by candidates who were formerly in the Jana
Sangh. There had been a slow sense of progress, of gradually finding
their feet in a Congress-dominated world. Crashing to two seats
interrupted this sense of progress and shattered the party's morale.[61]

Table 2: Lok Sabha Elections of 1984[62]

Political Party	LS 1980		LS 1984	
	Vote Share	Seats Won	Vote Share	Seats Won
Bharatiya Janata Party	-	-	7.74%	2
Indian National Congress(I)	42.69%	353	49.10%	404
Janata Party	18.97%	31	6.89%	10

In his presidential address in the party's executive committee meeting in March 1985, Vajpayee said, 'As the president of the party I take full moral responsibility on myself for the failure of our party in the assembly and Lok Sabha elections, and I shall be gladly willing to undergo any punishment that the party decides.'[63]

The adverse result demanded introspection and course correction. As Vajpayee put it, 'Firstly, was the party's defeat because of our decisions to merge Jana Sangh with the Janata Party in 1977 and to withdraw from the Janata Party in 1980? Secondly, should BJP go back and revive the Bharatiya Jana Sangh?'[64]

It seemed that the new name and the new symbol, the lotus, were more popular with members. Party workers who had moved ahead with the 'BJP and the *kamal*' did not want to go back to the 'Jana Sangh and the *diya*'. After long deliberations, the party decided to not go back but to stay with 'BJP and the *kamal*'.[65]

On Vajpayee's suggestion, the National Executive constituted a working committee to study the party's working style and prepare an action plan for the next five years. Krishna Lal Sharma was made the head of the committee to rethink the party's orientation and draw the roadmap for the next five years. The committee invited feedback from state offices. The working committee presented its report to the National Executive in Gandhinagar. To Vajpayee's question of whether the BJP should revive the Jana Sangh, the report stated: 'We are very much proud of Jana Sangh heritage; we benefited by our experience when we were in the Janata Party and that we will march ahead by building up BJP, towards our cherished objectives.'[66]

The report of the working committee also underlined the importance of ideology. It said, 'The statement that the BJP is a party with a difference means that the party, amongst other things, possesses an ideology which is not fully shared by others. In ultimate analysis the strength and spread of a political party will also depend upon its ideological appeal.'

Based on the analysis of the report, the National Council decided that the basic philosophy of the party would be centred on integral humanism, propounded by Pandit Deen Dayal Upadhyaya. It restated its commitments to Gandhian socialism, democracy, nationalism and national integration, positive secularism and values-based politics.[67]

The party decided to broaden its base, strengthen its cadre, focus on women and youth, and penetrate rural areas and weaker sections of the society. The new party did not have a dedicated voter base at the time. The BJP felt that the Congress enjoyed the support of the rural population and minorities through the politics of appeasement. The Communists had a base in working classes. The BJP needed to create a comparable constituency. To this end, the organizational structure of *morchas* and cells was adopted, which laid the foundations of the party's expansion in the years to come. People working in various fields are not able to associate themselves with politics because they are not able to figure out work, campaigns and specific tasks for themselves in mainstream political parties. The youth have a different approach to things, programmes and plans. They have different interests. Similarly, people who come from scheduled castes and scheduled tribes or other backward classes also have different expectations from politics. Morchas and cells within the party help accommodate the aspirations and interests of such groups. The Mahila Morcha helps women participate actively in politics and work on women-related issues. It ensures that women do not hesitate to join the political workspace. The morchas and cells are imperative to increasing political awakening and participation across various groups in the society.

The BJP set up Yuva Morcha, Mahila Morcha, Kisan Morcha and Morchas for Scheduled Castes and Scheduled Tribes, which would be homogeneous in some respects (for instance, Yuva Morcha would have only youth, Mahila Morcha only women, etc) and create a BJP network in that space. They were not meant to compartmentalize the party but to create channels to let different groups of people into the BJP. This arrangement allowed people who might have been uncomfortable with the BJP to associate with an extended element of a network of organizations.

Apart from the morchas, the BJP set up various cells such as Ex-Army Cell, Intellectual Cell, Economic Cell, Foreign Policy Cell, Cultural Cell and Legal Cell. This allowed professionals from various fields to associate with the party and strengthen the BJP on policy matters. While morchas were formed for mass-based programmes and agitational politics, cells were deliberative groups that devised strategies.

There was also a decision to regularly engage in activities like blood donation, tree plantation and literacy drives, so as to attract the common man to the BJP.

Deen Dayal Upadhyaya's death anniversary, 11 February, was chosen to be commemorated as Samarpan Divas. The party also decided to mark 6 April, the BJP's Sthapna Diwas (Foundation Day), and the week running up to 14 April—Dr B.R. Ambedkar Jayanti— as the Foundation Week. Given that the BJP had a round-the-year enrolment programme, a protocol was established where this week was focused solely on fund-raising. The idea was to get funds not from the BJP members or close sympathizers, who contributed on Samarpan Divas, but to obtain small donations from a broader range of sympathizers. The idea was that a sympathizer tended to cross over into becoming a supporter in the act of rationalizing a small donation.

Sharma's report said that the BJP's organization was its main strength and that the party should use this strength to realize its political goals. The working committee report set the roadmap to put together organization, ideology, leaders and cadre to move ahead from the 1984 debacle.

The Congress Party under Rajiv Gandhi

After the 1984 elections, the Congress government, led by Rajiv Gandhi, took office. Rajiv Gandhi was young and energetic. He was backed by a huge mandate. The new team that came in with Rajiv, however, had his close friends who were not too well versed with the Congress's culture and style of functioning.

Around the same time, the BJP was moving ahead with a new batch of young leaders—first under Vajpayee and then under Advani in 1986.

In the 1980s, some leaders from the Sangh joined the BJP. As the party took shape under Vajpayee and Advani, many young leaders emerged on the horizon and began doing groundwork for the newly formed party. Venkaiah Naidu, who joined as general secretary, came to the party through student politics. Hard-working Naidu was a polyglot. Rajnath Singh was associated with Yuva Morcha. Other leaders such as Pramod Mahajan, Kalraj Mishra, Kalyan Singh, Brahm Dutt Dwivedi and K.N. Govindacharya also came onboard the BJP. Among this battery of leaders was Narendra Modi, who joined the BJP's Gujarat unit.

It was a time when the Congress party needed to reflect on the difficulties of the Indira Gandhi years and pull back towards the older healthy traditions of the party. Instead, Rajiv Gandhi accelerated the process of centralization of power that had begun with Indira Gandhi, through which the Congress lost its impersonal institutional capacity. He functioned by minimizing the role of the organization with very centralized decision-making and power concentrated in the hands of a small coterie.[68]

Under Indira Gandhi, intra-party democracy had broken down, and obedient individuals loyal to her were placed at the head of Pradesh Congress Committees.[69] Rajiv Gandhi did not restore elections and intra-party dispersion of power: He merely replaced Indira Gandhi's coterie with his own. The Congress remained leader-driven and completely dependent on Rajiv Gandhi.[70] Advisors such as Arun Nehru and Arun Singh who came from private sector backgrounds became very powerful, but they were inexperienced in politics.

As is often the case, such an approach to decision-making created political blunders. By 1985, barely a year after the huge victory, the

Congress lost assembly elections in many states including Punjab, Assam, Karnataka, Andhra Pradesh, West Bengal and Tamil Nadu.

Corruption Scandals

The Rajiv Gandhi government soon saw the emergence of corruption scams. The serious charges of corruption that went right to the doorstep of the Congress prime minister made people think about a political alternative. The BJP, whose leaders came with a clean image, raised the corruption issues vehemently in public and that began to weaken the Congress's electoral roots.

On 16 April 1987, the Swedish Radio broadcast claimed that the Swedish arms manufacturer, A.B. Bofors, paid bribes to top Indian politicians and defence personnel to secure the 1986 deal for the supply of 400 155 mm Howitzer guns for the Indian Army.[71] The Government of India and A.B. Bofors denied the allegations. Four months later, a Joint Parliamentary Committee, headed by B. Shankaranand, was constituted to investigate the allegations. The Committee submitted its report in April 1988, concluding that there was no evidence to substantiate the allegations that commissions and bribes were paid to anyone, or any middlemen were involved in the acquisition process.[72] The report came under severe criticism for giving a clean chit to the Rajiv Gandhi government. The leader of the All India Anna Dravida Munnetra Kazhagam (AIADMK) in the Rajya Sabha, Aladi Aruna, who was also a member of the JPC, wrote in a dissenting note, 'The conclusions of the report conceal the facts of the deal and cover up the connivance of our government with Bofors and refuse to identify the recipients, who could be none other than Indians or Indian associates, or both.'[73][74] In January 1990, shortly after V.P. Singh became Prime Minister, the Central Bureau of Investigation (CBI), the central investigating agency of the country, lodged an official complaint with the police by registering a First Information Report (FIR) against Martin Ardbo, the then president of A.B. Bofors, alleged middleman Win Chadda and Hinduja brothers.

Another controversy erupted over a 1981 deal with the German company HDW [Howaldtswerke-Deutsche Werft] for the delivery of four submarines at the cost of Rs 465 crore by the end of 1987.[75] By 1987, only two submarines were delivered. In February 1987, V.P. Singh, the then defence minister, received information that HDW may have overcharged the Government of India. He ordered that the price of the remaining two submarines be renegotiated. The Indian Ambassador, J.C. Ajmani, informed Singh that the Germans were not inclined to renegotiate the price as it included a 7 per cent commission they had paid to secure the contract. In April 1987, Singh ordered an inquiry into the deal. These events created a rift between Rajiv Gandhi and defence minister, V.P. Singh. Ultimately V.P. Singh resigned from the government, owing to conflicts about the handling of corruption allegations in the HDW submarines deal.[76]

4

Decade of Growth (1986–1996)

Following the defeat of the Congress party in all state elections held between 1985 and 1986, Rajiv Gandhi was concerned about losing Muslim votes.[1] This resulted in a landmark event in the history of the Congress's relationship with Muslims, the Shah Bano case. Political scientist Zoya Hasan describes the events leading up to the Congress's 'excessive regard for Muslim sensibilities on personal law' as follows: 'Halfway through his five-year term as prime minister, Rajiv Gandhi had faltered in most of his major initiatives. What had, however, created the greatest problems for him and the Congress were the compromising overtures and tactics that he had been advised to adopt towards the demands of the various religious communities and their sundry anxieties.'[2] The first among these was when 'the prime minister, concerned about losing Muslim support, decided to enact the Muslim Women's (Protection of Rights on Divorce) Act (MWA) of 1986.' This was done to reverse the landmark Supreme Court judgment, which granted a maintenance allowance to Shah Bano, a seventy-three-year-old Muslim divorcee, to be paid by her husband under the Criminal Procedure Code (CrPc).[3]

The episode unfolded when the Supreme Court delivered its verdict in a 1978 case in which Shah Bano and her five children were thrown out of the house by her husband Mohammad Ahmad

Khan. Shah Bano then knocked at the doors of courts demanding maintenance. The case reached the Supreme Court. On 23 April 1985, the Supreme Court ruled in favour of Shah Bano and directed her former husband to provide her monthly maintenance.[4] Some religious leaders and public intellectuals opposed the Supreme Court verdict on the grounds that it interfered with Islamic laws.[5][6][7] Faced with a series of political difficulties, in what appears to have been an attempt to shore up support among Muslims, in 1986, Rajiv Gandhi used his massive majority in Parliament to enact a law to overturn the Supreme Court verdict. The Act, the Muslim Women's (Protection of Rights on Divorce) Act (MWA) of 1986, was clearly discriminatory as it denied Muslim women the right to maintenance from their husbands, a right that was given to non-Muslim women in the country.

Rajiv Gandhi's attempt to overturn the Supreme Court verdict was opposed even within the Congress party. Minister of state Arif Mohammad Khan resigned from his post following the government's decision.[8] Another section in the Congress opposed it on the grounds that the party's stand on the Shah Bano case might adversely affect support among Hindus. For many years, the BJP had claimed that the Congress was interventionist with regard to the reforms of Hindu personal laws, and comfortable with using state power to push towards a more liberal ethos, but at the same time it refrained from interfering with traditional Muslim customs. L.K. Advani had termed this one-sided approach 'pseudo-secularism'. The passage of the MWA gave the BJP a practical situation in which it could substantiate its long-standing view. This helped the BJP gain greater traction among the majority of India who had otherwise treated the BJP with caution. People came to realise that the Congress was no longer a reformist party and was merely doing vote-bank politics, while it was the BJP which was taking up reformist issues. Perhaps understanding this, Rajiv Gandhi once again played the pseudo-secularism card trying to win back the Hindu trust that he had lost.

Ram Janambhoomi Agitation

The movement for a temple in Ayodhya is based on the fact that the Ram Temple was built in Ayodhya at Shri Ram's birthplace. According to Hindu scriptures, Ram Lalla Virajman is the infant Lord Ram. Under Mughal ruler Babur, Ayodhya's Ram temple was destroyed in 1528 and the Babri structure was built on the ruins of the temple. It is believed that from 1526 to 1858, various cultural and religious festivals continued at the site under Mughal rule and that a wall was built for the first time in 1858, with Hindus praying in the Sita Rasoi area, and Muslims taking possession of the main site where Ram Lalla was born.[9]

The first litigation in the matter was filed in 1885 by Mahant Raghubar Das. Ram Lalla, a deity, is a juristic entity who has the right to sue and be sued in the Indian legal system. In 1934, after a struggle between the two communities, the area that the Muslims believed to be the mosque was abandoned. After Independence, the issue of rebuilding the Ram temple re-emerged. In the late 1980s, sensing a rising anger towards his government after the Congress's move to change Muslim Personal Law, Rajiv Gandhi became worried about losing Hindu votes.[10] The District and Sessions Judge of Faizabad, ordered the locks of the Babri mosque to be opened for Hindu worshippers on 1 February 1986.[11]

According to reports at the time, the Congress leadership, acting through Arun Nehru, ensured that the doors opened within an hour of the Faizabad district judge's ruling.[12] In 1989, a lawsuit was moved by former Allahabad High Court judge Deoki Nandan Agarwal for Ram Lalla, as the next friend of the deity.[13] In this suit, the deity, Ram Lalla, was seeking the title right. This was done on the grounds that the land itself had the character of the deity and of a 'juristic entity'.

In 1986, the BJP presidency had passed on from Vajpayee to Advani.[14] The BJP now started redesigning its strategy under the new leadership. Advani set three dimensions for the party—organizational, ideological and an orientation towards growth.

Organizationally, the party laid a lot of emphasis on expansion of membership. On the ideological front, the BJP brought the issue of nationalism to centre stage. This issue had been raised by Mahatma Gandhi but the vote bank politics of Congress overshadowed it after Independence. The BJP, under Advani, pushed forth cultural nationalism because the party believed India's nationalism was imbued in its cultural ethos.

The BJP emerged as the Congress government's principal opposition, attacking the Rajiv Gandhi administration on issues ranging from secularism to corruption and internal security. The party issued a 50-point chargesheet highlighting the mistakes and failures of the government and demanded that there be a time-bound investigation into all corruption-related cases, including Bofors. The BJP agitated on both the national and regional levels on a host of issues. Under Advani's leadership, young leaders such as Venkaiah Naidu, Kalyan Singh, Narendra Modi, Rajnath Singh, Arun Jaitley, Pramod Mahajan, Sushma Swaraj, Gopinath Munde, Uma Bharti and Mukhtar Abbas Naqvi were given important responsibilities.

For the first time, the party took a strong stance on the issue of Ram Mandir. A resolution was passed in June 1989, during the Palampur session in Himachal Pradesh. It said: 'The BJP holds that the nature of this controversy is such that it just cannot be sorted out by a court of law . . . The BJP calls upon the Rajiv Government to adopt the same positive approach in respect of Ayodhya that the Nehru Government did with respect to Somnath. The sentiments of the people must be respected, and Ram Janmasthan (Ram's birthplace) handed over to the Hindus—if possible through a negotiated settlement or else, by legislation. Litigation certainly is no answer.'[15]

In this resolution, the BJP asserted that when Mughal emperor Babur came to India in 1528, he demolished the temple that existed on Ram Janmabhoomi and built a mosque over it. The BJP argued that it was a pious site linked to the people's belief and Hindus had been living for years with the hope that a temple would be built on the site. The party contended that during the war of Independence against the British in 1857, Muslims had accepted the Hindu claim to build a temple on the site in view of their sentiments and that the British, who believed in the policy of divide and rule, did not let the agreement fructify.[16] The BJP's resolution also said Muslims should forgo their claim on the Ram Janmabhoomi, keeping in mind Hindu sentiments. The party declared that it would take the matter of the temple in its own hands. The BJP attacked the Congress for having a callous attitude towards the sentiments of the overwhelming majority in this country—the Hindus.[17] The party demanded that Ram Mandir be built at the site and included the temple construction on its agenda.

The Palampur session in 1989 was the turning point for the BJP's demand for the Ram Mandir. It laid the foundation for an agitational programme to take the BJP's message from cities to remote villages of India. The BJP's cells and morchas, meanwhile, provided platforms for people to join the party. The BJP had supported and demanded 33 per cent reservation for women in Parliament. The party had vehemently opposed Roop Kanwar's decision to perform sati in the Deorala village of Sikar district in Rajasthan. The party also criticised caste-based discrimination vehemently and expanded its base in Adivasi areas. This allowed the BJP to grow as a cadre-based mass party with progressive values.

In November 1989, the Vishwa Hindu Parishad (VHP) performed a *shilanyas* (foundation stone laying) ceremony at the Ram Mandir. The litigation in the Ram Janambhoomi case had been going on since 1949. In 1989, the Faizabad sessions court ordered the reopening of the Ram Janmabhoomi temple complex in Ayodhya so that Hindus could offer prayers. The VHP committed itself to building the Ram Temple in Ayodhya. In light of the reaction to his stance on the Shah Bano case, Rajiv Gandhi allowed the shilanyas to take place, hoping to turn Hindu votes in his favour.

As Zoya Hasan writes, 'For the Congress, the two decisions—the revocation of the Shah Bano verdict and the reopening of the gates to the mosque in Ayodhya—were part of a "grand" strategy to arrest its declining hold over Hindu and Muslim votes.'[18] This 'grand strategy' was a historic mistake for the Congress.

V.P. Singh Government and the Mandal Agitation

In April 1987, Rajiv Gandhi's cabinet minister, V.P. Singh had openly rebelled. On 12 April 1987, he had resigned from Cabinet.[19][20] He was expelled from the Congress(I) party. In 1988, Congress dissident leaders led by V.P. Singh formed the Janata Dal, along with two other political factions including the socialist parties led by Chandra Shekhar.[21] In 1989, the Janata Dal was formally recognised as a party in the Lok Sabha.[22] V.P. Singh brought together a spectrum of parties, ranging from regional -organizations such as the Telugu Desam Party, the Dravida Munnetra Kazhagam and the Asom Gana Parishad. The National Front had N.T. Rama Rao as the president and V.P. Singh as the convener with outside support from the BJP.

This consolidation of votes became important in the 1989 elections. Alongside this, the Rajiv Gandhi government was marred by numerous allegations of corruption. As a consequence, in the 1989 elections, while Congress got 39.53 per cent of the votes, it only got 197 seats.[23]

V.P. Singh's Janata Dal won 143 seats; the National Front Coalition, including the Janata Dal party, won 146 seats; the Communist Party of India (Marxist) won thirty-three seats; and the Communist Party of India got twelve seats.[24] The BJP, which had won just two seats in 1984, took everyone by surprise, winning eighty-five seats and emerging as the third-largest party. Its vote share increased to 11.36 per cent. With this, the BJP was finally back to a respectable performance that could compare with that achieved twelve years ago in 1977. After the 1989 election results, the BJP was no longer just a north Indian, upper caste, peripheral party as suggested by the party's detractors.

Table 1: Lok Sabha Elections of 1989[25]

Political Party	LS 1984		LS 1989	
	Vote Share	Seats Won	Vote Share	Seats Won
Bharatiya Janata Party	7.74%	2	11.36%	85
Indian National Congress(I)	49.10%	404	39.53%	197
Janata Dal	-	-	17.80%	143

This was the time when Congress had openly opposed backward class reservation. The BJP, on the other hand, had advocated social justice and an egalitarian society by including it as a promise in its election manifesto.

Simultaneously, the RSS was working for the welfare of tribals through its *Vanvasi Kalyan Ashram* programmes. This helped the BJP connect with tribal areas and connect them with its broader cultural nationalism programme. The base prepared by the RSS in these areas helped the BJP in later years gain success on Scheduled Tribes (ST) seats.

After this fractured mandate, the National Front coalition formed a minority government and came to power with outside support of the BJP and the Communist parties. For the BJP, support from the outside was viewed as a mechanism to avoid the earlier experiences of the Janata Party. The leader of the National Front, V.P. Singh, became the Prime Minister. This was a precarious situation as the ruling party had assured support from only 146 legislators out of 529 and relied on support from two ideologically distinct groups. These three groups had come together due to their antipathy for Rajiv Gandhi and the hope that they could parley their support for the administration for better electoral prospects in the future.[26] Since the government relied on outside support from the BJP on one end and the Communist parties on the other, it constantly required consensus from diverse groups.

Everyone at the time understood that this was a difficult situation for the ruling coalition. Political strategists of the ruling party looked for the big political move—akin to the Shah Bano case and Ram temple opening—that could shore up support for the government. On 7 August 1990, the V.P. Singh government decided to implement the recommendations of the Mandal Commission report that had been ignored for years. Going by the recommendations of the Mandal report, the government announced a decision to grant 27 per cent reservation to Other Backward Classes (OBCs). As with the other two big moves, the law of unintended consequences took over. Massive protests by members of the upper castes erupted across the country, resulting in many deaths, while the government hung on to the decision hoping to obtain votes from OBCs. In his Lok Sabha speech Rajiv Gandhi opposed the implementation of the Mandal report. He said, 'I charge you with this—you have taken the country to the edge of caste wars . . . Sir, Raja Sahib's policies are not very different from what the Britishers were doing. It was the British who tried to divide our country on caste and religion and today it is the Raja Sahib, sitting there, who is trying to divide our country on caste and religion.'[27]

The Congress had not implemented the recommendations of the Kaka Kalelkar Commission, aka the First Backward Classes Commission, which submitted its report in 1955. The party had implemented the recommendations of the Mandal Commission, which was set up during the Janata Party era in 1979 and had submitted its report in 1980. And, when the V.P. Singh government tried to implement the report, the Congress opposed it.

The Rath Yatra

The Mandal agitation was an important phase in the history of the nation. National politics had degenerated with each move made by the incumbent government, where the political leadership staved off unpopularity by using state power in order to appeal to one narrow constituency after another (Muslims, Hindus, OBCs). These moves were divisive; they tore the country apart on religious and caste lines. They were inconsistent with the BJP's vision of a unified country, a country tied by cultural nationalism. The RSS believed that a civilization cannot be negated. The civilizational values of all societies are important and progress of a society must be rooted in the same values. There needed to be removal of all ills, vices and discriminatory practices in the realization of this cultural nationalism.

In 1973, Madhukar Dattatraya Deoras, popularly known as Balasaheb Deoras, became the RSS *sarsanghchalak* (chief). He was a strong advocate of reservations.[28] During his seminal Pune speech of 1974, he said, 'If untouchability is not wrong, nothing is wrong.' When the issue of caste-based reservations came up for discussion in the RSS, Balasaheb Deoras said, 'Put yourself in a role of a dalit and then discuss if reservations are required or not.'[29]

Deoras was moderate. He understood the essence of the Ram Mandir issue agitation as linked to India's cultural nationalism. In the 1980s, the *Ganga Ekatmata Yatra* was organized by the Vishva Hindu Parishad on the insistence of Deoras for Hindu unity.[30] During the yatra, water from Ganga was carried in giant urns on cow-driven carts to different parts of the country.

The RSS ran a nationwide campaign in India when Eknath Ranade decided to set up Vivekananda Kendra at Kanyakumari in Tamil Nadu in 1972. From the common man to state chief ministers, everyone was invited to participate in the setting up of the Kendra.

The Meenakshipuram conversion of 1981 in which 800 Dalits converted to Islam had been taken very seriously by the RSS. Balasaheb Deoras asked the Sangh Parivar to work directly with marginalized Hindu communities. Under Deoras, the RSS gave a boost to *sewa karya* through its swayamsevaks and sister organizations. Deoras had decided to expand the RSS work to include the marginalized. Ram was seen as the cultural symbol of India and a mandir at his birthplace an issue of faith, which the RSS rallied behind.

In 1989, the RSS celebrated the birth centenary of Keshav Baliram Hedgewar. Despite being unwell, Balasaheb travelled extensively for the preparations. As many as 50,000 committees were formed for the centenary celebrations. The idea was to galvanize Hindus as one people through the events held to mark the occasion. So, even as the BJP was gaining ground, the RSS was growing in its reach.

It was against this background that Advani decided to go on a Ram Rath Yatra (Lord Ram's chariot procession) hoping to bridge the divides that had been created in Hindu society and increase consciousness against the Congress' 'pseudo-secularism'.[31] The BJP said it would take the whole society together without caste divisions. This yatra began on 25 September 1990 from Somnath in Gujarat and ended on 30 October 1990 in Ayodhya in Uttar Pradesh, over a period of thirty-six days. While the shortest distance between the two cities is 1,750 km, a much more circuitous route of 10,000 km was adopted, so as to cover more districts and important population centres. The BJP leaders, workers and sympathizers showed up in force to amplify the impact of the yatra.

Narendra Modi, who had been a humble RSS *pracharak*, emerged on the national stage for the first time. He had first come to notice after the 1985 assembly elections in Gujarat, where the BJP did badly, close on the heels of the failure in the 1984 parliamentary elections. Against this backdrop, Modi was given the responsibility of organizing the BJP's campaign for the city elections in Ahmedabad in 1987. He built a highly systematic approach to fighting these elections, and the BJP won two-thirds of the seats. This approach was, in a way, a prelude to the booth-level management that the BJP came to be known for many years later. After this success in 1987, Modi was drawn into organization work for Advani's yatra, working out its first leg through 600 villages in Gujarat.[32]

This was still an age where video delivery into homes through television sets was not mainstream, which meant that media coverage was primarily through print. The BJP succeeded in capturing the imagination of the print media which played up the significance of this yatra. It began with a prayer at the Somnath temple, where prominent politicians like Vijayaraje Scindia and Sikander Bakht were present, along with many other BJP dignitaries.

At every stop, Advani gave speeches. He said that the Ram Rath Yatra was a symbol of power and aspirations of the 70 crore Hindus of the country. In reality, for the BJP, the issue of Ayodhya was not about a land dispute; it was a mission to unite India with the thread of cultural nationalism. The BJP stood for appeasement for none. The Congress, which was attempting a balancing act between Muslim appeasement and small enticements for the Hindu community, accused the yatra of raising anti-Muslim sentiment. Countering this, while addressing a mass gathering in Bhopal's Imami Gate, Advani said that though he had completed a journey of 4,000 km, he had not said a single word hurtful to the Muslims or any other community.[33] He emphasized that the yatra was 'a crusade against pseudo-secularism and minorityism which I regard as a political issue.'[34]

The yatra kicked off a greater political mobilization than was anticipated, making the V.P. Singh government uneasy.[35][36] On 23 October 1990, when the yatra reached Samastipur in Bihar, Advani was arrested on the orders of the then chief minister of Bihar, Lalu Prasad Yadav. As a consequence, the BJP withdrew support to the government. V.P. Singh lost the vote of confidence in Parliament on 7 November 1990.[37] In May 1991 the country went to polls again. The elections were held against the backdrop of the assassination of Congress party's prime ministerial face Rajiv Gandhi.

When results of the 1991 Lok Sabha elections were declared, though the Congress got back to power with 232 seats that gave India leadership of a coalition, the BJP emerged as the main Opposition party with over 120 seats. The Janata Dal with sixty-nine seats, emerged as the third-largest party.

Table 2: Lok Sabha Elections of 1991[38]

Political Party	LS 1989		LS 1991	
	Vote Share	Seats Won	Vote Share	Seats Won
Bharatiya Janata Party	11.36%	85	20.11%	120
Indian National Congress	39.53%	197	36.26%	232
Janata Dal	17.80%	143	11.84%	59

With a 20.11 per cent vote share, the BJP had almost doubled its vote percentage in comparison to the 1989 general elections when it had won 11.36 per cent votes.[39] This proved that the new political strategies of the BJP were successful. The party won fifty-one of the eighty-five Lok Sabha seats in Uttar Pradesh where emotions about the Ram temple ran high. The Ram temple was also an emotional issue in adjoining regions of north India. After Advani's arrest at Samastipur, the Ram Janmabhoomi movement continued through kar sevaks (volunteers) who proceeded with the march.[40] On 2 November 1990, some kar sevaks offered prayers to Ram Lalla in the morning and then proceeded to the Babri structure. Fearing violence, the police used tear gas and baton charges to disperse the crowd. Nevertheless, some groups of karsevaks reached the mosque.[41] In response, the police opened fire and chased karsevaks through the alleys around Hanumangarhi in which many were killed.

The violence by UP Police had a major impact on Uttar Pradesh and on Indian national politics. The chief minister of Uttar Pradesh, Mulayam Singh Yadav, was accused by the BJP of being pro-Muslim.[42] Yadav described his decision to order firing on the crowd in Ayodhya as 'painful yet necessary as it was ordered by the high court to maintain peace, law and order till the judgment came out'.[43] Hindu activists arranged a memorial meeting for the deceased on 4 April 1991, at the Boat Club, New Delhi. They also launched a nationwide programme displaying the *asthi kalash* (funeral urns) of the dead.[44] Passions about the Ram temple were mightily stirred and there was anger in the country.

In the meanwhile, assembly elections were held in Uttar Pradesh. For the first time in its history, with slogans like '*Ram Lalla hum aayenge, mandir wahin banayenge*', ('Lord Ram, we will come and the temple will be made in the same place'), the party campaigned for votes aggressively. The BJP came to power winning 221 of the 425 seats in the 1991 Uttar Pradesh assembly election.

Table 3: Uttar Pradesh Assembly Elections of 1991[45]

Political Party	AE 1989		LS 1991		AE 1991	
	Vote Share	Seats Won	Vote Share	Seats Won	Vote Share	Seats Won
Bharatiya Janata Party	11.61%	57	32.82%	51	31.45%	221
Indian National Congress	27.90%	94	18.02%	5	17.32%	46
Janata Dal	29.71%	208	21.27%	22	18.84%	92
Bahujan Samaj Party	9.41%	13	8.7%	1	9.44%	12

Kalyan Singh, a Lodh leader belonging to the OBC category, was elected the chief minister of Uttar Pradesh on 24 June 1991. There had been a decline in law and order under the previous Samajwadi Party rule, and Singh worked on restoring the peace. Immediately after taking oath as the chief minister, Singh visited Ayodhya and vowed to build a Ram temple on the site. Four months later, in October 1991, his government acquired land around the Babri complex. He gave the Supreme Court an assurance that the mosque would not be demolished.

But on 6 December 1992 the Babri structure was brought down. Kalyan Singh resigned from chief ministership that evening, taking moral responsibility. The union government dissolved the

assembly and banned the RSS, the VHP and the Bajrang Dal. The
union government used this opportunity to dismiss the elected BJP
governments in Rajasthan, Madhya Pradesh and Himachal Pradesh.

In a conversation with the author (Bhupender Yadav), Arun
Jaitley once said that when the Babri structure was demolished there
was no scope for a decision on how to react. When the group of
karsevaks started marching, the leaders present at the site urged them
to stop. H.V. Sheshadri, joint general secretary, in fact, appealed
them to stop in many languages.

A special CBI court in 2020 that heard the matter observed that
the Babri Mosque demolition incident 'was not pre-planned'. The
court said that the accused people were, in fact, trying to control the
crowds.[46]

On 16 December 1992, P. V. Narasimha Rao set up the Liberhan
Commission to inquire into the demolition. This commission,
which was formed under a Congress government, submitted its
report seventeen years later to a Congress government in 2009,
and was largely ineffectual. Speaking on the debate in Lok Sabha,
Rajnath Singh said: 'The commission has taken recourse to
deductive logic to arrive at a pre-determined conclusion.'[47] In the
Rajya Sabha debates, Arun Jaitley called the report 'a national joke'
and said 'He (Justice Liberhan) errs on basic facts . . . gets the date
of Mahatma Gandhi's assassination wrong . . . puts M.A. Jinnah's
words in the mouth of Deen Dayal Upadhyaya and you want
the country to take the report seriously? . . . The only person the
commission had been kind to was its own appointing authority—
Shri P.V. Narasimha Rao.'[48]

The Ram temple movement got the BJP enormous popular
support. It brought the party firmly into the mainstream,
particularly in north India where Ram is an important element of
everyday religious practices and beliefs. It got the party into the
position of winning elections in a major state, Uttar Pradesh, which
kicked off organizational strengthening there and attracted party
workers to join the BJP in many states. BJP's support to the Ram

temple movement reduced the influence of the Congress, which lost support of both Hindus and Muslims, and never regained salience in the Hindi heartland.[49]

Coalition Governments

This was an era in which family and caste-based parties were rising in Uttar Pradesh and Bihar. In addition, small regional parties in UP and Bihar, like the Rashtriya Janata Dal, the Samajwadi Party and the Bahujan Samaj Party, started emulating the Congress's strategy of trying to win the Muslim vote bank. Over a decade, the vote share of the Congress collapsed through a loss of voters to the BJP and these new parties.

On the national front, however, as the V.P. Singh government fell, Chandrashekhar became the Prime Minister with the support of the Congress on 1 December 1990. Chandrashekhar told Rajiv Gandhi that Congress should join the government. Rajiv Gandhi, in turn, assured Chandrashekhar that his party leaders would join over the next two–three months.

The Congress did not keep its promise of joining it. On the contrary, in March 1991, the party abruptly withdrew its support. The Congress alleged that the Chandrashekhar government was using the Haryana Police to conduct surveillance on Rajiv Gandhi.

Some believe that the real reason why the Congress withdrew support from the government was that Chandrashekhar was close to resolving the Ram temple issue and this was unacceptable to Rajiv Gandhi. According to a book written by Rajya Sabha deputy chairman Harivansh titled *Chandra Shekhar—The Last Icon of Ideological Politics*, the former Prime Minister, along with then chief ministers Sharad Pawar, Mulayam Singh Yadav and Bhairon Singh Shekhawat, had mediated between VHP and Muslim leaders on the temple issue in 1990. Quoting veteran journalist Ram Bahadur Rai, a close associate of Jaiprakash Narayan, the book says that it is widely believed that the Chandra Shekhar government was 'on the cusp of solving the Babri mosque-Ram Janmabhoomi dispute by promulgating an ordinance'.[50]

According to Harivansh, after getting the information on preparation of such an ordinance, then Congress president Rajiv Gandhi and his 'coterie of advisers' panicked as they 'did not want Chandrashekhar to gain in stature' by resolving such a complex problem. Harivansh further says that Chandrashekhar, during his tenure as prime minister, did not hesitate in taking some of the boldest initiatives to reduce the overt belligerence between the purported leaders of the Hindu (VHP) and Muslim communities (BMAC—the Babri Mosque Action Committee). He adopted a straightforward approach to look for a peaceful and permanent solution to the dispute by engaging openly with the conflicting parties.[51]

In the event, after the Congress withdrew support, no majority coalition was feasible, and the ninth Lok Sabha was dissolved. Barely sixteen months after an election, the country faced another election. The election for the tenth Lok Sabha was held in three phases. In a shocking turn of events, the day after voting in the first phase of the elections was completed, on 20 May 1991, Rajiv Gandhi was assassinated while campaigning in Sriperumbudur, Chennai, in Tamil Nadu. His assassin, a suicide bomber, Dhanu, was a member of the Liberation Tigers of Tamil Eelam (LTTE). The LTTE was opposed to India's intervention in Sri Lanka.

Rajiv Gandhi's assassination once again created a sympathy wave in favour of the Congress. Despite the wave, however, the BJP managed to perform well and was in the Opposition, reaching the three-digit mark at 120 seats for the first time.

The BJP had been limited to two seats in 1984 owing to the sympathy wave in favour of Congress. The BJP's ideological commitment set the party on the path of a steady rise. The climb to 120 seats was an organic growth for the party and was a result of the work that had been done at the organizational and ideological levels. Having suffered a setback as a constituent of the Janata Party, the BJP finally emerged successful at restructuring itself as a new party and found the organizational and political pathways to power.[52] Over the next five years, the BJP played the role of a responsible Opposition.

The death of Rajiv Gandhi left the Congress with having to choose a new leadership. There was no clarity if someone from the Gandhi family could immediately take over. Under these circumstances, Narasimha Rao, who had almost retired from Central politics, emerged on the centre stage of national politics.

P.V. Narasimha Rao had been a minister in both Rajiv Gandhi and Indira Gandhi's Cabinets. Before Rajiv Gandhi's death, P.V. Narasimha Rao was at the end of his political career. It is said that Rao had packed his bags from Delhi and was planning to return to his village in Andhra Pradesh, exiting active politics.[53] After the demise of Rajiv Gandhi, the leadership of the Congress fell upon him.

With 232 seats, Congress did not have a majority; Rao had to navigate the landscape of finding and retaining coalition partners. Indeed, it is said that Rao initiated the power sharing arrangements for a stable coalition in the union government, which was carried forward by Vajpayee in the NDA-1 period, and later termed 'coalition dharma'. While this balancing act was adroitly maintained through the five years, it did suffer from allegations about bribes paid by Rao to MPs from the Jharkhand Mukti Morcha and Janata Dal for their support when faced with a no-confidence motion in 1993.[54]

When Rao took office from Chandrashekhar, the Indian economy was in doldrums. The economic crisis was a consequence of the socialist policies followed by the Congress for many decades. The licence-permit-raid raj built under these policies had induced economic stagnation, and the country was not able to cope with the consequences of the Kuwait war of 1990-91. By March 1991, the current account deficit in India's balance of payments had touched a record level of nearly US$ 10 billion. This was more than 3 per cent of GDP. During this period, despite falling imports, there was a further decline in gross official reserves to US$ 1.7 billion which was equivalent to about three weeks of imports by the end of June 1991.[55] India's short-term external debt shot up while foreign currency reserves were barely a billion dollars. The situation was so bad that in order to tide over the balance of payment crisis, the Chandrashekhar government mortgaged forty-seven tonnes of gold, which was well reported in newspapers and electronic media.

The task of pulling out the economy from this mess was a huge challenge facing the Rao government. Alongside this, India also faced a foreign policy problem, when the collapse of the USSR in 1989 deprived it of an important geo-strategic partner with whom a stable arrangement had been established for the 1971–1989 period. Owing to the Gulf crisis, there was also a sharp increase in oil prices at the start of September 1990 coupled with depleting remittances.

The response to this situation could have been to try to muddle through, as is the wont of many governments in India. Rao chose to play on a bigger scale. He turned India away from Nehruvian socialism in favour of economic liberalization.

The reforms at the time carried forward the liberalization of the economy which had begun in 1977 when the Janata Party took charge. In July 1991, the rupee was devalued by 18 per cent and a structural adjustment programme under the International Monetary Fund (IMF) was announced. The transition to a market-determined exchange rate system had begun. Industrial and import licensing was virtually abolished and the need for clearances was removed. Barriers to cross-border activity were reduced. For the first time, foreign investment was automatically allowed in a wide range of industries. A programme of disinvestment of government equity in public sector enterprises was initiated.[56] These decisions had a significant impact on growth. They also put India on a different trajectory in terms of the philosophy of economic policy. This strategy for economic policy was carried forward by downstream administrations and generated a remarkable phase of growth.

There was a long-term impact of these reforms on the political economy of the country: There was a shift in the balance of power between the union government and the state governments. When the union government controlled industrial licensing, it determined who would get a licence, and where a factory would be set up. These decisions were made by the political parties in command at the union government to suit their own interests. Once industrial licenses were not required, and the Ministry of Finance largesse was less important in financing, state governments could attract investment projects on their own.[57] Regional parties could now have both power and money. State governments could provide better governance and welfare and get rewarded by the market economy with increased investment.

Another important long-term impact of economic liberalization was the rise of the middle class in India. Poverty elimination took place on a vast scale following liberalization, with the share of the population below poverty line coming down sharply.[58] Hundreds of millions of people graduated to the middle class. As new businesses and professions started emerging in response to growing demand both domestically and due to India's integration with the world economy, an aspirational class emerged. Higher economic growth increased the size and political influence of this middle class. For many in the middle class, there was a special appeal in traditional social values, religion, vernacular expression, and a mistrust of the westernized, English-speaking elite. The BJP with its focus on preserving Indian culture, languages and traditions found a natural support base in this class.

At this time, the Rao government filed charges against Advani through the Central Bureau of Investigation accusing him of being involved in a 'hawala' transaction. The BJP believed this was mere political vendetta, which came from the control of the CBI in the hands of the ruling party. Writing of the hawala allegation Advani noted, 'To be accused of corruption was an unsettling new experience. Never in my entire political life had even my adversaries made allegations of bribery or financial frauds against me . . . I took two immediate decisions. Firstly, I would tender my resignation from membership of Lok Sabha. Secondly, I would announce that I would not contest the Lok Sabha elections until I was exonerated by the courts of this false accusation.'[59] Once charges were framed, however, Advani also stepped down as party president and was succeeded by Murli Manohar Joshi.

Joshi was born in 1934 when India was a British colony. He was a student at the University of Allahabad. He was deeply influenced by the thoughts and works of the likes of Golwalkar and Deen Dayal Upadhyaya. Another person who had considerable influence over Joshi was his teacher Prof. Rajendra Singh, who went on to become the RSS *sarsanghchalak*. Joshi joined the RSS in 1944 when he was just ten years old. In 1949, he joined the Akhil Bharatiya Vidyarthi Parishad and the Bharatiya Jana Sangh in 1957. He was among the founding members of the BJP.

In keeping with the BJP's tradition of establishing a public connect through yatras, Joshi decided to embark on Ekta Yatra for national integration. The yatra would begin from Kanyakumari, the place where Swami Vivekananda found the purpose of life, and end with the hoisting of the tricolour at Lal Chowk in Srinagar. The forty-seven-day yatra began in December 1991. The yatra ended with Joshi, Modi and other BJP leaders and workers hoisting the national flag at Srinagar's Lal Chowk. Modi remembers the yatra thus: 'What happens is that the separatists used to burn the Indian flag. We were not allowed to hoist the flag in Srinagar. And they challenged that whosoever wanted to hoist the flag in Srinagar, we will kill him. We took on the challenge: yes, we will come there and we will hoist the flag.'[60]

For the BJP workers and sympathizers this was a proud moment and a tribute to Syama Prasad Mookerjee who had lost his life fighting for Kashmir's full integration with India. While Advani's Ram Rath Yatra of 1989 was centred on cultural nationalism, the Ekta Yatra was focused on national integration.

The BJP's yatras bore fruit in the 1995 assembly elections held in Maharashtra, Gujarat and Bihar. In Maharashtra, the BJP won sixty-five seats and 12.8 per cent votes against forty-two seats and 10.7 per cent votes it got in 1990.[61] In Bihar, the party won forty-one seats with 12.96 per cent votes against thirty-nine seats and 11.61 per cent votes of 1990.[62]

The most significant victory came from Gujarat where Modi had been instrumental in strengthening the party foundation. The BJP won an absolute majority with 121 seats and 42.51 per cent votes. In 1990, the party had won sixty-seven seats with 26.7 per cent votes. The Congress secured forty-five seats and 32.8 per cent votes against thirty-three seats and 30.7 per cent votes it got in 1990. The Janata Dal was wiped out.[63][64]

Table 4: Gujarat Assembly Elections of 1995[65]

Political Party	AE 1990		LS 1991		AE 1995	
	Vote Share	Seats Won	Vote Share	Seats Won	Vote Share	Seats Won
Bharatiya Janata Party	26.69%	67	50.37%	20	42.51%	121
Indian National Congress	30.74%	33	28.99%	5	32.86%	45
Janata Dal	29.36%	70	3.42%	0	2.82%	0

Modi supported Keshubhai Patel as the chief ministerial candidate. He was a RSS veteran who joined the Sangh cadres in the 1950s and was one of the founder members of the Jana Sangh. Modi was appointed state general secretary in 1994 and given the task of training about 1.5 lakh party workers, using the model of organization-centred elections. Modi dedicated himself to this ground-level work. The party even went on to win district-level panchayat polls with thumping majorities. So, when Modi supported Keshubhai for the CM's post, the party accepted.[66] This did not go down well with Shankersinh Vaghela who threatened to split the party. Vaghela was also a former member of the Jana Sangh and an RSS veteran who was responsible for organizing and strengthening sister organizations of the RSS, the Bharatiya Kisan Sangh and the Akhil Bharatiya Vidyarthi Parishad. On 28 September 1995, Modi wrote his resignation letter, saying, 'I cannot see my party cut into two pieces. So it is better that I give this party to you and I am leaving.'[67]

Advani was mindful of the work Modi had done to strengthen the party in Gujarat. He had not only strengthened the organization, helping the BJP form its first ever government in the state on its own, but also brought various sections of the Sangh together. Modi was made the BJP national general secretary in November 1995. The party rebellion in Gujarat continued.

The 1996 Suraj Yatra (march for good governance) had continued amid this turmoil. The third major yatra in the BJP's history after Ram Rath Yatra (for cultural nationalism) and Ekta Yatra (for national integration), Suraj Yatra was about bringing issues of governance to centre stage.

To spread awareness about the goals of the yatra, Advani said, 'Through this Suraj Yatra we will take the BJP's message of suraksha (national security), shuchita (probity in public life), samrasta (social harmony) and swadeshi (self-reliance), and its ideology of cultural nationalism (Hindutva) to the people. (sic)'[68] These messages also formed a part of the BJP Election Manifesto of 1996.

The concept of 'social engineering' was worked upon by K.N. Govindacharya, the party's former general secretary, to describe the strategy to strengthen the electoral base of the party by appealing to backward classes.[69] The Suraj Yatra contributed to achieving this aim, with careful messaging that was fashioned for the desired target audience. The Suraj Yatra ran from 9 March to 24 April 1996.

Vajpayee as PM

A BJP 'Maha Adhiveshan' (big public rally), was held on 11–13 November 1995, in Mumbai's central suburb Dadar. On 12 November a public gathering was organized at Shivaji Park with all senior leaders present. It was incumbent BJP president Advani's turn to address the gathering. Having spoken about the party's traditions and policies, what Advani said next left everyone surprised: 'We will fight the next election under the leadership of Shri Atal Bihari Vajpayee and he will be our candidate for prime minister. For many years, not only our party workers but also the common people have been chanting the slogan *Agli bari, Atal Bihari* (next time, Atal Bihari Vajpayee). I am confident that the BJP will form the next government under Atalji's premiership.' The gathering erupted in applause. Later when Vajpayee asked Advani, 'What did you do? You should have at least asked me once,' Advani replied, 'Would you have agreed had I asked you?'[70] Advani had started from a very difficult situation, and built a powerful political machine, but he understood that the right path to the top lay in the moderate, popular and well-loved Atal Bihari Vajpayee. Advani knew that in his political journey of decades, Vajpayee had come to be an acceptable face across parties. The BJP had managed to increase its seats tally, but it needed a face that would be acceptable to all allies. The BJP needed to expand geographically and Advani knew that it was possible only under Vajpayee at that point. He was a mild-mannered, affable personality.

Vajpayee's oratory skills had played a huge role in the BJP's rise through the Jana Sangh days. He became Prime Minister after nearly forty years of being a member of Parliament and travelling to almost every district of the country. He had an understanding of all issues of governance and even understood the nuances of foreign affairs. He was a poet at heart but a decisive and visionary leader at the same time.

Vajpayee had been a parliamentarian since 1957 and had been a strong voice in Parliament since the Jana Sangh days. In 1980, he had decided to part ways with the Janata Party due to his commitment to nationalist ideology and association with the Sangh. Vajpayee valued his association with the RSS and his decision to walk out of the Janata Party government was proof of this bond. In the age of coalition politics, Vajpayee was also the more acceptable face. The decision to present Vajpayee as the PM candidate was unanimous in the BJP.

Despite not enjoying a full majority, the Rao government completed the full five-year term. At this time, the BJP, which was fast emerging as an alternative to the Congress, in national politics, raised issues that had a bearing on the political, economic and social structure of the country. The clouds of Mandal and Kamandal had not withdrawn from the political atmosphere. The full picture was hazy. During the Rao government's tenure many social and economic changes were taking place in India. These changes were automatically going to have an impact on national politics. The BJP repeating its cultural nationalism call said, 'We are committed to promoting social harmony instead of social conflict.'[71]

In its 1996 manifesto, the BJP presented before the nation four foundations—security, purity, swadeshi and harmony. The BJP also vociferously raised the issues of electoral reforms, corruption-free governance, rural economy and self-reliance. Jana Sangh had laid a strong base for the BJP to build its foundation upon. The organizational, ideological and electoral structure existed, and the BJP had to build upon it. The high number of candidates who won the 1977 elections, making the Jana Sangh the biggest section of Janata Party, gave the BJP several leaders with administrative experience and varying degrees of hold in their states.

Bhairon Singh Shekhawat and Sunder Lal Patwa in Madhya Pradesh, Kailashpati Mishra in Bihar, Kalyan Singh in Uttar Pradesh, Sahib Singh Verma and Madan Lal Khurana in Delhi, Keshubhai Patel and Narendra Modi in Gujarat, Uma Bharti in Madhya Pradesh, Shanta Kumar in Himachal Pradesh, Gopinath Munde in Maharashtra, B.S. Yediyurappa and Ananth Kumar in Karnataka were among the leaders who had administrative experience and helped build the BJP's foundations in states from the party's early years to 1996.

A battery of younger leaders also surfaced during this time. Sushma Swaraj came up as a gifted orator in Parliament and other public platforms, Arun Jaitley provided the BJP heft with his legal acumen, while Venkaiah Naidu strengthened the organizational structure. In Uma Bharti, the BJP found a firebrand leader.

K.N. Govindacharya built a strong base by way of his social engineering, while Pramod Mahajan helped the BJP get well-versed with surveys and electoral tools to make political contests more systematic and result-oriented. Meanwhile, Modi worked on the BJP's organizational structure first at the state level in Gujarat and then at the national level during this crucial period for the party. His experience proved handy in preparing a new generation of motivated BJP *karyakartas* whom Modi led by example. The BJP had the guidance and leadership of Vajpayee and Advani to keep the flock together and build the party's base.

What also helped broaden the BJP's base on the ground was its ideological association with the RSS. The period from 1980s–1990s saw an expansion in the activities of RSS affiliates such as the Akhil Bharatiya Vidyarthi Parishad, the Vishwa Hindu Parishad, the Bharatiya Mazdoor Sangh and the Bharatiya Kisan Sangh. Many people from these organizations joined the BJP and many others provided the party support on the ground.

By the time the 1996 elections arrived, the BJP had emerged as a national political alternative. Advani decided to undertake a Suraj Yatra to mark the occasion. He said this was not merely about an election campaign. He compared the yatra to Subhash Chandra Bose's 1943 'Dilli Chalo' call and Adi Shankara's pilgrimage to the four corners of the country.[72]

In the eleventh Lok Sabha elections in 1996, the BJP won 161 seats with the party emerging as the single-largest party. On the other hand, the Congress won 140 seats. The Janata Dal won forty-six, CPM won thirty-two and CPI won nine seats. President Shankar Dayal Sharma invited the BJP to form the government. For the first time in India, a BJP government was formed. Atal Bihari Vajpayee, the widely accepted face of the BJP, known for his gentle politics, firm policies and popular oratory, was sworn in as the tenth prime minister of India. The government however could not gather the

requisite numbers to remain in power. On the floor of Lok Sabha
Vajpayee said, 'We bow down before the stronger alliance . . . but
rest assured that we won't rest until we finish the work we have
begun in the nation's interest.'[73]

* * *

Between 1980 and 1996, the BJP moved from being a peripheral
party to a cadre-based mass party, which was a convincing national
alternative. In just sixteen years, the party took shape as one that
could win elections and not just exist as an ideological block.

The BJP had reached a huge milestone in Indian politics, but
despite the coalitions and alliances the BJP was part of, the propensity
to isolate the party by treating it as an untouchable did not change.
The expanding base of the BJP had become a headache for many
parties, and they had become insecure. And that is why Vajpayee's
government was made a victim of the same political isolation
and the government survived only thirteen days—the shortest in
India's history.

Table 5: Lok Sabha Elections of 1996[74]

Political Party	1991		1996	
	Vote Share	Seats Won	Vote Share	Seats Won
Bharatiya Janata Party	20.11%	120	20.30%	161
Indian National Congress	36.26%	232	28.80%	140
Janata Dal	11.84%	59	8.10%	46

5

BJP in Government (1996–2004)

After the fall of the Vajpayee government, thirteen parties came together as the 'United Front' to form a government with the support of the Congress from the outside.[1] The new administration started with H.D. Deve Gowda as the Prime Minister, on 1 June 1996. The coalition depended on Congress support. However, the Congress began to soon feel uncomfortable with the decisions of the Deve Gowda administration. For one, Gowda showed a lack of interest in post-poll adjustments in the run-up to the 1996 UP state elections. Further, he announced the creation of Uttarakhand as a separate state in his Red Fort speech on 15 August 1996, without consulting the Congress. He was also unhelpful towards the Congress leaders who had pending cases against them with the agencies. Issues such as these led to a change of heart in the Congress and the party withdrew its support to the Deve Gowda government.[2]

On 11 April 1997, Gowda had to face a floor test after the Congress withdrew support. When Gowda spoke during the floor debate, he referred to Kesari's prime ministerial ambitions, describing the Congress president Sita Ram Kesari as an 'old man in a hurry'.[3] As expected, the Gowda government lost the trust vote by 292 to 158 votes.[4]

After Gowda was voted out, Congress supported another coalition, and a new Prime Minister was sworn in. Inder Kumar Gujral, who was foreign minister in Gowda's government, became the Prime Minister, again with outside support of the Congress.

However, Gujral's term was also short-lived. Following a hung Assembly in the Uttar Pradesh elections of 1996, a power-sharing agreement had been reached between the BJP and BSP in April 1997. It was decided that for the first six months, BSP leader Mayawati would be the state's chief minister and for the next six months, Kalyan Singh from the BJP would head the state.[5] However, during Kalyan Singh's tenure, the BSP decided to withdraw its support due to disagreement over certain issues. This led to considerable friction and some violence in the streets, which prompted the BJP government led by Kalyan Singh to call for a vote of confidence. In response to BSP's decision, BJP state leader Rajnath Singh announced that if the BSP wanted to withdraw its support, it could do so. He was optimistic about the BJP winning the vote of confidence as it was the single-largest party in the state.[6]

Prime Minister Gujral responded to this by recommending the imposition of President's Rule in the state. In a rare act of autonomous decision-making by the office of the President, President K.R. Narayanan did not act on this; he asked the government to review its recommendation.[7] To avoid a confrontation with the President, the United Front government was forced to reverse its decision to dismiss the Kalyan Singh government. While most allies in the United Front agreed that a confrontation was best avoided, the Congress wanted the BJP government to go. The Congress felt that the BJP was gaining ground in Uttar Pradesh and could become the major force in the state. In stark opposition to the Congress party, prime minister Gujral did not want President's Rule to be imposed in UP. However, as his government was in place with the Congress's support, his decision not to dismiss the BJP government in UP made the collapse of his government imminent.[8]

Table 1: Uttar Pradesh Assembly Elections of 1996[9]

Political Party	AE 1993		LS 1996		AE 1996	
	Vote Share	Seats Won	Vote Share	Seats Won	Vote Share	Seats Won
Bharatiya Janata Party	33.30%	177	33.44%	52	32.52%	174
Indian National Congress	15.08%	28	8.14%	5	8.35%	33
Bahujan Samaj Party	11.12%	67	20.61%	6	19.64%	67
Samajwadi Party	17.94%	109	20.84%	16	21.80%	110

It was, however, the investigation into Rajiv Gandhi's assassination that brought the coalition government led by I.K. Gujral to a premature end. The inquiry commission's report on the assassination of Rajiv Gandhi, led by Justice Milap Chandra Jain, said that the conspiracy to assassinate Rajiv Gandhi had a connection to the DMK. The Jain Commission report concluded that the DMK had provided sanctuary to the Liberation of Tamil Tigers Eelam (LTTE) and was thus an accomplice in the assassination.[10]

These explosive findings triggered a chain reaction that shattered reputations, forced realignments and brought down Gujral's fragile government.[11] When the Gujral government did not dismiss the DMK from the Cabinet, despite these allegations, Congress president Sita Ram Kesari announced the withdrawal of support from the government. Gujral's time as prime minister lasted eleven months.[12]

In his resignation letter, Gujral wrote, '. . . My Council of Ministers and I hereby submit our resignation from my Government. In my communication to the Congress President [Kesari], I have said that it is unfair and unethical to tarnish the fair name of a party only because the Jain Commission's Interim Report—without any substantiated data—has chosen to blame the party and, I say with sadness, the entire Tamil people . . . My Council of Ministers and I hereby submit our resignation.'[13]

After the fall of the Gujral government, fresh elections to the twelfth Lok Sabha were announced. This was the third time that the Congress initially participated in a majority coalition in Parliament, and then withdrew support. Earlier, the Congress had done the same to the Charan Singh and the V.P. Singh governments. This behaviour started adversely affecting the extent to which its allies felt they could trust the Congress to be part of a coalition or to support it.

In the meantime, the BJP leadership was cleared of the false hawala charges against them. In April 1997, the Delhi High Court ruled on the allegations against Advani in the CBI chargesheet. It found no evidence of favours or money flows between Advani and the Jains. The charge sheet was quashed.[14] There could not have been a better new year's gift for Advani.[15] Amid these political developments, the country was set to celebrate the fiftieth Independence Day on 15 August 1997. The BJP decided to build on its successes with yatras and planned a 'Swarna Jayanti Rath Yatra' (golden jubilee chariot journey).

The golden jubilee yatra was launched by Advani at Mumbai's August Kranti Maidan on 18 May 1997. Each yatra had a central theme, and for this one, Advani later wrote, 'I wanted to project the BJP as a party committed to good governance. Although India had attained swaraj or self-governance in 1947, it had not been transformed, even after fifty years, into suraj or good governance.'[16]

This positioning was particularly important at a time when the excitement of the reforms of the early 1990s had subsided, and many voters had started perceiving all politicians as unprincipled, unscrupulous, self-seeking and power-hungry. The messaging of the yatra helped the BJP achieve a better connection with the people and portray the party as an organization of principled politicians, who stood for more than just obtaining and wielding power.[17] The yatra covered 15,000 kilometres over fifty-five days, traversing through nineteen states and through the far-flung Andaman and Nicobar Islands.[18] By this time, the BJP's yatra system was well established, familiar organizational capabilities were rolled out one more time, with mature processes put into motion on a larger scale, harnessing the growing support for the party.

Mid-term Lok Sabha elections were held in 1998. The BJP built on its growing success in elections and scaled up its methods. A large-scale mobilization of voters had been accomplished through numerous yatras at the national stage and within many states. By this time, measurement of the populace through polls had become an important activity, both within the media and as an information system to support decision making in election campaigns. The BJP brought in greater professionalism to do the number crunching in order to chalk out winning strategies.

The results were consistent with the long journey of the BJP towards growing influence. Its strength in Lok Sabha went up from 161 seats in 1996 to 182 seats, while the Congress only got to 141 seats.[19] For the first time, the BJP became the single-largest party, and was invited to form the government. While the BJP's vote share rose by 5 per cent from the 1996 elections to 25.59 per cent, it still remained short of the 50 per cent mark which the Congress had obtained in the 1980s.

Table 2: Lok Sabha Elections of 1998[20]

Political Party	LS 1996		LS 1998	
	Vote Share	Seats Won	Vote Share	Seats Won
Bharatiya Janata Party	20.30%	161	25.59%	182
Indian National Congress	28.80%	140	25.82%	141
Communist Party of India (Marxist)	6.12%	32	5.16%	32

With the support of the AIADMK, the Biju Janata Dal, the Janata Party, the Lok Janshakti Party, the Shiromani Akali Dal, the Shiv Sena, the Samata Party, the West Bengal Trinamool Congress, the Telugu Desam Party, the Haryana Vikas Party, the Telangana Rashtra Samithi and the Pattali Makkal Katchi, Vajpayee once again became the Prime Minister on 19 March 1998. The coalition he led was named National Democratic Alliance (NDA).

The breadth of the coalition underlines the mainstreaming of the BJP. Just two years earlier, in 1996, only the Shiv Sena, the Samata Party, the Haryana Vikas Party (HVP) and the Akali Dal had joined forces with the BJP taking the combined tally to 194 seats. This configuration had not worked; Vajpayee resigned in thirteen days. But in 1998, the BJP had more seats (from 161 to 182), and more political parties were willing to work with Vajpayee as Prime Minister. It was striking to see that socialist figures like George Fernandes were willing to partner with Vajpayee and the BJP, as this was in stark contrast with their opposition towards the dual membership of the Jana Sangh members in the Janata Party and the RSS in 1977.[21] Fernandes was also instrumental in the formation of the NDA and later became the official convener of the alliance. The Pokhran II tests were conducted during his tenure as defence minister in the BJP-NDA government between 1998 and 2004.[22] These developments symbolized the fact that the political isolation of the BJP had ended and the party was now considered the principal Opposition party to the Congress.

The BJP-led NDA, which gained power in 1998, after having its share of ups and downs, lasted for thirteen months. The experiment ushered in an era of non-Congress coalition governments as a viable political option in India. This undercut the claim that only the Congress could successfully create a stable administration.

While a key dimension of this new political culture was the growing significance of coalition politics, another equally crucial dimension was the increasing role of regional parties in the national coalition. National parties could no longer afford to ignore regional parties because of their growing role in providing the required numerical strength in Parliament.[23]

1998 Nuclear Tests

Less than two months after Vajpayee became Prime Minister for the second time, in a major move, the government conducted nuclear tests on 11 May 1998. Making India a nuclear power had been a commitment made by the BJP in every election manifesto since 1967 (when it was the Jana Sangh). After the tests, on 27 May, outlining India's right to nuclear power, Vajpayee spoke in Parliament on the issue of the tests. 'India is now a nuclear weapons state . . . It is not conferment we seek, nor is it a status for others to grant . . . It is India's due, the right of one-sixth of humankind,' he said.[24]

The underground nuclear tests of May 1998 were conducted during a period when the Indian economy was under considerable stress.[25] Part of the problem was the global economic situation. The East Asian financial crisis which began in July 1997 continued to impact the world economy. The contagion spread to Russia and major parts of Latin America. There was global uncertainty, with prospects of large-scale decline in GDP of major economies, and a fall in world trade.[26] Although the contagion effect of the crisis did not affect India much, its foreign exchange reserves fell between April 1998 and July 1998.[27] The rupee depreciated sharply between November 1997 and July 1998.[28] This was alarming. However, there was some consolation for India. The economy experienced a decline in external debt and in the current account deficit.[29][30] These managed to insulate the Indian economy from the adverse effects of the crisis.

Vajpayee was certain all major superpowers, including the United States of America, would condemn India's action, sooner or later.[31] So, India was prepared for a backlash and wasn't caught unawares. As expected, the US condemned India for carrying out the nuclear tests and imposed economic sanctions.[32] India faced suspension of fresh multilateral lending, downgrading by some international credit rating agencies and reduction in net foreign institutional investment. This was bad news for India as its economy was already in a state of disorder having been hit by the decline in global trade. As a consequence, the domestic economy experienced a creeping rise in inflation primarily caused by supply shocks in food.[33]

The Vajpayee government had to come up with a quick and effective solution to reinstate the economy. The government was faced with a question of how to manage the sudden decline in foreign exchange reserves. To counter the decline caused by imposition of the economic sanctions, on 1 June 1998, the government launched the Resurgent India Bond (RIB) scheme. The aim was to raise foreign exchange through RIB by offering it exclusively to non-resident Indians (NRIs). To make the bonds attractive, the government made them fully repatriable and provided tax concessions.[34] The scheme worked well. Though the government expected to attract about $2 billion from these bonds with high returns, NRIs ended up investing $4.2 billion in the scheme.[35] [36] This addressed the issue of large exchange rate depreciation and helped the Vajpayee government tide over the potential negative impact of the sanctions.

Import Duties

As part of the 1998–99 Budget, the government decided to raise import duties by 8 per cent. In general, the BJP's economic philosophy was influenced by the spirit of 'swadeshi'. However, this time, the decision was influenced by demands put forward by a cross-section of the industry. The government intended to address the issue of taxation of domestically produced goods vis-à-vis imported goods. The measure was proposed keeping in view that although domestic production was subject to sales tax, other local taxes and levies, the import sector escaped the same. In addition, the government's proposed levy of 8 per cent duty on imports was approximately equal to the burden of local taxes on domestic producers. This duty, according to the government, was not a protectionist measure, but a response to the demand for a level-playing field.

The initiative, however, pushed up costs and received a backlash from businesses across various industries.[37] It was perceived as a measure to discourage foreign direct investment (FDI) and joint ventures in industries that use imported components in their production process. The initiative was opposed by the user industry in need of imports as raw materials and other intermediaries as well as industry associations like the Confederation of Indian Industry (CII).[38] Even though producers welcomed this measure, there was significant pressure to roll back.[39] Eventually, on 12 June 1998, the government was forced to roll back the import duty of 8 per cent to 4 per cent.[40][41]

Economic Policy

From the days of the Jana Sangh, the party had opposed the Nehruvian model of development. It stood against both communism and capitalism and had said, 'The party has rejected Capitalism and Socialism on the ground that both these ideologies lead to centralization, monopolization, and alienation of the individual.'[42]

The Bharatiya Jana Sangh had outlined its own vision for the economy as follows: 'Bharatiya Jana Sangh envisages a socio-economic order which guarantees equal opportunity and freedom to every individual to fulfil his material needs and achieve moral and spiritual progress. The Jana Sangh rejects both Capitalism as well as Stateism as both lead to concentration of economic power and monopoly. The evils flowing from private monopoly can be checked through State regulation. But concentration of political as well as economic authority in the hands of the State is incompatible with democracy.'[43]

In its opposition to the Nehruvian model, the BJP felt that industrialization should not be rushed. It should grow in an organic manner with small industries leading the way. The skills, arts, crafts and methods of production developed in traditional crafts and in rural India should not be destroyed to make space for machine-led growth. The economic resolution of the party at Bangalore, in December 1958, had said, 'Bharatiya Jana Sangh has always felt that economic planning should always be viewed in the background of the country's social, cultural and political objectives. As such a Socialistic Economy which invariably leads to greater concentration of power in the State, is not compatible with democratic ideals. The aim of Planning should mainly be to create conditions wherein more and more people have the initiative and facilities for engaging themselves in gainful economic activities. This, however, should not lead to the concentration of power in a few hands.'[44]

While the swadeshi movement opposed foreign capital, the government moved ahead on removing excessive bureaucratic interferences in economic and financial activities even when they concerned foreign capital. One of its important contributions was to decriminalize cross-border restrictions. In 1998–99, the government proposed to repeal the Foreign Exchange Regulation Act (FERA) and replace it with a new Foreign Exchange Management Act (FEMA), which would be consistent with the needs of a modern economy. FEMA would later come into operation from 1 June 2000.[45]

An Eventful Year

The year 1999 was an eventful year for the government. After the nuclear tests, Vajpayee undertook a bus yatra to Lahore on 19 February 1999 as part of the BJP's commitment to peace and stability in the region. Vajpayee's journey marked the inauguration of a Delhi to Lahore cross-border bus service named *Sada-e-Sarhad* (call of the frontier). Vajpayee signed a bilateral treaty known as the Lahore Declaration with Pakistan's Prime Minister Nawaz Sharif to end the tension in the region. The treaty was widely acclaimed both in India and abroad as a historic move to bring peace. This combination of 'talk softly and carry a big stick', and force projection through nuclear tests, coupled with peace initiatives through the bus yatra, raised Vajpayee's stature and popularity.

In 1999, the Congress moved a no-confidence motion against the government. The vote on the motion was set for 17 April 1999.

The Vajpayee government was at first confident that the Congress would lose. Mayawati had assured the BJP that the Bahujan Samaj Party (BSP) would vote in its favour. However, she reneged on her promise and voted against the government. This made it a tough contest.

The BJP, which had by now established itself as an alternative to the Congress in thirteen months, expanded its organization alongside. The nuclear test had added to the BJP's heft as a viable national alternative. The Congress was obviously unsettled and hence brought in the no-confidence motion. In his Lok Sabha speech on the motion, Vajpayee said, 'The House has many single-member parties which are grouping together to remove the BJP. The BJP isn't a party that has cropped up like a mushroom, it has worked for forty years among the masses to make its place . . . Today, I have been accused of lusting after power and of doing whatever it takes to be in power . . . But, I have been in power before and I have never done anything immoral for power . . . If breaking up political parties is the only way to form a coalition that stays in power, then I do not want to touch such a coalition with a barge pole.'[46]

Political analysts have been trying to identify the individuals who were decisive in swinging the vote against the NDA. Giridhar Gamang, Odisha's chief minister from the Congress party, who was still a member of Parliament, voted against the government and this one vote—269 ayes to 270 noes—led to the fall of the Vajpayee government. However, Pranab Mukherjee, in his book *Coalition Years* 1996–2012, argued that Gamang did not have a choice to vote any other way as he was bound by anti-defection laws.[47] Gamang, in turn, believed the vote that mattered was that of Saifuddin Soz, a member of the Jammu and Kashmir National Conference Party (JKNC), who defied his party leadership to vote against the Vajpayee coalition government.[48]

While resigning from the Congress in 2015, in an interview to the *Economic Times*, Giridhar Gamag said, 'It was not my vote which turned the tables against the Vajpayee government but the cross-voting of Prof. Saifuddin Soz. The Vajpayee government lost the confidence motion by one vote for the cross-voting of Prof Soz as he had gone against the whip of his party and voted against the motion'.[49] For this defiance, Soz was expelled from the JKNC. He later joined the Congress in 2003. As a consequence of the no-confidence motion against the government, the Lok Sabha was dissolved on 26 April 1999 and the next election was due in five months. In the interim, a caretaker government was installed.

The caretaker government did not have the luxury of quietly winding down its work. Over a fortnight after losing the trust vote, the Vajpayee government was informed about 'some strange movement of unidentified people crossing the LoC in Kargil district in the Ladakh region of Jammu and Kashmir'. The information had come to the Indian Army from its local informers in the Batalik sector. When the Army sent patrol teams, it found the intrusions extended beyond Batalik to Drass, Mushkoh and Kaksar sectors. Defence Minister George Fernandes visited the troubled area on May 12–14, and Vajpayee was apprised of the situation. The Cabinet Committee on Security came to the conclusion that Indian troops should mount attacks along the Line of Control.[50] The counter-offensive operation codenamed 'Operation Vijay' was launched on 26 May. After the Indian armed forces recaptured most of the infiltrated territory, Pakistan, which also faced huge international criticism, withdrew its forces from the remaining areas. On 26 July, Indian forces declared the complete withdrawal of Pakistani forces and the Kargil War officially ended.

The Kargil War stirred nationalistic sentiments and Vajpayee's popularity rose. The BJP had always believed that in the face of external threat, the nation must speak in one voice. During the 1962, 1965 and 1971 wars, the Jana Sangh had fully backed the government in power on foreign policy and military affairs.

The results of the thirteenth Lok Sabha elections were satisfying for the BJP. While it had contested 388 seats in 1998, it only contested 339 seats in 1999. As a consequence, its apparent vote share dropped from 25.59 per cent to 23.75 per cent. But it won 182 seats and its allies got 124 seats. The decline of the Congress continued, where it went down to 114 seats and 28.3 per cent of the votes.

Table 3: Lok Sabha Elections of 1999[51]

Political Party	LS 1998		LS 1999	
	Vote Share	Seats Won	Vote Share	Seats Won
Bharatiya Janata Party	25.59%	182	23.75%	182
Indian National Congress	25.82%	141	28.3%	114
Communist Party of India (Marxist)	5.16%	32	5.40%	33

NDA-1

Vajpayee was once again sworn in as Prime Minister. The composition of the NDA government from 1999–2004 was much more diverse in regional and cultural terms than the Janata Party which won seats essentially from the north and west. The NDA had all-India representation.[52] Vajpayee's Cabinet members included L.K. Advani, Ananth Kumar, Sikander Bakht, Surjit Singh Barnala, George Fernandes, Jaswant Singh, Murli Manohar Joshi, Kashiram Rana, Naveen Patnaik, Pramod Mahajan, Suresh Prabhu, P.R. Kumaramangalam, K. Ramamurthy, Ram Jethmalani, Satyanarayan Jatiya, Ramakrishna Hegde, Arun Shourie and Yashwant Sinha. Describing the concepts of 'coalition dharma', Advani said, 'Ours is a coalition government which places certain obligations and responsibilities—what can be called the dharma of coalition—on all partners in the alliance. As far as the BJP is concerned, I would like all our colleagues, especially those in responsible positions in the state units, to realize that the interests of the coalition at the centre are paramount. The party's strategies in states must be subordinate to its national strategy. As a broad policy, it should be our endeavour to develop the right coalition chemistry with our allies by constantly enlarging the area of common interests and shrinking, or, at any rate, inactivating, the area of differences.'[53]

The post-1999 environment was new in many respects. For the first time since 1977–1980, a non-Congress incumbent government returned to power through a democratic process. The social base of the BJP represented a collection of upper castes, tribals and OBCs, many of whom were previously Congress supporters. Secondly, the BJP embarked on an agenda of economic reforms, playing a leadership role in the direction of the Indian state in a way that, in the past, had only been played by the Congress.

When Advani moved to government in 1998, Kushabhau Thakre became the party president. Kushabhau had joined the RSS as a pracharak in 1942. Before he became the president of the Janata Party unit in Madhya Pradesh, Kushabhau spent nineteen months in jail during the Emergency. Kushabhau, who was an exceptional organizer, had emphasised at various points during his tenure that for all its supportive role, the party should not become overly dependent on the government, that it should have an identity and organizational capital of its own.

On the growth strategy of the party, he said, 'We now know that the BJP cannot move ahead if we do not include everyone. The growth of the party must not be merely geographical. There must also be social growth.'[54] The BJP began on the path of expanding out from a relatively narrow support base in the west and north, towards a greater diversity of supporters spread all over India.

Much like Kushabhau, the BJP's organization was moulded by those who spent time as pracharaks in the RSS. Sunder Singh Bhandari, Kailashpati Mishra, Jagannathrao Joshi, Krishna Lal Sharma and Jana Krishnamurthi are examples of people who entered the BJP after having served the Sangh for many years and strengthened the BJP's organizational foundations when they entered the party. The list of RSS pracharaks who joined the BJP from the Sangh is in fact endless. This keeps the party bound to its ideological moorings and provides ground-level support in disseminating the party's messages to the people.

What guided the BJP in its search for alliances was the fact that regional aspirations had been ignored by the Congress. The party felt that the emergence of regional parties, post 1980, was a phenomenon that had resulted from the Congress's disregard for regional aspirations.

It, therefore, attempted alliances with parties that felt their issues had not been accorded due importance by the Congress. These parties included the Biju Janata Dal, the Shiromani Akali Dal, the AIADMK and the PMK. Looked upon as an essentially north India-based outfit, the BJP could easily forge new alliances in areas where the Congress faced difficulties because it was the dominant party, and smaller parties that were emerging were opposing the Congress. These parties were more comfortable with an alliance with the BJP. It was Vajpayee who brought together varying groups as a joint national alternative. Unlike the earlier coalition experiments that aimed at toppling the Congress government or keeping it out of power, the new formation was the first to emerge as a coalition with the aim of forming a government. This coalition had a Common Minimum Programme to run a government effectively.

By adopting this strategy, the BJP became a partner for regional parties which were structurally opposed to the Congress or to a Congress-led coalition. This approach generated the natural strategy for the BJP in Punjab, Maharashtra, Tamil Nadu, Karnataka, Haryana and Orissa, and with the Trinamool Congress of West Bengal against the Left Front government. As part of the strategy of pulling in different ideological parties, the BJP at the time followed the Common Minimum Programme of the NDA.

Economic Policy 1999–2000

When the BJP government came to power again at the Centre following the 1999 elections, the economy was facing difficulties.

On the one hand, the South East Asian economic crisis continued to hurt the world economy.[55] On the other, economic sanctions continued in the form of commercial and financial penalties imposed by certain developed countries following India's nuclear tests at Pokhran. The question on everyone's mind was how to mitigate these adversities and critical economic challenges which had emerged from decades of corruption, inefficiencies and faulty economic policies of the Congress government. Under Vajpayee, the newly formed government adopted multiple measures and policy reforms to revive the economy.

Among the most important reforms undertaken by the government were those in telecom, power, finance and tariffs that laid the foundations for India to become a leading software exporter in the world. There was a huge opportunity for India to export services and software based on offices located in India which hired people in India who worked for global firms. However, that could not be achieved owing to the lack of telecom facilities. Investment in telecom required allowing the private sector to invest. It also required lower tariffs for equipment, availability of stable power sources and the ability to raise capital. The government undertook a series of reforms that enabled a telecom revolution.

First, in the 1999–2000 Budget, the government announced proposals for rationalization and reduction of customs duties. Specifically, there was a significant reduction in import duty on a number of critical inputs in the telecom sector, such as ICs and micro assemblies, storage devices and CD-ROMs, telecom equipment and optical fibres. The government repeatedly emphasized the importance of the telecom sector for the country's development in the new century and millennium.[56] In 1999, the New Telecom Policy (NTP) was introduced by the government. It led to major structural reforms in the telecom sector and enabled investment in this much needed but neglected sector. In the 1990s, telecom services had been restricted to government departments. There was a minuscule number of telephones in India, mobile telephony was missing, and internet connectivity was abysmal. The telecom reforms enabled private entry into domestic long distance and international connectivity.

The government also changed the power policy, laying the foundations for an increase in power investment and production and a reduction in power shortages in India. In May 2003, Parliament enacted the Electricity Bill.[57] The government undertook several reforms in equity markets and capital controls. These allowed companies to raise capital. At the same time, it allowed Indian companies to invest abroad and acquire foreign firms. This helped Indian software businesses raise capital and buy up small software companies in Europe and the US. Through this they managed to increase their customer base and adopt new technology. The telecom and financial sector reforms allowed large Indian companies to export software and become world leaders in this field. This agenda of self-reliance with national pride fitted with the party's economic ideology.

With its swadeshi philosophy, the party preferred encouragement of domestic industry, and its views on foreign direct investment in India were cautious. The party's view was that greater flow of FDI should be allowed in areas where FDI was necessary. However, it felt that the government should make sure that foreign companies set up greenfield units, and not be allowed to acquire existing Indian companies; that too, with money raised from the Indian capital market.[58] The Vajpayee government struck a balance between globalizing and inviting FDI into India. This was also characteristic of policies in subsequent BJP governments.

The approach also entailed removing red tape for FDI in sectors where it was being welcomed. In Budget 1999–2000, the government announced an expansion of the list of automatic approvals for FDI. It was decided that wherever specific approvals were required, the decision would have to be taken in thirty days. A Foreign Investment Implementation Authority was set up in 1999 to expedite approvals into actual investment inflows. The objective was to understand

and solve the problems of foreign investors and help them get faster approvals.

At the same time, the government announced the decision to introduce VAT, a precursor to a system-wide Goods and Services Tax (GST). VAT was implemented in 2003. To reduce corruption and leakages in the direct tax system, the government designed and implemented the Tax Information Network (TIN).

When the party came to power, it recommended that the government speed up the disinvestment process. It wanted the government to release the huge funds blocked in PSUs for investment in the social and infrastructure sectors. It said the government must accord the highest priority to turning huge industrial assets into productive assets that would spur industrial growth to a new level.[59] On 10 December 1999, the NDA government established the Department of Disinvestment under the Ministry of Finance. In 2001, it became the Ministry of Disinvestment. The union government completely sold off companies (e.g. VSNL, Modern Foods) and assets (e.g. hotels belonging to ITDC). When these assets went into private hands, the same labour and capital generated higher output. In addition, the continuous flow of budgetary expenditure to pay for the losses of some of these PSUs ended. Also, with the aim of improving utilization of mines and minerals the government privatized many mining companies.

Infrastructure and Pension Reforms

The need to improve rural infrastructure was a recurrent priority for the BJP for many decades. The National Executive reiterated this stand in many of its meetings. Right from its inception the party demanded that top priority be given to programmes aimed at reduction of rural poverty and creation of mass employment, like construction of rural roads and small irrigation schemes. It argued in favour of public works programmes, such as roads, minor irrigation, social forestry, rural water supply, housing, etc. The party emphasized the philosophy of integrated rural development with an accent on non-farm rural industries, agroforestry, social forestry, rural roads, rural electrification, rural health care and drinking water.[60]

The government launched the Pradhan Mantri Gram Sadak Yojana (PMGSY) on Vajpayee's birthday on 25 December 2000, to improve rural road connectivity. A centrally sponsored scheme, PMGSY was launched with the objective to provide all-weather road access to unconnected habitations in rural regions.

On a country-wide level, one of the largest road infrastructure projects was launched under the National Highways Authority of India (NHAI) in 1999. The main objective of the National Highways Development Project (NHDP) was to build roads of international standards and highways of four and six lanes on major national routes. This route connected four major metros: Delhi, Mumbai, Chennai and Kolkata. Over the next few decades, the NHAI created a good network of highways and roads across the country.

Another recurring theme of the BJP was a small government. The party had consistently believed in fiscal prudence and was against large government spending. In December 2000, the government introduced the Fiscal Responsibility and Budgetary Management (FRBM) Bill in Parliament.

One of the major initiatives of the NDA government was to reduce the dependence of pension provisions on the government budget and to lay the foundations of a healthy budget in the future. The government announced a roadmap for a new pension scheme for civil servants in Budget 2001. In August 2003, the Cabinet approved the formation of an interim regulator, the Pension Fund Regulatory and Development Authority (PFRDA), and in December, Vajpayee signed off on the implementation of the New Pension Scheme (NPS) starting 1 January 2004. The pension reform for civil servants as a first step towards a population-wide pension system that could cover millions of India's informal workers was a practical move. It was based on the understanding that by building the NPS for civil servants, and by having civil servants become the first adopters of the new system, foundations were being laid for the future extension of the NPS to the larger population.

The defined benefit system was intrinsically inequitable. Almost the entire pension liability of the government was going to a handful of civil servants while other workers had no old age security. If Indian society had to ensure old age security to the bulk of workers, India needed a pension system in which the pension expenditure of the government was not exhausted by civil servants. In a defined contribution system, each worker would put aside money for old age with some contribution from employers and/ or the government. This money would be invested for the working life of the person and continue to grow. The pension of the individual would come from this money.

The pension liabilities of the government were rising and expected to become unsustainable. It was clear that the country could never afford a fully defined benefit pension programme. The New Pension System was a step towards addressing this huge potential burden in the future.

Expanding the Party's Sphere of Influence

While on the one hand the government was implementing economic reforms that had long been on the agenda of the Jana Sangh and BJP and laying the foundations for an increased role for private investment in the economy, on the other, the party organization was also increasing its support base. The growing expansion of the BJP was, according to political analysts, 'intertwined with a distinct three-tiered growth in its social appeal'.[61] The first-tier growth involved the BJP extending its sphere of influence beyond its traditional support base of upper caste Hindus. In the Hindi heartland, besides this core support base, the category that was mobilized was the Scheduled Tribes. In the Hindi heartland, this upper caste Hindus coupled with STs coalition was a direct competition to the traditional Congress coalition of upper caste, scheduled castes, scheduled tribes and Muslims.

The second tier consisted of OBCs, who were brought in through poll alliances with regional parties that were trusted by OBCs.[62] The third and most difficult tier for the BJP to obtain support was the SCs and Muslims.

What many commentators did not understand was the essence of the BJP and RSS's position on caste. Even during Golwalkar's days, the Sangh had denounced *varna vyavastha* (varna system). In 1969, VHP's Dharma Sansad was held in Karnataka's Udupi. The Dharma Sansad, in the presence of Golwalkar, passed a resolution to eradicate untouchability. The resolution said, '*Hindavah sahodara sarve, na hindu patiyo bhave* (All Hindus are born out of the same womb [of Mother India])'. Later, Dev Dutt, who was a tribal, became the president of the BJP's Gujarat unit. Suraj Bhan, a Dalit leader, was the Haryana BJP chief. The BJP's ideology of cultural nationalism was rooted in the philosophy that all Indians are equal.

Traditionally, regional parties became important in state governments, but national politics remained the preserve of the Congress and the BJP. The NDA represented a break from this idea, with significant power sharing with many regional parties. This brought regional perspectives into the union government's decision-making and attenuated the behaviour of regional parties by bringing union government considerations into their policies and positions. Through this, it generated a deepening of the federal character of the republic.[63][64]

Although the NDA led by the BJP was not as fragile as was projected, it did experience occasional hiccups due to ideological differences among its constituents.[65] The net result of the 1999 and 2004 national polls was a deepening of the rhythm of coalition governments. It resulted in moderate behaviour of the government, where many were consulted on all decisions, and large national parties accepted the need to share power with a variety of partners, many of which were regional parties.[66]

In this period the BJP had shown ingenuity by winning the confidence of regional parties. With the TMC in Bengal, the TDP in Andhra Pradesh, the AIADMK in Tamil Nadu, the Asom Gana Parishad in Assam, the Bodoland People's Front in Assam, the Akali Dal in Punjab, the Shiv Sena in Maharashtra or the Janata Dal United in Karnataka, the BJP had succeeded in aligning disparate groups against the Congress. Some of these were long-standing ideological fellow-travellers but some were unexpected allies, such as Bihar's Samata Party.

The BJP was growing as a party not only in terms of making new alliances, but also in numbers. In the party's National Council held in Nagpur in 2000, then party general secretary Venkaiah Naidu said, 'The BJP had 1.81 crore primary members in 1998. Today, there are nearly 3 crore primary members. As against 98,000 active members in 1998, we have 2.43 lakh active members now.'[67]

The foundation of successful political parties is the enthusiasm of small donors. The BJP also felt that it did not want to be dependent on external sources for funds. The BJP built organizational strength under the Aajeevan Sahayog Nidhi programme in 1997, where workers and sympathizers were asked to make an annual contribution of Rs 1,000, Rs 5,000 or Rs 10,000. By 2000, this process had gathered momentum.[68] In 1999, the BJP adopted the Chennai Declaration, a document that guides the BJP members to rededicate themselves to the BJP's commitment to value-based politics and make it an instrument to deliver good governance. Through these donations and commitments, the party sought to bind new members closer to the party and its objectives and activities. The party intensified its training camps. Since the BJP is a cadre-based party, inculcation of ideology was an important element of the strategy for new party members. The BJP held *sammelans* (conferences) and media training programmes at the organizational level.

India's Position at WTO

The Vajpayee government and the BJP largely worked in sync with other elements of the Sangh Parivar. However, sometimes differences emerged with the government in spheres of economic policy. While the Vajpayee government was more open to foreign capital, other organizations of the RSS such as the Swadeshi Jagaran Manch disagreed. Issues such as tariffs, FDI and multilateral trade agreements were among the areas of contention.

After the BJP had come to power, during the World Trade Organization (WTO) Ministerial Conference in Doha, Qatar held between 9 and 13 November 2001, India made major headway with respect to its key concerns: agriculture, Singapore issues regarding multilateral rules on investment and the Trade-Related Aspects of Intellectual Property Rights (TRIPS) agreement. The Doha Round began on a note of dissatisfaction among developing countries with respect to the conclusions reached during the Uruguay Round that took place prior to Doha.

Beginning with the declaration on Trade Related Aspects of Intellectual Property Rights (TRIPS) and Public Health, India pushed for measures to protect public health and promote access to medicines for all.

India's stand with respect to agriculture involved negotiating for greater market access, reduction in trade distorting domestic support and reduction of export subsidies on part of developed nations. Apart from this, India also brought to attention the issue of non-agriculture market access (NAMA). India's stance focused on tariff reduction and other non-tariff barriers. Particularly, the country raised the issue of using the Swiss formula for tariff reductions. As a result of this formula, developing countries would have committed to higher tariff cuts than developed countries.[69]

The Commerce and Industry Minister Mr Murasoli Maran expressed India's opposition towards including them in the development agenda at the Doha Round thus: 'In the areas of investment, competition, basic questions remain even on the need for a multilateral agreement. Most importantly, do the developing countries have the capacity to deal with them? Will we be able to say that they do not impinge strongly on domestic policies that are well removed from trade? . . . . We are doubtful that we can give affirmative replies to all these questions. In any case, the Singapore Declaration requires an explicit consensus for any decision to move to negotiations. Let us therefore wait till an explicit consensus emerges on these issues.'[70]

Following the Doha Round, the Fifth Ministerial Conference was held in Cancun, Mexico, between 10 and 14 September 2003. The mandate for Cancun was to review the progress made with respect to negotiations concerning agriculture, non-agriculture market access (NAMA) and the four Singapore issues that were still ongoing since the Doha Round concluded.[71] Even though two years had passed since Doha, deadlines on all core issues concerning developing nations, namely, TRIPS and Public Health, Implementation issues, Special and Differential Treatment, were not met.[72]

Against this backdrop, Arun Jaitley, who was the minister of commerce and industry at the time, led India into the Cancun ministerial meeting. Ahead of Cancun, Jaitley commented on various issues concerning India, 'We are going to be firm on getting a commitment from the European Union to reduce trade-distorting agricultural subsidies . . . we have the support of countries like China and can also count on other countries like Brazil and Australia.'[73]

He also made a statement on the issue of agriculture: 'There can be no movement on reforms unless the developed countries are prepared to accept deeper cuts in agricultural subsidies.'[74]

* * *

By 1999 the impact of the economic liberalization of 1991 had run out its steam. It was evident that economic reforms needed to continue. The Jana Sangh and the BJP's agenda of improving the standard of living of the 'last man in the line' could not be achieved in a country of shortages, without roads or telecom and where the government continued to run hotels and businesses. Achieving the objective of a decent standard of living for India's poor required investment. Before a government could promise to give people access to basic facilities such as roads, power, communication, pensions, etc., there needed to be investment in these sectors. The Vajpayee government undertook several important reforms that laid the foundations for higher economic growth. The reforms aimed at greater investment in infrastructure such as power, roads, telecom as well as manufacturing. The reforms opened these sectors up to private investment, reduced the role of bureaucracy and politicians and laid the foundations of higher growth and improved standards of living. Many years later, under the leadership of Narendra Modi, when the party won again, and was able to offer India's poor digitally-based direct benefit transfers through JAM (Jan Dhan, Aadhaar, Mobile) and every home with a phone, Internet and electricity in the remotest parts of the country. This became possible because of the foundations laid during the first BJP regime.

6

The Loss of 2004

Under Vajpayee, India had adopted a three-pronged strategy to deal with Pakistan. The fight against cross-border terrorism in J&K and other parts of the country intensified. In Pakistan, General Pervez Musharraf became the President following a military coup. Vajpayee was of the opinion that the differences between the two countries could be resolved through dialogue. The Agra summit talks, for which Musharraf was invited to the Taj Mahal city in July 2001, was an outcome of Vajpayee's belief in resolving outstanding issues through dialogue. The talks failed. When the 9/11 attacks happened in America, it drew the world's attention to terror and Pakistan, and helped persuade the international community to come closer to the Indian position on Pakistan as a state sponsor of terrorism.

The Vajpayee government declared that unless Pakistan stopped aiding terrorism, talks would not be held. The efforts to stop terrorist infiltration from Pakistan were also stepped up. Simultaneously, India began strengthening the diplomatic offensive by trying to make the world understand how Pakistan was fomenting terror on Indian soil.

On 13 December 2001, the Indian Parliament was attacked by terrorists. The Indian Army subsequently started Operation Parakram which involved mobilising 7,00,000 troops at the border.

The forces remained deployed for ten months. Meanwhile, Pakistan also increased its troop deployment along the borders with India. This build-up of military on both sides of the border led to tensions. The international media focused attention on it as fears of tension between two nuclear nations grew. The de-escalation took place in 2002 after both sides withdrew the large number of troops along the border.

These years were also tumultuous for the party and saw three rapid changes in party presidents.

Party Presidents

Politics in southern Indian states are typically dominated more by regional parties than by the larger national political parties such as the BJP or the Congress. However, both the BJP and the Congress have had some success in forging alliances with regional parties. During the NDA's tenure, attempts were also made by the party to shun its 'cow-belt party' tag and seek a foothold in southern states in particular. Keeping this in mind, the BJP elected three party presidents from the southern belt in quick succession. In 2000, Bangaru Laxman, who hailed from Andhra Pradesh, was elected BJP president. Laxman had been a trade union leader and came from a scheduled caste community.

Bangaru Laxman's tenure came to an end in 2001 when a private TV network, Tehelka, released video footage that appeared to show him allegedly taking bribes. At the National Executive in New Delhi in March 2001, Advani underlined how the allegations against Bangaru Laxman were politically motivated. 'The situation arising out of the publication of the Tehelka tapes clearly shows that there is a sinister conspiracy to destabilize the Vajpayee government by anti-democratic means. The true purpose of the campaign of lies and slander against the BJP and the NDA government launched by the Congress Party, using the Tehelka tapes as a pretext, is now out in the open . . . The Congress Party's refusal to have a debate in

Parliament and its demand for the government's resignation are a pointer to its utter frustration. Its frustration is also rooted in the fact that the BJP has not only emerged as the dominant political party but has also succeeded in winning the support of more and more allies.'[1]

After Bangaru Laxman's resignation, K. Jana Krishnamurthi, who hailed from Tamil Nadu, became party president. He had given up his law practice and became a full-time worker of the Jana Sangh. He was among the founding members of the BJP. A former Union law minister and member of Parliament, Krishnamurthi was the second person from Tamil Nadu to head a national party in India after Kamaraj. In 1977, when the Jana Sangh merged with the Janata Party, he became the general secretary of the party's Tamil Nadu unit. On 14 March 2001, he took over as the president of the BJP from Bangaru Laxman. He, however, had health issues that prevented him from travelling extensively. So, ahead of the 2002 assembly elections, Venkaiah Naidu took over the party command.

Naidu, a *swayamsevak*, came into the spotlight for his role in the Jai Andhra Movement of 1972. While the movement was called off a year later, Naidu became the convener of the anti-corruption Jayaprakash Narayan Chhatra Sangharsh Samiti of Andhra Pradesh. Naidu, also known for his oratory since his youth, was jailed along with other Opposition leaders during the Emergency. He served as the party's national president from 2002 to 2004. On 18 October 2004, the first major change of leadership within the BJP after the general election results took place when Venkaiah Naidu resigned from the post of the party's national president. Advani succeeded Naidu as the party president.

After coming to power at the centre, the BJP felt that it needed expansion in terms of geography and social base. During deliberations within the party on the ways to achieve the goal, it was felt that the party must move ahead with a Gandhian perspective in the social and economic sphere rather than adopt Gandhian socialism. This was a time of debates around reservations and religion. By then these debates had been going on for about a decade and the party decided to have better representation of all sections in the party. The party felt that the politics of appeasement and vote bank had compromised social justice. Thus, the BJP fought against corruption on the one hand, and strived for cultural nationalism by way of yatras on the other.

The BJP gained more than any political party from the decline of the Congress as a dominant pan-Indian force. It was able to project itself in new geographic areas and social segments as a result of holding power at the Centre. However, the extent of this geographic and social expansion was subject to continuous power play at all levels of the political process. One state in which the BJP expanded support during that period—that would stay with it for many years— was Gujarat where a new leader had emerged.

Modi in Gujarat

Starting as an RSS pracharak in Gujarat, Narendra Modi played a major role in the campaigns and expansion of the BJP in the state. He had been associated with the party's organization before helping the BJP develop deep and strong roots there. In February 1987, Modi was given the responsibility to organize the party campaign for the Ahmedabad municipal elections. His methodical planning helped the BJP win two-thirds of the seats in Ahmedabad municipality. During an interview in 1996 when asked about the speculation that he could become CM one day, Modi had said, 'I am connected to the mission and not ambition. In my life, mission is everything, not ambition.'[2]

Modi subsequently rose within the party ranks to be named as a member of the BJP's National Election Committee in 1990. He helped organize L.K. Advani's 1990 Ram Rath Yatra and Murli Manohar Joshi's 1991–92 Ekta Yatra. Narendra Modi was appointed the BJP national secretary and he moved to New Delhi in 1994, where he assumed responsibility for party activities in Haryana and Himachal

Pradesh.[3] He was promoted to the position of BJP general secretary (organization) in May 1998.[4]

Modi was involved in expanding the party's membership in Gujarat. In 2001, the state was struck by the Bhuj earthquake. In 2001, chief minister Keshubhai Patel's health was failing and the BJP lost a few state assembly seats in the by-elections. Patel's standing had been damaged by his administration's handling of the earthquake which had killed about 20,000 people. The central leadership of the BJP responded by appointing Narendra Modi as chief minister in October 2001. Barely a few months after Modi took charge, on 27 February 2002, a train with several hundred passengers was set on fire near Godhra by a mob, killing approximately sixty people. The train carried many *karsevaks* who were returning from Ayodhya after performing a religious ceremony. The Vishwa Hindu Parishad gave a call for a bandh. During the bandh riots broke out.[5]

The Modi government imposed a curfew in twenty-six major cities, issued shoot-at-sight orders and called for the army to patrol the streets, but the violence still escalated.[6] Modi's detractors used the violence as an opportunity to launch a smear campaign against him.

In April 2002, the BJP's National Executive was held in Goa. Upon reaching Goa, Advani spoke to Modi regarding his resignation. At the end of the National Executive, after delineating the events in detail, Modi made an offer for resignation. This was rejected by the National Executive. Instead, a resolution appreciating Modi's administrative swiftness in controlling and stopping the riots was passed. It said:

'In the best traditions of the party, so as to assist the party in discussing the happenings in Gujarat threadbare, and so that it may take a decision without any inhibition, Shri Modi offered to step down as chief minister. In a democracy there is only one way to put the issue, and the calumny to rest: The people are the ultimate arbiters, and so the people of Gujarat are the ones who can and must decide. Accordingly, the National Executive unanimously rejects

Shri Modi's offer to resign his post. It is confident that Shri Modi can meet every challenge, that by effective action he can counter every canard.'[7]

The public mandate that the National Executive was referring to had been won by Modi. However, Modi decided to answer his adversaries by seeking a fresh mandate by calling for a midterm election in the state, seeking to either exit or obtain legitimacy through elections. In the 2002 assembly elections, the BJP secured 127 seats and 49.85 per cent votes against 117 seats and 44.81 per cent votes garnered in 1998.[89] The Congress won fifty-one seats and 39.28 per cent votes in 2002 against fifty-three seats and 34.8 per cent votes polled in 1998. Hence, Modi returned to power as people voted for his model of development.

During his tenure as CM of Gujarat, Modi often heard about farmers who were constrained by bad roads in getting their products to market. He was passionate about building better roads. Gujarat had suffered for decades with poor water availability. Addressing this issue became his priority. He also started projects to divert the surplus water of Narmada to parched areas and brought clean drinking water to Adivasi areas. In the meanwhile, Modi transformed the Sabarmati riverfront. He ensured roads were built from cities to Adivasi areas. In an initiative to drive investment in the state, he started the 'Vibrant Gujarat' shows to drive investment into the state. He worked on ending crime in Gujarat. In Ahmedabad, temple yatras had come under attacks in the past. As CM, Modi worked on tackling these issues. Modi asked party MLAs to ensure children in their areas reached schools. During the admission season, all the BJP MLAs would work in villages, talking to parents where dropout rates were high to ensure children, especially girls, went to school.

The Semi-Finals: State Elections in 2003

Around September–October in 2003 when winter came knocking, the political temperature in the country was rising. Four states,

Delhi, Rajasthan, Madhya Pradesh and Chhattisgarh, were headed for elections. The media called it the semi-final that would be followed by the finals, the Lok Sabha election. The government had performed well so far, and this was evident in the 8.2 per cent GDP growth in 2003.[10]

In Madhya Pradesh, the Congress had remained invincible since 1993 under the leadership of Digvijaya Singh and it was expected that the party would once again win the 2003 elections. Taking a lesson from the internal differences over not announcing a chief ministerial face in the previous elections, the BJP declared Uma Bharti as its CM candidate.

The party made development an issue for the elections, claiming that Digvijaya Singh's government, despite being in power for ten years, had failed to bring progress for Madhya Pradesh, particularly in critical areas such as power, water and roads. Two consecutive victories had made the Congress government overconfident. The BJP, on the other hand, had gauged the discontent among the people, and made promises to work on the fronts where there was unhappiness.

Both the BJP and Congress contested on all 228 seats of the state and while the BJP won 173, the Congress was limited to thirty-eight seats.[11] This was a huge defeat for the Congress. The BBC compared the Congress party's loss to its defeat in 1977. It said that the Congress had not lost so badly even in 1977.[12]

Table 1: Madhya Pradesh Assembly Elections of 2003[13]

Political Party	AE 1998		LS 1999		AE 2003	
	Vote Share	Seats Won	Vote Share	Seats Won	Vote Share	Seats Won
Bharatiya Janata Party	39.28%	119	46.58%	29	42.50%	173
Indian National Congress	40.59%	172	43.91%	11	31.61%	38
Bahujan Samaj Party	6.15%	11	5.23%	0	7.26%	2

The newly formed state of Chhattisgarh faced its first elections in 2003. Ajit Jogi was the Congress chief minister then. Right before elections, a problem cropped up for the BJP when a video of Dilip Singh Judeo surfaced. It was claimed that Judeo had taken a bribe. Judeo was the BJP MP from Bilaspur and was the minister of state for environment and forests in the Vajpayee government. Later in 2016, a special CBI court posthumously cleared Judeo of the charges levelled against him. The CBI said in the court that the sting was done at the behest of Amit Jogi to ensure political dividends for his father Ajit Jogi. When the controversy erupted, Judeo was a front runner to become the BJP's chief ministerial face for the Chhattisgarh elections. The controversy changed the situation just ahead of elections.

The party was now looking for a leader who not only had a strong base among the people of Chhattisgarh, but also enjoyed a clean image. The BJP chose Raman Singh, who was at the time the Union minister of state for commerce and industry. In 1999, Raman Singh had entered Parliament by defeating veteran Congress leader Motilal Vohra from Rajnandgaon in Chhattisgarh. He was now entrusted with the responsibility of strengthening the party organization in the state by taking everyone along and ensuring a victory for the BJP in the upcoming state elections.

Under Singh's able leadership, the BJP won fifty of the ninety seats. The Congress won thirty-seven.[14] Raman Singh's taking over as the chief minister ushered in a political era in the newly carved-out state that continued for over a decade.

As in Chhattisgarh, in Rajasthan also, the BJP sent a leader from the Centre. In November 2002, Vasundhara Raje took over the reins of the party as the state unit chief. The BJP decided to launch a 'Parivartan Yatra' in the heat of May–June. The BJP won 120 seats in the 200-member Rajasthan assembly. The Congress won just fifty-six.[15]

One important aspect of the BJP's victory in all three states was the support of tribal voters. Of the thirty-four seats reserved for tribals, the BJP won twenty-nine in Chhattisgarh. In Madhya Pradesh and Rajasthan also, the BJP won a majority of the seats reserved for tribals.[16] Their support for the BJP made it clear that the group remained neglected by Congress governments and this neglect turned them towards the BJP. On 10 December 2003, the *Business Standard* wrote, 'BJP won semi-final on tribal power'.[17] The traditional Congress coalition was the combination of upper caste Hindus, tribals, Harijans and Muslims. The BJP had made major inroads by expanding its voter base across all sections of society.

Lok Sabha Elections 2004

The BJP's strong performance in the three elections infused the party with greater confidence. It was decided to prepone the Lok Sabha elections that were due in September 2004. The BJP started to feel if the national elections were held before the due date, the party would be able to return to power easily. Buoyed by this confidence, the BJP in its National Executive meeting held in Hyderabad on 11– 12 January 2004, decided to go for early elections.

In his address Vajpayee said, 'The recent NDA meeting has authorized me to take a final decision about preponing elections. Now, the responsibility is on me. The NDA is ready. The BJP is ready. The hour of deciding has come. The decision can be only one.'[18]

On the request of Prime Minister Atal Bihari Vajpayee, President A.P.J. Abdul Kalam dissolved the thirteenth Lok Sabha on 6 February and the Election Commission of India announced that fresh elections would be held in four phases between 20 April and 10 May for the fourteenth Lok Sabha.

Opinion polls conducted in the media also strengthened the party's confidence in an impending victory. In an opinion poll conducted for the *Indian Express* and *NDTV*, Nielsen predicted that the NDA would get between 287 and 303 seats. Another opinion poll, India Today–ORG Marg Mood of the Nation Poll, predicted 330 to 340 seats for the NDA. While the popularity ratings of Vajpayee shot up to 47 per cent, Sonia Gandhi's ratings stood at 23 per cent.[19] The India Shining slogan was born out of the same confidence. The government felt that people were happy with its functioning, and that its achievements had managed to reach the people of India.

In its election manifesto 'Vision Document 2004', the party proclaimed to have ended political instability as well as successfully maintained a coalition for the past five years. The manifesto highlighted the party's effort to broker peace talks with Pakistan, conduct free and fair elections in Jammu and Kashmir and initiate conflict resolution in the northeast. It also emphasized the party's achievements on the macroeconomic front, achieving a GDP growth rate of 8 per cent and crossing the $110 billion mark in forex reserves. The manifesto made 'development, good governance and peace' the central issues for the 2004 Lok Sabha elections.

As a part of the party's election campaigning activities, voters received a pre-recorded telephone message that began with *Main Atal Bihari Vajpayee bol raha hun*' (This is Atal Bihari Vajpayee speaking), urging voters to vote for him.[20] There were various ad campaigns launched which included innovative advertisements on billboards across the country.[21]

Leading up to the elections, Vajpayee was seen as more popular among the youth than Sonia Gandhi. A survey on youth sentiment prior to the election, conducted by Aaj Tak–Dainik Bhaskar–India Today–ORG Marg found that 55 per cent of eighteen to twenty-four-year-olds preferred Vajpayee as Prime Minister. A similar trend was detected for twenty-five to thirty-four; 52 per cent of them supported Vajpayee. The exit polls gave out similar results: 51 per cent of the eighteen to twenty-four-year-olds voted for the BJP whereas 41 per cent voted for the Congress.[22]

A month before the elections, the party revised its strategy after it received below-the-par feedback on its campaign. The strategy for the second phase of the campaign was altered and the focus shifted to highlighting the party's achievements on the development front. Hard-hitting statistics on the BJP-led NDA government's social welfare programmes like the food security programme, Pradhan Mantri Gram Sadak Yojana and Indira Awas Yojana were aggressively advertised to showcase that the party had been successful in achieving its social reform agenda.[23]

However, the India Shining campaign did not appeal to every section of voters. Many felt that it was targeted towards urban voters and completely ignored the plight of voters in rural India who could not fully relate to the growth agenda that was being promoted by the party.[24]

In its first ad campaign against the BJP, the Congress resorted to sloganeering and challenged the incumbent's promise of job creation. It also countered BJP's 'India Shining' slogan with its very own 'Aam aadmi ko kya mila?' (What did the common man get?).[25] The Congress party strategized to direct its campaign towards highlighting the NDA's failures on the unemployment and agriculture front and putting the spotlight on the various scams that had taken place during the incumbent's tenure. It also dismissed the 'India Shining' campaign in rural regions. Similar to the BJP's phone call campaign, the Congress party sent out inspirational text messages to voters such as, 'Some only feel good, some have good feelings for you.'[26]

The BJP was so sure of its victory that a day before the election results were to be announced, Pramod Mahajan used the Indian map to try to explain to Vajpayee how the BJP was headed to win more seats than in the 1999 elections. When Mahajan was done, Vajpayee told him to pack his bags and get ready to sit in the opposition benches.

In 1998, when the BJP formed its first coalition government at the Centre, Pramod Mahajan's skills at number-crunching and coalition management made him indispensable to Vajpayee. Mahajan, a member of the RSS, got actively involved in BJP politics when he became the sub-editor of its Marathi newspaper *Tarun Bharat*. When BJP formed its first government in Gujarat in 1995, Mahajan was the party's in-charge for the state. Both worked. Mahajan introduced the BJP to surveys and phone calls to reach out to voters in a big way. His media-friendly approach and communication skills came in handy in pushing the BJP ahead. During his stint as parliamentary affairs minister, he also built alliances across party lines.

Vajpayee did not participate in the election campaign for the 2004 polls because he had undergone a knee surgery, and the campaign was being led by Advani. With an aim to establish public connect, a 'Bharat Uday Yatra' was undertaken under the leadership of Advani. The government's achievements of the last five years were highlighted all through the yatra that lasted for thirty-three days and covered 8,500 kms and 121 constituencies.[27] During his public meetings, Advani talked about how the public was impressed with the performance of the government on BSP that is, Bijli, Sadak and Paani (power, roads and water). He also raised issues like Ram Mandir and Uniform Civil Code.

Having seen the impact of Advani's previous yatras, the Opposition was alarmed. When the yatra reached Andhra Pradesh, the Opposition knocked on the doors of the Election Commissioner Narayan Rao with the concern alleging that the yatra could create and deepen the communal divide in the country. In an all-party meeting, CPI, which was backed by the Congress, said, 'Advani's yatra would bring back bitter memories of communal trouble triggered by his earlier campaigns.'[28] The yatra had heated up the politics of the country and left the Opposition jittery.

With 145 seats, the Congress emerged as the largest party when the 2004 Lok Sabha election results came in. After its win in three states, the BJP had gained confidence. Even as the BJP managed to expand its reach and base, the Congress still enjoyed an edge as it was an old party and still was the default voting option for many. Vajpayee's term was historic, but it was seen that wherever the party cadre weakened, the party failed to gain a base.

Leaders such as Pramod Mahajan felt that the India Shining slogan would catch the nation's fancy. But the more experienced and

politically astute Vajpayee felt that the campaign was not a practical
public outreach campaign. The results of 2004 were in sync with
Vajpayee's expectations. The Congress won seven seats more than
the BJP. The lesson the BJP learnt was that public participation is
important in issues of governance.

The BJP contested on 364 seats but won only 138. The NDA
coalition had also weakened over time and together the NDA stood
at 186 seats. In comparison, the Congress and its allies won 216.
Though the Congress emerged as the largest party, even with its
allies, it was 57 short of the majority mark to be able to form the
government. At this time, the Communist parties emerged as the
Congress's saviour helping it to form the government by extending
support.

The party lost many important seats in 2004.[29] The party also
suffered the loss of crucial seats held by its cabinet members.
Human Resource Development Minister Murli Manohar Joshi lost
his Allahabad seat to Rewati Raman Singh from the Samajwadi Party
while the Foreign Minister, Yashwant Sinha, lost his Hazaribagh
seat in Jharkhand to B.P. Mehta from the CPI. Other BJP ministers
who lost their seats in 2004 were Ram Naik, Jagmohan Malhotra,
Syed Shahnawaz Hussain, Sahib Singh Verma, Vijay Goel, Kariya
Munda, C.P. Thakur and Shanta Kumar. For the BJP, this defeat was
a stinging blow, the first break from a long period of electoral gains.

Table 2: Lok Sabha Elections of 2004[30]

Political Party	LS 1999		LS 2004	
	Vote Share	Seats Won	Vote Share	Seats Won
Bharatiya Janata Party	23.75%	182	22.16%	138
Indian National Congress	28.3%	114	26.53%	145
Communist Party of India (Marxist)	5.40%	33	5.66%	43

The 2004 elections were fought on the India Shining slogan with the confidence that emanated from the BJP's victories in three states. The slogan was an attempt by the BJP to connect the enthusiasm within the party for the country's development and progress with the people of the nation. This did not work. Since Pramod Mahajan was identified with the India Shining election campaign, after the debacle in 2004, he took the blame for its failure.

Advani, however, said that there was no single reason for the BJP's defeat. First, the appeal for votes on the basis of the commitment to 'development and good governance' was not a nationwide emotional appeal that impacted voting at the regional level. While it worked in Karnataka, where the BJP won eighteen of the twenty-eight seats, it did not work in a state like Uttar Pradesh, where the party won just eleven of the eighty seats.[31] In UP, the bad performance was due to weak organizational structure. In Bihar, the caste and religious arithmetic did not work out.

Second, he felt that shortcomings in managing the coalition had proven costly in Andhra Pradesh where the party allied with the Telugu Desam Party, and in Tamil Nadu where it had hurriedly formed a coalition with the AIADMK. In Jharkhand, Haryana, Jammu and Kashmir and Assam, the party did not have effective coalitions. On the contrary, the Congress's electoral victory was driven mostly by the way it formed alliances.

Third, the negative campaign run by the party's opponents overpowered the BJP's positive campaign as not all sections of the society had been able to benefit from the progress that was made. The government failed to take the full benefits of development to the poor and marginalized sections of the society.

Fourth, there was an anti-incumbency sentiment against sitting MPs that contributed to the BJP's performance in 2004. This resulted in ninety sitting MPs not getting re-elected. Advani believed that he was responsible for this loss as he was away from Delhi for a long period of time during the Bharat Uday Yatra and could not lend support during crucial decisions related to election campaigning.[32]

Advani also strongly felt that slogans like 'Feel Good Factor' and 'India Shining' harmed the BJP in the 2004 elections. They were not suited for the campaign as the Opposition successfully raised questions on issues like poverty and unequal development, unemployment among the youths and the problems facing the farmers.

* * *

As Advani pointed out, there was no single reason for the defeat. There were failures in managing the alliance and that had cost the BJP. The negative campaign of the Opposition also impacted it adversely.

From 1998 to 2004, the BJP had run the first non-Congress government for a full term. A communication gap between the BJP's organization and the government proved costly. During this period, the party saw a regular change of presidents, and this did not bode too well for the organization. So despite organizational capacity the party could not take the positive message of the government's work to the people.

It is also noteworthy that this was the time when the party focused more on advertising but was failing to connect with the people on the ground. Many reforms had taken place during the NDA government, but the BJP had not been successful in effectively communicating them to the people.

When the party formed the coalition government in 1998, new inductions did not happen, and a new team could not take shape. The government worked well but the BJP could not build the next generation of leadership to take the party forward. It was from 2004 onwards that the party once again brought its focus back to new inductions and began building a new generation of leaders.

7

Building the Party (2004–2008)

On 14 May 2004, the BJP lost the elections, and the UPA pre-poll alliance led by the Congress formed the government with the support of the Left from the outside (no Left representatives occupied cabinet positions). While we tend to think of the 2004 elections as a major win for the Congress, the shift in seats was actually modest. The Congress only won 145 seats in 2004. It was four seats ahead of where it had been in 1998, and seven seats ahead of the BJP's tally of 138 seats. The Left block had sixty seats; a little less than half of the Congress.[1]

The elections had been fought through the convention of competing parties without anointed Prime Ministers, hence the new coalition had to choose its prime minister. President Abdul Kalam invited Sonia Gandhi for a discussion on government formation since she was the leader of the single-largest party. A conflict was brewing on the subject of Sonia Gandhi's foreign origin with many parties being opposed to her taking over as Prime Minister.

Sonia Gandhi instead chose Manmohan Singh as Prime Minister, while she remained Congress president. This was a different arrangement compared with the previous Congress governments; for instance, wherein Indira Gandhi, Rajiv Gandhi and P.V. Narasimha Rao were in the position of both Prime Minister and party president. The Singh/Gandhi arrangement involved an unusual dynamic where political power was vested with the party president while the leadership of the executive branch was with a Prime Minister who was not a directly elected leader and therefore did not enjoy the mandate to rule.

Somnath Chatterjee of the CPI(M) was chosen as the Speaker. The CPI(M) was a powerful partner, with the ability to bring down the government if it withdrew from the coalition. The UPA-1 government was thus a balancing act between three power centres: the executive branch led by Manmohan Singh, which included the Planning Commission led by Montek Singh Ahluwalia; the Congress and the National Advisory Council (NAC) led by Sonia Gandhi, and the CPI(M) Politburo.

The CPI(M) had ideological differences with the Congress, and with the new path of economic policy that had been built by successive prime ministers from Rao to Vajpayee. A key person who wove the coalition together, until his death in 2008, was Harkishan Singh Surjeet, the CPI(M) general secretary. As an example, it was Surjeet who acted as the mediator between the Samajwadi Party and the Congress by taking Amar Singh to meet Sonia Gandhi. The relations between the two parties had soured after Amar Singh accused the Congress party and Sonia Gandhi of tapping his phone back in 2006.[23]

The UPA government established a new advisory committee, the NAC led by Sonia Gandhi. Its stated objectives were to monitor the implementation of the Common Minimum Programme—the agreed upon agenda for the UPA, to provide inputs for the formulation of policy by the government, and to extend support to the government in its legislative business. This was an experiment in institutional arrangements for living within the coalition arrangement, the mechanisms of power sharing for five years of stability under a coalition government such as achieved by Vajpayee and Rao. But there was also the possibility, as with the Planning Commission, of NAC becoming an extra-constitutional centre of power.

The BJP was crestfallen by the election results of May 2004, and only gradually got back to rebuilding its political position. On 6 April 2005, BJP president Advani spoke at the party's National Council. He listed five tasks for the party, including expanding the BJP's base in regions where the party's presence was marginal making the BJP *sarva vyapi* (spread in all corners) and a party of good governance bridging the gap between India's potential and her actual performance; reorienting the agenda of economic reforms to benefit gaon (village), garib (poor), kisan (farmer), and mazdoor (worker); strengthening the appeal of the party among the youth by promoting young leaders and espousing their issues; and making constructive work an integral part of the BJP activity.[4]

Two months later, in June 2005, Advani visited Pakistan. Born in Karachi in 1927, he described his visit as both 'personal and political'. During his Pakistan tour, Advani visited Mohammad Ali Jinnah's mausoleum, he offered flowers at the site and while leaving, made an observation in the visitor's book:

'Many people leave an imprint on history, but very few people actually create history. Qaid-e-Azam Mohammad Ali Jinnah was actually one of those few people. In his early years, Sarojini Naidu, a leading luminary of India's freedom struggle, described Mr Jinnah as an "ambassador of Hindu-Muslim unity". His address to the Constituent Assembly of Pakistan on 11 August 1947, is really a classic, a forceful espousal of a secular state in which, while every citizen would be free to practise his own religion, the state shall make no distinction between one citizen and another on grounds of faith. My respectful homage to this great man.'[5]

Advani calling Jinnah a secular leader and the flag-bearer of Hindu-Muslim unity led to consternation in the party and the larger Sangh Parivar. The BJP had always considered the Partition of India an unfortunate and avoidable political blunder and had held Jinnah responsible for it. The media had a field day. On 4 June 2005, the *Telegraph* carried the headline, 'Advani salutes 'secular' Jinnah'. The media reported that Sudheendra Kulkarni had faxed the full text

of his remarks to Prakash Javadekar who took them to Venkaiah
Naidu, Sushma Swaraj and Arun Jaitley, and they, in turn, decided
to not publish them on the web or disseminate them to the press.
When Kulkarni insisted they be published, he was rebuffed. It took
Advani's return on Monday for these to be made available on the
party website.[6]

The RSS and the VHP spoke openly against Advani's praise
of Jinnah.[7] Vajpayee, however, stood behind Advani. He said, 'His
remarks on Jinnah are being misinterpreted.'[8] However, most
party leaders tried to distance themselves from these statements.[9]
The Sangh Parivar, especially the VHP, strongly attacked him and
demanded that he retract the statements.

Advani, however, stood firm and said, 'I have not said or
done anything in Pakistan which I need to retract or review.'[10]
He demanded that the party draft a resolution categorically
supporting his stand on Jinnah. Advani said that due to the
media's misreporting, his statements were misrepresented. He
believed that on TV news especially, the reportage was aimed at
creating sensationalism and headline-grabbing news. Further, he
felt that either knowingly or unknowingly, the media did not pay
attention to the historical context, the nuances of the statement,
the subjective arguments, the people related to the story and the
complexity of issues involved.[11]

Advani resigned as BJP president on 7 June 2005 upon his return
to India. However, on 8 June, a unanimous request was made after
discussions within the party asking Advani to stay in his position.
On 10 June, a meeting of the BJP National Executive was held and
the following statement was issued after a resolution to the effect was
passed:

'The BJP praises its President's out of league and unprecedented
visit to Pakistan . . . Without calling Jinnah a secularist, he reminded
the people of Pakistan of the speech that Pakistan's founder
delivered in the country's Constituent Assembly, in which Jinnah
laid emphasis on religious freedom and asked everyone to refrain

from religious discrimination. The BJP reiterates that no matter what Jinnah's vision for Pakistan was, the country he established is not religiously secular. Even the idea of two nations for Hindus and Muslims is an antithesis to the principles that the BJP stands by. The BJP has always been critical of the division of the country based on religion and will continue to do so and will continue to reject the two-nation theory propounded by Jinnah and supported by British rulers. We can't ignore the reality that Jinnah led a communal campaign to create Pakistan as a result of which thousands of innocent people were killed and lakhs of them became homeless and lost their livelihoods.'[12]

After this resolution was passed, Advani continued to serve as the BJP president but said he would not continue in the position after the upcoming Mumbai meeting. When the National Council of the party met in Mumbai in December 2005, Rajnath Singh was elected party president. On 31 December 2005, Rajnath Singh took over as the party chief.

Rajnath Singh was born in a family of farmers in Bhabhaura village which falls in UP's Varanasi district. He was deeply influenced by his father Ram Badan Singh. Rajnath Singh had been part of the RSS since his childhood when he was still in school. When he joined the University of Gorakhpur for masters, Singh actively participated in student politics and became a member of the ABVP. His rural background gave him a good understanding of the issues concerning agriculture. In 2000, he became the chief minister of Uttar Pradesh. He had held many portfolios, including agriculture and food processing ministries, in the Vajpayee government. He had been elected to the Rajya Sabha for a second term in 2003 and was reappointed national general secretary of the BJP in 2004. He was in-charge of Jharkhand and Chhattisgarh for the state elections of 2003 and was credited for the first BJP government in Chhattisgarh in 2003.

Rajnath Singh became party president at a time when the party's morale was low, following the electoral loss of 2004, the Jinnah controversy and then Advani's departure as party president. He initiated a series of organization-building activities. After taking over as party president, Singh recognized that with the emergence of new groups and constituencies, both at the local and national levels, the party needed to focus on growing deep roots through setting up of new party cells. He emphasized a back-to-basics approach, to get back to the difficult work of building a party while in the Opposition in Parliament.

Born in 1951, Singh represented the next generation of the BJP politicians, when compared with Vajpayee (born in 1924) or Advani (born in 1927). In this sense, his elevation was an important milestone, establishing a new leadership team for the BJP after the 2004 debacle. Alongside him, the next generation of BJP politicians such as Arun Jaitley (b. 1952), Sushma Swaraj (b. 1952), Pramod Mahajan (b. 1949) and Vasundhara Raje Scindia (b. 1953) started coming to the fore. Later, that BJP generation saw the rise of Narendra Modi (b. 1950). Rajnath Singh's new team had Pramod Mahajan, Rajiv Pratap Rudy, Dharmendra Pradhan, Ananth Kumar, Mukhtar Abbas Naqvi, Smriti Irani and many other young leaders. As many as 80 per cent of the people in his team were below sixty years of age.

This, inevitably, led to friction with senior politicians such as Kalyan Singh, Uma Bharti, Madan Lal Khurana and Keshubhai Patel. Of particular importance was Kalyan Singh, who had served as the UP chief minister twice, in 1991–92 and 1997–99. He had parted ways with the BJP once before, which had led to his ouster from the party in November 1999. While he had returned to the BJP in 2004, his dissatisfaction with the new BJP led to his departure in 2009, when he formed a new party, the Jan Kranti Party (Rashtrawadi). This departure was also reversed in January 2013. Kalyan Singh's return to the BJP was a big boost for the party. He was an important OBC leader and significantly helped the party win the 2017 assembly elections.

A similar story unfolded with Uma Bharti, the politician from Madhya Pradesh. She stormed out of a meeting of the party leadership, which was chaired by L.K. Advani in November 2004.[13] Bharti had earlier started a *padyatra* (foot march) protesting the nomination of Shivraj Singh Chouhan as the chief minister of MP by the party's parliamentary board despite the party having asked her to not undertake the yatra. Her walkout from the party meeting was seen as an extreme act of indiscipline. After this, she was sacked as party general secretary and suspended from party membership for a month, and then expelled from the party in 2005. She stepped out to start a new party, the Bharatiya Janashakti, which was closed down in 2010 and Bharti returned to the BJP in 2011. Similarly, Madan Lal Khurana was expelled from the BJP in August 2005, when he criticized Advani, and was brought back in September after he apologized. He was ousted again in March 2006 when he joined in the rebellion led by Uma Bharti.

Rajnath Singh's task in the post-2004 period was to stabilize the party amid these rebellions and bring focus back to building the party as an organization. He formed a committee led by Sushma Swaraj, with Kiren Rijiju, Najma Heptulla and Sumitra Mahajan, to propose changes to the BJP's constitution that would allow the party to have 33 per cent reservation for women at the organizational level. These changes were implemented in 2007.[14]

In this period the BJP also protested terrorist activities. In July 2005, the Ram Janambhoomi in Ayodhya and a Shramjeevi Express train in Jaunpur were attacked by terrorists. Later that year, blasts happened in New Delhi and at the Indian Institute of Science in Bangalore. In 2006, the Sankat Mochan temple and Cantonment railway station in Varanasi came under attack. Rajnath Singh planned a 'Bharat Suraksha Yatra', drawing on the familiar yatra-based mobilization strategy where the BJP had strong organizational capabilities, through which these events would be harnessed to portray the BJP's stance on the need to be tough on terrorism. He started the yatra from Puri in Orissa, while Advani started another leg of the yatra from Gujarat's Rajkot. Together the yatra was supposed to cover about 12,000 km across ten states.

Shortly after coming to power in 2004, the UPA government commissioned the Sachar Committee to look into the issues being faced by Muslims and their representation in Indian society. The BJP saw this as Congress's attempt to once again play one religion against another for votes. In its National Executive held on 17 September 2005, the BJP adopted a resolution saying, 'The UPA was established in May 2004 after the general election on the basis of anti-BJPism ... The UPA government's obsession with vote bank politics has, predictably, degenerated into minorityism. The extension of reservation in education, employment and local government to Muslims in Andhra Pradesh, and the 50 per cent reservation for Muslims in Aligarh Muslim University signal the beginning of a process that will have hideous consequences on national unity ... The BJP also rejects as preposterous a surreptitious attempt to introduce Islamic Banking and Islamic Company Law. It is deplorable that neither the Prime Minister nor the UPA chairperson cared to visit the Ramjanambhoomi complex after the terrorist attack, so insensitive are they to Hindu sentiment.'[15]

'The Government's appeasement of minorities is directed at Muslims alone. When it came to anti-Sikh riots of 1984, the Government showed its lack of sincerity. The ATR [Action taken report] on the Nanavati Commission Report is a vivid example of its unwillingness to prosecute Congress leaders who had a hand in the killings.'[16]

The Bharat Suraksha Yatra raised issues of Congress appeasement, along with misuse of the office of the governor in Goa, Jharkhand and Bihar to keep the BJP out of power. On 22 April 2006, after Singh had covered about 3,738 km and Advani had travelled 4,700 km, news came in that Pramod Mahajan had been shot by his brother Pravin.[17] With the senior BJP leader battling for life, the yatra was called off.

Running parallely, a problem came up about Sonia Gandhi's chairmanship of the NAC. Under Article 102(1)(a) of the Constitution, a person is disqualified as MP for holding any office of profit under the Government of India or the government of a state, other than a narrow class of positions declared by Parliament by law not to disqualify its holder. In the establishment of the NAC, the government had not amended the law on office of profit to include the NAC chairman as one of the exempted positions. Alongside Sonia Gandhi, there were numerous other positions which were occupied by members of Parliament, which were incompatible with the office of profit law. When this came to light, the BJP protested the impropriety. NDA leaders led by Vajpayee, marched to Rashtrapati Bhavan urging President A.P.J. Abul Kalam Azad not to give consent on any ordinance on this issue.[18] On 23 March 2006, Sonia Gandhi resigned from the Lok Sabha. Later she was re-elected and the bill was passed amid an NDA walkout.

State Elections

In 2004, elections were held in six states: Andhra Pradesh, Arunachal Pradesh, Karnataka, Maharashtra, Orissa and Sikkim. Of these, a BJP government was formed, in alliance with the BJD, in Orissa alone.

Rajnath Singh's reconstruction of the BJP as an organization started generating results in the elections. From 2004 to 2007, the NDA allies led by the BJP won in eight states. They made new progress in the states of Karnataka, Bihar and Punjab and obtained support from backward castes. The 2007 Gujarat elections underlined the emergence of Narendra Modi.

There was a surprising result in Karnataka, where the BJP won seventy-nine seats and emerged as the single-largest party.[19] This was the first time the BJP became an important party in the south. The JD(S) and Congress joined hands to 'keep the communal forces in check'.[20] This once again was reminiscent of the political isolation that the BJP had been facing since the days of the Jana Sangh. The Congress and some other opposition parties wanted to brand the BJP as communal to make the party a political pariah even as they turned into family enterprises and got mired in corruption.

Dharam Singh of the Congress party became the chief minister. But this coalition did not work out. In January 2006, twenty months after the coalition was formed, the JD(S) withdrew support from the Dharam Singh-led government and formed an alliance with the BJP.[21] The new arrangement between the JD(S) and the BJP lasted twenty months, paving the way for fresh elections in 2008. The BJP won an absolute majority in this election, with 110 seats, and formed its first government in Karnataka and southern India.[22]

In 2005, elections were held in three states, Bihar, Haryana and Jharkhand. The BJP formed governments in two states, Bihar and Jharkhand. In Jharkhand, the BJP won thirty seats and emerged as the single-largest party.[23] Alongside, the party had the support of its NDA ally, JD(U), which won six seats, as well as five independent candidates. However, the BJP faced a formidable pre-poll alliance between the Shibu Soren-led JMM [Jharkhand Mukti Morcha] and the Congress, as well as a hostile governor who chose to invite Shibu Soren to form the government.[24] Soren was now faced with a vote of confidence in the Assembly, but the JMM–Congress alliance, with twenty-six seats, did not have sufficient numbers to prove a majority. The Congress sought to poach the five independent candidates aligning with the BJP, albeit unsuccessfully.[25] Ultimately, the JMM and the NDA formed a coalition government in Jharkhand.

In Bihar, the BJP and the JD(U) formed a coalition government in 2005. Between 1990 and 1995, Bihar was the only state in the Hindi heartland where the BJP's vote share declined. This decline was because of the rise of OBC politics. The BJP formed an alliance with Nitish Kumar and the George Fernandes-led Samata Party in 1996. The Samata Party, which merged into the JD(U) in 2003, was the BJP's third alliance after the Shiromani Akali Dal in Punjab and the Shiv Sena in Maharashtra. It marked a new style of BJP alliances, going beyond traditional partnerships grounded in religious outlook, with the Akali Dal and the Shiv Sena, reaching out to a respected secular/socialist partner in the form of George Fernandes.

The 2005 election results in Bihar in February threw a fractured mandate with the JD(U) winning fifty-five seats and the BJP getting thirty-seven.[26] Since no party was in a position to form a government, President's Rule was imposed. Elections were held again in October that year. The NDA alliance came to power with the JD(U) winning eighty-eight seats and the BJP winning fifty-five.[27] Nitish Kumar became the NDA chief minister.

Before the 2005 elections, the Lalu Yadav-led RJD had ruled the state for fifteen years. Through the alliance with the JD(U), the BJP was able to wean away Lalu Yadav's traditional voter base comprising backward classes. Political scientist Milan Vaishnav notes: 'The BJP–JD(U) alliance forged a powerful political coalition that exploited the BJP's popularity among Hindu upper castes and the JD(U)'s constituency made up of the lower rungs of the OBCs, a new grouping that came to be known as Extremely Backward Castes (EBCs). The construction of the EBC identity was a savvy attempt to strip votes of non-Yadav backward castes from the RJD. Kumar's JD(U) also fractured the vote of Bihar's Dalits by again targeting the most backward among them, fashioning a new Mahadalit category and directing welfare benefits to this new group.'[28]

Table 1: Bihar Assembly Elections of 2005[29]

Political Party	AE 2000		LS 2004		AE 2005	
	Vote Share	Seats Won	Vote Share	Seats Won	Vote Share	Seats Won
Bharatiya Janata Party	14.64%	67	14.57%	5	15.65%	55
Indian National Congress	11.06%	23	4.49%	3	6.09%	9
Janata Dal (United)	6.47%	21	22.36%	6	20.46%	88
Rashtriya Janata Dal	28.34%	124	30.67%	22	23.45%	54

In 2007, elections were held in seven states: Goa, Himachal Pradesh, Punjab, Uttarakhand and Uttar Pradesh. The BJP governments got through in two of these states: Uttarakhand and Himachal Pradesh. In Punjab, the BJP–SAD coalition came to power. Punjab was an unexpected victory for the BJP–SAD alliance, ousting the incumbent Congress party. Significantly, the alliance made substantial inroads in the SC constituencies, with the BJP winning four seats and the SAD party winning sixteen seats. In comparison, the BJP had not won any SC seat in the preceding elections.[30]

Towards the end of the year when elections were held in Gujarat, Narendra Modi once again returned as the chief minister. This was a major victory because Modi had faced baseless criticism from several quarters over the 2002 Gujarat riots.[31] Modi had travelled across Gujarat as an RSS pracharak in the 1980s and helped build the organization. Madhavsinh Solanki's Kshatriya, Harijan, Adivasi, Muslim (KHAM) project had created divisions along caste and religious lines in the state. Modi had worked towards bridging the divides when he became chief minister in 2001. When he took over, the effects of the Kutch earthquake of 26 January 2001 were still being felt. Modi pushed hard on the agenda of private investment-led economic growth. He argued that officials should play a supportive role, to create conditions where private persons felt safe, and therefore brought investment to the state. Modi knew that merely investment wasn't enough and that equal and equitable social upliftment of people was also important. From 2003, the biennial Vibrant Gujarat Summit began as a major event that brought the business community together and galvanized investments into Gujarat. The phrase 'Gujarat model of development' came to be used widely.

This approach to economic policy, and the refashioning of the role of the state, was popular with the urban middle class, which obtained immediate rewards in terms of greater prosperity and safety. In the run up to the 2007 elections, the opposition parties decided to present a common front. Interestingly, the state unit of the Congress party and the national presidents adopted contradictory strategies. While the state unit steered clear of the 2002 riots, the national leaders repeatedly spoke about that time. During the campaigning,

Congress president Sonia Gandhi called Modi *'maut ka saudagar'* (merchant of death). Modi focused on maintaining peace and security in Gujarat during his tenure. He published a placard in the English press: 'In 4 years, acts of terror claimed 5,619 lives in India. But in Gujarat, only 1.'[32]

Table 2: Gujarat Assembly Elections of 2007[33]

Political Party	AE 2002		LS 2004		AE 2007	
	Vote Share	Seats Won	Vote Share	Seats Won	Vote Share	Seats Won
Bharatiya Janata Party	49.85%	127	47.37%	14	49.12%	117
Indian National Congress	39.28%	51	43.86%	12	38%	59
Bahujan Samaj Party	0.32%	0	1.48%	0	2.62%	0

In January 2008, the BJP's National Executive meeting was held at Ramlila Grounds in New Delhi. The party's political resolution emphasized two issues: internal security and the Sethusamudram project. In 2007, in an affidavit, the Congress had told the Supreme Court that Lord Ram did not exist. The BJP which has always held Lord Ram as the symbol of India's cultural nationalism registered a strong protest. The BJP resolution said, 'The stand adopted by the UPA government on the construction of Sethusamudram project was an onslaught on India's culture and sentiment of a vast majority of Indian people. To deny the existence of Bhagwan Ram and seek a judicial mandate on the subject is an indication of the UPA towards the sentiments of the country. In step after step the UPA has sought to denigrate the beliefs of majority of Indians.'[34]

At another national executive meeting of BJP's minority wing a few months later, the party spoke against the divisive spirit of the Sachar Committee report. 'If Muslims are poor, unemployed and backward today, it is because of the Congress which has ruled this country for majority of the years. It has done nothing for the uplift of Muslims.'[35] The Committee made various recommendations in favour of minority communities. Some of these recommendations included revision of procedures for delimitation of constituencies where certain constituencies with a large share of SCs, particularly comprising Muslims, were still under the 'un-reserved' category. The Committee also recommended that appropriate state level laws be enacted to ensure minority representation in local bodies to encourage Muslim participation.[36]

Nuclear Deal

The give and take between the Congress and the Communists reached a difficult point in 2007 when India and the US began discussing the nuclear deal. In July 2007, both governments announced that they would be giving final touches to the nuclear agreement and in August, the details were made public. When this happened, the Communist parties issued a threat that if the government went ahead with the deal, they would withdraw support.

On 13 September 2008, the BJP's National Executive passed a resolution on the Indo-US nuclear deal in 2014. It said, 'The entire argument of Dr Manmohan Singh's government in favour of the Indo-US nuclear deal made in the last three years stands completely exposed in the light of the letter sent by the Bush administration to the Chairman of The House, Foreign Affairs Committee of the US Congress about the condition of the deal. The stand of the BJP that the deal in the present form, seriously compromises India's strategic sovereignty and the right of nuclear tests stands, completely vindicated. In fact, many assurances given by the Prime Minister before Parliament about the merits of the deal turn out to be patently false and misleading as far as India's strategic interest is concerned. In fact, as recently as July 2, 2008, the Prime Minister's Office issued a statement that the 123 Agreement clearly overrides the Hyde Act and this position would be clear to anyone who goes through the provisions.'[37]

It further said, 'The text of the nuclear agreement and the statements of the Bush administration establish that the proposed 123 Agreement is in full conformity with the Hyde Act and in the event detonated a nuclear explosive device then the USA has the right to cease all nuclear co-operations with India immediately including the supply of fuel as well as to request the return of any items transferred from USA including fresh fuel. The text of the nuclear agreement and the statements of the Bush administration establish that the UPA government has perpetrated a mega fraud on both the Parliament and the people of the country . . . The BJP would like to clearly reiterate that any compromise on India's right to nuclear tests is wholly unacceptable.'[38]

The discussion around the deal continued for about a year and so did the disagreements between the Communist parties and the UPA government. Finally, on 8 July 2007, the Communist parties announced they would withdraw support from the government on the issue of India going to the International Atomic Energy Agency to seek its approval for the nuclear deal. On 9 July, the Communist parties submitted a letter to the President declaring the withdrawal of their support. The Congress now faced the challenge of proving its majority in Parliament. The government won the support of 275 MPs in comparison to the 256 who voted against it.[39] This was viewed with great euphoria in the world of finance and the economy, as they felt this would set the stage for an untrammelled leadership by Manmohan Singh and his colleagues, without the interference of the Left. With the benefit of hindsight, we know that this date (July 2007) was the high point of the UPA after which it saw a decline.

The Congress had survived the test in the Lok Sabha by obtaining the help of the Samajwadi Party. There were allegations of horse-trading to win support for the no-confidence motion. In 2008, the then Uttar Pradesh chief minister and the Bahujan Samaj Party leader Mayawati alleged that this agreement was in the personal interest of Mulayam Singh Yadav.[40] In 2009, BJP general secretary Arun Jaitley said that the UPA government had misused the CBI to shield Mulayam Singh Yadav in a 2007 disproportionate assets case, in return for his support.[41] On the other hand, Mulayam Singh Yadav claimed that the CBI, at the behest of the UPA government, was preparing fake documents to implicate him in a 2007 disproportionate assets case.[42] He said, 'The government takes support by issuing threats through the CBI. I supported the government through its tough times, but it sent the CBI after me.'[43]

The Election Management Committee of the BJP laid out a plan on 14 September 2008, for the Lok Sabha elections of 2009. It said that the task of formation of eight committees—state election committee, state election management committee, publicity committee, resource mobilization committee, media management committee, tours and travels committee, legal committee for election related work and data collection committee—should be immediately completed. A senior party functionary who was not contesting elections was nominated as 'prabhari' (in-charge) for each Lok Sabha constituency. Relevant state-level issues were identified for the national campaign. It was also decided to identify suitable women candidates so that women were adequately represented.

Alongside this, there were major changes taking place in the country. On 15 September 2008, Lehman Brothers declared bankruptcy in the US, triggering a global financial crisis, and imposing great turmoil in the Indian economy. On 26 November 2008, terrorists from Karachi carried out India's worst terrorist attack, killing 166 people in Mumbai and holding India's financial capital hostage for over three days.[44] The security response of the authorities, after the first deaths were reported, was remarkably slow. In response to widespread criticism, the UPA moved P. Chidambaram from the ministry of finance to the ministry of home affairs, and Pranab Mukherjee became the finance minister. Five years later, National Security Adviser M.K. Narayanan said, that the government had sufficient inputs about a terrorist attack on Mumbai's five-star hotels but did not believe that someone would come in so brazenly as the terrorists of 26/11 did. Consequently, no timely action was taken.[45]

Corruption Scandals

Concerns about corruption had first been pushed into the limelight by the Baba Ramdev campaign. In 2011, Baba Ramdev proposed a fast against corruption and black money. A Congress delegation comprising Pranab Mukherjee, Kapil Sibal, Pawan Kumar Bansal and Subodh Kumar Sahay went to Delhi airport to receive Yoga guru Baba Ramdev and urge him to call off the fast. This was an embarrassing sight for the Congress. Just days later, Baba Ramdev started his hunger strike at Delhi Ramlila Maidan. As the crowds swelled, the Congress began to get nervous. It ordered a midnight crackdown on the protesters. The police fired teargas shells and lathi-charged the protesters who were sleeping. The UPA was plagued with allegations of corruption in the Commonwealth Games, the 2G auction and coal block allocation. People were angry and Baba Ramdev had given vent to the pent-up anger.

Delhi had a Congress government at the time. The Commonwealth Games held in New Delhi in October 2010 were embroiled in a controversy over graft in its organization. The Central Vigilance Commission (CVC) and the Comptroller and Auditor General of India (CAG), investigated the various projects being undertaken, and found serious discrepancies in the organization of the event.[46] [47] There were issues with the quality of construction for various games, irregularities in contracts that were awarded for this construction, misappropriation of funds, financial bungling and loss of revenue.[48] Not only were organizers of the event charged with corruption, but many public officials in the state and centre were also held responsible.[49]

The 2G scam was revealed when the CAG presented its report on the Issue of Licences and Allocation of 2G Spectrum on 16 November 2010.[50] Vinod Rai served as CAG from 2008 to 2013.

The CAG estimated that there was a loss of revenue worth Rs 1.76 trillion from the way the auction was done. This was mainly attributed to issuing of low-cost telecom licenses based on 2001 market prices.[51] Apart from the issue of pricing of the 2G spectrum, there were procedural irregularities in allocation of licences. The Department of Telecom (DOT), which was responsible for carrying out allocation of 2G spectrum in a transparent and fair manner, flouted multiple rules and processes. The CAG report said that important guidelines were not followed; for instance, of the 122 licenses issued eighty-five were ineligible.[52] The cut-off date for submitting applications was said to have been changed arbitrarily in favour of certain companies over others and licenses were said to have been issued on a first-come-first-served (FCFS) basis.[53] In April 2011, the CBI filed a 80,000 page chargesheet, accusing some telecom officials as well as A. Raja who was the Telecom Minister at that time.[54]

However, in 2010, these allegations of corruption had a considerable impact upon the reputation of the UPA government.

Another scam that surfaced after a draft report was leaked in March 2012 by Vinod Rai, CAG, was the 'Coalgate' or the coal blocks allocation scam.[55] CAG's audit covered the period during the Eleventh Five Year Plan as well as allocations made under the ministry of coal since 2004. The report revealed that between 2004 and 2009 there was inefficient allocation of coal blocks which led to a loss of Rs 10.76 trillion.[56] This estimate was later revised to Rs 1.86 trillion in August 2012 when the final report was tabled in Parliament.[57]

The CAG report revealed that even though the criteria for coal block allocation was changed to competitive bidding in January 2004, the ministry chose to allocate coal blocks with the help of an 'inter-ministerial screening committee' that further took suggestions from other state governments and national level ministries like power and steel. Hence, the government exercised its discretionary power and allocated coal blocks to select private players.[58]

As described in the CAG audit report, the 35th meeting of the Screening Committee in September 2007 noted: 'Based on the data furnished by the applicants and the feedback received from State Governments and the Ministry of Power, the Committee assessed the applications having regard to the matter such as techno-economic feasibility of the end use project, status of preparedness to set up the end use project, past track record in execution of projects, financial and technical capabilities of the applicant companies, recommendations of the State Governments and Administrative Ministry concerned.'[59]

Maharashtra also had a Congress government at the time. In November 2010, the Adarsh Housing Society scandal in Mumbai was exposed. A 31-storey residential complex was built in a prime location in Mumbai, on land that belonged to the defence ministry.[60] Originally built with the intention of allotting flats in the complex to 1999 Kargil war heroes and their widows, it was revealed that top-level bureaucrats, military officials, politicians, and their respective family members were allocated these flats as bribes in return for concessions.[61] As disclosed in the CAG report on the scandal, various rules and regulations were flouted. For instance, eligibility rules were not followed as seen with allotment of flats; environmental clearance was not obtained, thereby violating the Coastal Regulation Zone laws; breaching the FSI rules, additional floors were built.[62] After the CBI filed an FIR against army officials, bureaucrats and politicians in January 2011, a charge-sheet was also filed in a special court set up by CBI in July 2012.[63] A senior member of the Congress party and then chief minister of Maharashtra, Ashok Chavan, was forced to resign.[64]

This procession of scandals added up to an overall credibility crisis that damaged the UPA government. Political opponents of the government mobilized street protests on corruption.

These developments reinvigorated the BJP which felt that voters were growing tired of UPA's unresponsive and weak leadership, which was corrupt all through. The BJP's National Council meeting was held on 6 February 2009, in Nagpur, Maharashtra. The political resolution adopted at the meeting said, 'Terrorist strikes at will and with impunity. They have amongst others attacked New Delhi, the political capital of India; Mumbai, the commercial capital of India; Bengaluru, the scientific capital of India; Varanasi, the spiritual capital of India. Be it north, south, east, or west, no part of the country is secure from the killing spree of terrorists. The terrorist attack in Mumbai on 26th November was the worst in the series.'[65]

Amid these developments, the country was moving towards the fifteenth Lok Sabha elections.

8

The Road to Resurgence (2009–2014)

When political parties were fighting the 2004 Lok Sabha elections, Vajpayee was battling his ailments. It had, by then become amply clear that he wouldn't be able to actively participate in elections in the future. It was incumbent upon the BJP to choose a new leader. L.K. Advani was a big leader in the BJP back then and was the party's natural choice to be projected as the prime ministerial face. In December 2007, an official decision about projecting Advani as the PM candidate was taken by the BJP's parliamentary board meeting held under the chairmanship of Rajnath Singh.

Speaking of the decision, Singh said that the parliamentary board had unanimously decided that Lal Krishna Advani would lead the party in elections. He further added that Vajpayee believed it was better to nominate Advani since his health prevented him from playing an active role in the party.[1]

During its campaign for the 2009 polls, the BJP raised the issue of terrorist attacks in different parts of the country highlighting the UPA government's failure on the front of national security. The party also made the UPA's politics of appeasement an election issue. The issue of India losing on the growth front was also part of the BJP's election agenda. On the issue of farmers, the BJP said, 'Successive Congress governments have not done justice to the farmers. They never provided remunerative prices for their produce. Even today,

141

60 per cent of the farmers do not get access to the institutional credit and are forced to take loans from money lenders. 85 per cent of the farmers do not get proper insurance cover.'[2]

The fifteenth general elections to the Lok Sabha were held in five phases spread over a month in April and May 2009, with its outcome declared on 16 May 2009. The election results brought a surprisingly strong victory for the UPA.[3] In terms of vote share, the NDA recorded a decline of 4.98 per cent, while the UPA vote share rose by about 4 per cent. As is well known, in first-past-the-post election systems, modest changes in the vote share tend to generate large changes in the number of seats. While the UPA had won 214 seats in 2004, they reached a tally of 262 seats. The Congress alone won 206 of these 262 seats. The BJP, on the other hand, won 116 seats and its coalition NDA won 159 seats.[4]

Table 1: Lok Sabha Elections of 2009[5]

Political Party	LS 2004		LS 2009	
	Vote Share	Seats Won	Vote Share	Seats Won
Bharatiya Janata Party	22.16%	138	18.80%	116
Indian National Congress	26.53%	145	28.55%	206
Communist Party of India (Marxist)	5.66%	43	5.33%	16

Rajnath Singh said that the results of the election would be analysed and there was no question of fixing responsibility on anyone in the party.[6] On the same day, Advani told the party's parliamentary board that he did not want to continue as the leader of Opposition, but the board did not accept his decision.[7] Two days later, Advani was convinced to become the leader of Opposition.[8]

The BJP's National Executive meeting was held in New Delhi on 20 June. A resolution on the loss was moved by then national spokesperson Ravi Shankar Prasad. It said, 'In many states of the country, whether ruled by the BJP by itself or in alliance with other political parties, the results were indeed commendable while in some states it was satisfactory. Karnataka, Chhattisgarh, Bihar, Jharkhand, Madhya Pradesh, Gujarat and Himachal Pradesh gave us assurance that the people therein trusted the BJP in a convincing manner. There are states where the performance was poor while in many states the party could not win even a single seat. Obviously, there have been shortcomings, which the party needs to address. We have to acknowledge, identify and rectify these with a very open mind.'[9]

The defeat led to criticism of the BJP's election strategy from within the party, as well as from the NDA members and the RSS. Senior BJP leader Murli Manohar Joshi felt, 'Perhaps the party's campaigning could not reach the grassroots. Our efforts did not reach the common man.'[10]

The most severe criticism came from within, with several articles in the *Organiser* analysing the BJP's defeat in the 2009 Lok Sabha Elections. It criticized the party's overdependence on the Internet rather than on grassroots constituency level management, as well as its failure to read the national mood for parties with a pan-India vision and presence. The article said, 'Overdependence on hi-tech and affluence more than that on the grassroots constituency-level management damaged the party prospects . . . There is a disconnect between the party and its mass base. The BJP is often seen as a victim of adverse publicity . . . The desperate BJP has developed a self-defeating obsession for media endorsement. Perhaps this was one of the reasons for the party losing most in urban constituencies.'[11]

The party's failure to build bridges with the Dalits in UP, its silence over the Singur agitation in West Bengal, internal bickering in UP, Rajasthan and Uttarakhand, and its reliance on 'coalition dharma' in Andhra Pradesh, Punjab, Orissa and Bihar, were also said to be factors that led to its defeat.[12] It was said that the BJP's over-emphasis on security issues above all other issues further dented its electoral prospects, especially in light of the 1999 Kandahar incident.[13] For example, the party had no credible response to the

employment guarantee scheme. It was felt that many BJP leaders
had abandoned Hindutva to appear 'liberal'. The BJP, it was felt, was
perceived to be reactive, rather than setting the agenda.[14] On 20 June
2009, the BJP Executive Committee passed a resolution recognizing
that the country has moved towards a bipolar polity, and reiterated
its commitment to the ideas of Hindutva.[15] It was felt that India had
two distinct ideological poles. These were represented by the BJP
and the Congress. The parties attached to these poles had a broad
agreement on their respective ideological formats.

The BJP's performance in state elections was also mixed. In the
Maharashtra assembly elections held in October 2009, the Congress
won just eighty of the 288 seats, while the Nationalist Congress Party
won sixty-two seats. The BJP won forty-six, while the Shiv Sena won
forty-four.[16] This was the first time the BJP had won more seats than
the Shiv Sena in the state. In the Haryana elections held simultaneously,
while the Congress got nine of the ten Lok Sabha seats, it won forty
seats in the assembly elections. The BJP managed just four of the ninety
seats.[17] The state election results accentuated the disappointment over
the electoral performance of the post-Vajpayee BJP.

A discussion began in the BJP over a new leadership to mould
itself for the future. Rajnath Singh had completed his tenure as the
party president and there was a need to elect a new leader. The BJP
national president is elected in accordance with its Constitution and
rules made by the National Executive Committee. In order to be
eligible for the post, a person must have been an active member of
the BJP for at least four terms of the National Executive and been a
member for fifteen years.[18] The president is elected by members of
the national and state councils, on nominations made by members of
state electoral colleges.[19] An eligible person can serve as the president
for a maximum of two consecutive terms of three years each.[20]

Voices in the BJP and the RSS, which were a little disheartened
after many years of poor electoral performance, suggested that it
was time for the next generation to take up the leadership mantle.
The RSS leadership was also changing at the time. After Balasaheb

Deoras, Rajendra Singh, popularly known as Rajju Bhaiya, had become the RSS sarsanghchalak in 1994. The Ram Janmabhoomi negotiations during the Rao government were held while Rajju Bhaiya, who had been a professor at Allahabad University, took over as sarsanghchalak. The matter moved to court when no solution could be found. Meanwhile Rajju Bhaiya had to leave the chair of the RSS chief because he was unwell. After Rajju Bhaiya, K.S. Sudarshan, who was an engineer, took over the RSS mantle in 2000. Sudarshan hailed from Kuppalli village of Mandva district in Karnataka and was a gold medallist in Bachelor of Engineering in Telecommunications from Sagar University. Sudarshan attended his first shakha when he was nine. The *sah-sarkaryavah* (general secretary) at that time was H.V. Seshadri. Together Sudarshan and Seshadri worked on invigorating the RSS with fresh energy. The new dimension of work led the RSS to establish organizations such as Sewa Bharti for service, Sanskar Bharti for artists, Sanskriti Bharti for literature, Akhil Bharatiya Adhivakta Parishad for lawyers and Vigyan Bharti for science. The two were also clear that a young leadership was important to run the RSS more efficiently with newer ideas. Sudarshan passed on the leadership mantle to a younger Mohan Bhagwat in 2009.

Simultaneously, the BJP too was moving towards a younger leadership. Goa chief minister Manohar Parrikar and Maharashtra BJP president Nitin Gadkari were considered for the BJP's presidency. Even though Gadkari was not very active in Delhi politics, the party chose him, on 19 December 2009, as the ninth and youngest president. He was just fifty-two years old at the time. From the Sangh to the BJP, younger leaders were being given leadership roles. Gadkari's team also had younger people from across India to ensure a rich mix of experience and expertise.

This principle of bringing in younger people into leadership roles was carried forward. Politicians like J.P. Nadda, Piyush Goyal, Devendra Fadnavis, Dharmendra Pradhan, Ravi Shankar Prasad, Nirmala Sitharaman, Smriti Irani, Bhupender Yadav and Anurag Thakur were among those brought to the forefront. This leadership team brought a new energy into the working of the party as an organization.

Revival in the States

Meanwhile, on the electoral front, the BJP did well in the 2010 Bihar assembly elections. Out of a total of 243 seats, the BJP got ninety-one seats, the JD(U) got 115, the RJD got twenty-two and the Congress got four.[21] The NDA formed the government with 206 seats.

In 2011, the BJP's National Executive was held in Guwahati on 8–9 January. It was decided here that the BJP would expand in the northeast.[22] The agenda for the meeting was to discuss issues of corruption under the UPA government, the infiltration of Indian land by Bangladeshis and most importantly, setting the agenda for its expansion into the northeast. The party announced that steps were being taken to deport illegal immigrants from the region as well as appealing to the Election Commission to delete the names of illegal infiltrators from the voter list.[23] Criticizing the UPA government for not doing enough to maintain peace and ensure infrastructure development in the region, the party announced key measures that it would undertake to promote overall development in the region. The resolution stated that it would be preparing a document, the 'North-East India 2025 Vision Document'. The party created the North-East Samparka cell, which was launched in 2010. Through this cell various activities and projects would be organized, including an informal help centre for students.[24]

A year later, the two-phase elections to the Gujarat assembly were held in 2012, on 13 and 17 December. Voter turnout came to 71.32 per cent. The BJP did well, with 115 seats in the 182-member assembly. For the third consecutive time, Narendra Modi became the chief minister of the state. By this time, stories about the successful functioning of the Gujarat state government had begun to circulate widely. Three consecutive election wins created conditions for Modi to play a bigger role at the national level.

Meanwhile, central investigative agencies were used to target the Gujarat government and falsely implicate Amit Shah. There were concerns about the extent to which these agencies were acting against the political opponents of the ruling party in the union government. Then finance minister Pranab Mukherjee also had his office bugged as an example of the government's misuse of institutions. Under Sonia Gandhi, the new team of Congress leaders was working only on manipulation as a means to stay in power. Mired in corruption, the party was losing legitimacy.

In a blatant misuse of constitutional agencies, charges were filed against Narendra Modi in the 2002 Gujarat riots case, and against Amit Shah in an encounter case. In March 2008, the Supreme Court reopened several cases related to the 2002 riots, including that of the Gulbarg Society massacre, and established a Special Investigation Team (SIT) to investigate the issue. In 2012, the Supreme Court cleared Modi of complicity in the violence. Further, when a charge-sheet was filed, Amit Shah resigned as Gujarat home minister and presented himself before the investigating agencies. He was incarcerated for ninety days. When he got bail, a petition was filed in Gujarat saying Amit Shah could influence witnesses in the case. Amit Shah was thus compelled to spend time away from Gujarat. Through this phase, which was the most difficult in his life, Shah remained composed because he knew the cases were politically motivated.[25]

The Special Investigation Team constituted after the Gujarat riots and the Supreme Court of India gave Narendra Modi a clean chit against all charges.[26] Similarly, Amit Shah was cleared of all charges.[27] It was clear that investigation agencies had been turned against Narendra Modi and Amit Shah as a political weapon by the Congress.

Anti-incumbency against the UPA II

By this time, news about corruption in the government had become part of everyday public discourse and people's anger against the

Congress-led UPA government was rising. That anger spilled onto the streets when social activist Anna Hazare launched a protest against UPA corruption, demanding the passage of the long-pending Lokpal Bill in April 2011. During this period, Baba Ramdev joined the anti-corruption movement by raising the issue of black money. The Lokpal Bill was introduced in Parliament on 22 December 2011, and passed in the Lok Sabha on 27 December 2011. Among other salient features, the bill aimed to establish an anti-corruption institution called 'Lokpal' at the central level and 'Lokayuktas' at state level. On receipt of a claim of corruption against a public servant, the Lokpal (or Lokayukta, as the case may be) had to enquire about the complaint within sixty days and could initiate departmental proceedings, if warranted. While the investigations were allowed to be completed within six months, if the complaint proceeded to trial, it would have to be completed within two years.[28]

Many political opponents of the UPA mobilized support for this campaign. Anna began an indefinite hunger strike on 5 April at Jantar Mantar.[29] In June, Delhi's Ramlila Maidan saw Baba Ramdev protest against black money.[30] He was subsequently detained and forced to leave the city.[31] These actions ended the protests, but the anger against the government rose. The BJP announced it would hold nationwide protests against corruption and police brutality.

A day after Baba Ramdev's arrest, BJP president Nitin Gadkari said, 'The incident that took place yesterday at midnight at the Ramlila ground is one that has blemished democracy. Those people were protesting against corruption and black money through democratic means. But Prime Minister Manmohan Singh and Sonia Gandhi ordered the atrocities on these people.' Sushma Swaraj, leader of the Opposition in the Lok Sabha, said the police action was carried out at the directions of the prime minister. Swaraj said, 'This is not democracy . . . the police cannot alone have taken such a step alone. It had the approval of the prime minister and full approval of the Congress President.'[32]

After the government failed to meet promises made to Anna Hazare, he announced that he would restart his agitation again on 16 August 2011. Hazare was arrested along with many of his supporters who were to join him in the protest. As a consequence, protests intensified, and the Anna agitation spread across the country. For the next twelve days, sit-ins and demonstrations were held across India.

The agitation was finally called off on 28 August when Parliament passed a resolution accepting three of Anna Hazare's demands. The government, however, did not deliver on any of the assurances and promises that it had made. In November 2012, Arvind Kejriwal's Aam Aadmi Party was born out of the agitation.

The slew of corruption scandals along with the widespread perception of policy paralysis towards the end of UPA II became a significant issue in the 2014 Lok Sabha elections. A major reason for this was the expansion of the Indian middle class after 1991. Political scientists, Pradeep Chibber and Rahul Verma, note that the Indian middle class grew five-fold between 2008 and 2018: 'This demographic shift is significant, because middle-class voters are more likely to be aware of the discourse around state regulations and thwarted business development. They are also more likely to believe that subsidies can be economically harmful.'[33]

In the run-up to the 2014 Lok Sabha, this shift in mood created an advantage for the BJP. The BJP was joined in its protests by civil society activists who were unhappy with the preferential treatment and widespread corruption in its criticism of the Congress. With the 2011 anti-corruption movement led by Anna Hazare and Supreme Court interference in the 2G scam, the debate on the special influence of business groups on the government became a part of mainstream discourse. It also undermined the idea that the UPA government could actually deliver goods and services to the public.

The next big protest against the UPA government happened over the Delhi gang rape and murder case in 2012. People were shocked at the brutality and came out to protest at India Gate. A group of six men gang raped and brutally assaulted a twenty-three-year-old paramedic student in a bus in Delhi. She died a few days later. Once again, the government cracked down on peaceful protesters turning India Gate into a battleground.[34] As the Lok Sabha elections approached, the protests born out of people's anger against the UPA showed no signs of abating.

By this time, the 2014 elections were beginning to occupy the imagination of political parties. In the BJP, Nitin Gadkari, who had been serving as the party president since 2009, was set to get another term. However, a controversy surrounding a group of companies with links to Nitin Gadkari was created by BJP's detractors. The allegations were part of a malicious campaign against Gadkari and the BJP. The party was convinced that this controversy was created by the Congress. Advani said that Gadkari was the victim of a UPA strategy to 'paint the entire political class with the same brush to minimise and escape its unpardonable sins . . . This is more to neutralise the unprecedented charges against the ruling UPA.'[35]

Gadkari, who during his tenure had infused within the party a fresh energy and strengthened the organization, decided to step down. He resigned on 22 January 2013. A day later, Rajnath Singh was again elected party president.[36]

Modi for PM

Right after Rajnath Singh took over as the BJP president, demands to anoint Modi as the candidate for PM began. With anger against the UPA rising, people were looking for a viable political option. There were media reports that the BJP was initially in a dilemma over Modi's acceptability within the NDA combine. The BJP decided not to allow external interference in its internal matters. As Modi's popularity rose, the party made a unanimous decision. In 2009, when journalist Vijay Trivedi had raised questions about the possibilities in Parliament, Modi had said that he only wanted to see Advani become prime minister.[37] But now it was clear that Modi was the most popular face of the BJP.

This issue played out in the BJP National Executive meeting in June 2013 at Panaji, Goa. The possibility of Narendra Modi being given a greater responsibility for the 2014 elections, if not being named as the party's prime ministerial candidate, was discussed. BJP's democratic practices allowed many ideas to be deliberated. The Sangh too was part of the informal deliberations. The party eventually decided that Narendra Modi's charisma and track record as an able administrator could propel the BJP towards victory.

The rousing welcome that Modi received upon his arrival, which also included a public announcement of support by Goa chief minister Manohar Parrikar, set the tone for the meeting. On 9 June 2013, Narendra Modi was made the BJP's campaign committee chief. Within the party there were some discussions over the choice, but it was unanimously accepted that the way Narendra Modi had presented a model of good governance in Gujarat, he had emerged as a skilled and efficient leader. Despite many efforts to malign his image and politically motivated cases, Narendra Modi continued his work as the chief minister of Gujarat. He brought a combination of administrative experience as chief minister of Gujarat alongside practical work in building the party as an organization.

There was a sense in the party that because of his age, Narendra Modi could work towards strengthening the foundation of the party for a long time. So it was decided to make him in-charge of the party's campaign committee instead of having him canvass for the party. By taking this step, the party made it clear that it would fight the Lok Sabha elections under his leadership. Eventually, in September 2013, the BJP's parliamentary board decided that Narendra Modi would be the party's prime ministerial candidate in the next Lok Sabha elections. Rajnath Singh announced the decision. The decision to project Narendra Modi as the PM candidate helped the party gear up for the elections by starting work on organizational consolidation and build up. To begin with, a few leaders did not support the move wholeheartedly, but later they agreed, and it went down well eventually.

BJP's ally in the NDA, the JD(U), opposed the decision to project Narendra Modi as the PM candidate. The BJP was firm on its stand to not let external factors impact internal decisions. Nitish Kumar decided to part ways with the NDA over the issue.

Meanwhile, a controversy was unfolding, on the Representation of the People Act. In June 2013, the Supreme Court declared Section 8(4) of the Representation of the People Act as unconstitutional. The verdict said that if a public representative was proven guilty of an offence and served at least two years of imprisonment as punishment, then they should be deemed unfit to continue in their position. This created bars against convicts as legislators, but there were also residual concerns based on the extent to which innocent people are convicted in India.

The UPA decided to overrule the court order using an ordinance. However, when the ordinance reached Pranab Mukherjee, he called Union Law Minister Kapil Sibal, Parliamentary Affairs Minister Kamal Nath and Home Minister Sushil Kumar Shinde to question the need for the ordinance. The BJP took a tough stance against the government over the ordinance.

On 27 September 2013, while Congress leader Ajay Maken was holding a press conference to defend the ordinance, Rahul Gandhi suddenly reached the venue, said it was trash and must be thrown in the dustbin. Ajay Maken, who had until minutes ago been defending the Bill, suddenly changed track and started speaking the same language as Rahul Gandhi on the legislation.[38] While this was unfolding in Delhi, Prime Minister Manmohan Singh was abroad to attend the United Nations General Assembly. On 2 October, during a Cabinet meeting, the UPA government decided to withdraw the Bill. This episode highlighted the lack of internal coordination within the Congress.

On 9 June 2013, Narendra Modi was appointed chairman of the BJP's 2014 Lok Sabha election campaign committee.

Rajnath Singh greeting Narendra Modi after the latter was chosen to head BJP's 2014 Lok Sabha election campaign committee.

Rajnath Singh, L.K. Advani, Sushma Swaraj, Arun Jaitley and Venkaiah Naidu congratulate Nitin Gadkari on taking over as BJP president in 2009.

Arun Jaitley greets Rajnath Singh on being chosen BJP president in 2013.

The Mahasampark Abhiyaan team with PM Narendra Modi on 1 May 2015 before starting the mission.

PM Narendra Modi with former US President Barack Obama at the Republic Day parade in 2015.

The BJP juggernaut tramples the last of the Left's bastion, Tripura.

Narendra Modi in Varanasi to file his nomination.

PM Narendra Modi with former UN General Secretary Ban Ki-moon at the UN General Assembly on 27 September 2014.

BJP leader J.P. Nadda greets Amit Shah as he takes over as BJP president in 2014.

PM Narendra Modi with former President Pranab Mukerjee at the launch of GST on 1 July 2017.

PM Narendra Modi with former Israeli PM Benjamin Netanyahu in 2018.

PM Narendra Modi with Russian President Vladimir Putin in 2018.

PM Narendra Modi with then BJP president Amit Shah at the BJP headquarters on 24 May 2019.

PM Narendra Modi brings his own tiffin to lunch with BJP booth workers in Varanasi on 22 December 2016.

Amit Shah during the BJP membership drive.

The BJP headquarters.

PM Narendra Modi congratulates J.P. Nadda (centre) on being elected BJP president as former party presidents (left to right) Rajnath Singh, L.K. Advani, Amit Shah and Nitin Gadkari look on.

Jammu and Kashmir BJP in-charge Narendra Modi with senior leaders at the Ekta Yatra in Jammu.

Atal Bihari Vajpayee facing a lathicharge in Delhi's Connaught Place, near the Embassy Hotel, in 1986.

Constituents of the Janata Party in 1988.

Atal Bihari Vajpayee addressing the crowd at Ramlila Ground.

Atal Bihari Vajpayee and L.K. Advani worked closely to take the BJP to greater heights.

(From left to right) V.P. Singh, Harkishan Singh, Atal Bihari Vajpayee and L.K. Advani at Haryana Bhawan in Delhi.

In February 1968, Pandit Deen Dayal Upadhyaya was given a tearful farewell.

Atal Bihari Vajpayee, Balraj Madhok, Sundar Singh Bhandari, Bhai Mahavir and other Jana Sangh leaders demanded a judicial inquiry into the death of Pandit Deen Dayal Upadhyaya.

Second RSS sarsanghchalak M.S. Golwalkar with Dr Syama Prasad Mookerjee.

Pandit Deen Dayal Upadhyaya returning from Russia.

Eknath Ranade, Pandit Deen Dayal Upadhyaya, J.P. Mathur, Atal Bihari Vajpayee.

Syama Prasad Mookerjee at Pathankot railway station on his way to Jammu.

Pandit Deen Dayal Upadhyaya and M.S. Golwalkar at the ashram of Prabhu Dutt Brahmachari in Vrindavan.

Jaiprakash Narayan and Acharya Kripalani addressing the media at the swearing-in ceremony of the Janata Party government in 1977.

Campaigning for 2014

Narendra Modi, as campaign in-charge, had started the preparations for the Lok Sabha elections early. He laid the foundation for a 182-foot statue of Vallabhbhai Patel to be built in iron. On 31 October 2013, Modi said, 'We request all village panchayats to donate a part of the iron from the tools they use in their fields.'[39] A campaign was organized to gather scraps of iron from all across the country which would contribute to the statue. This drew on the familiar BJP strategy of mass mobilization.

Assembly elections were held in five states in late 2013—Delhi, Madhya Pradesh, Rajasthan, Chhattisgarh and Mizoram. As is customary, the media called the elections the 'semi-finals' for the upcoming Lok Sabha elections. The elections were keenly fought. When the results of these elections came out on 8 December, the BJP governments returned to power in Madhya Pradesh, Rajasthan and Chhattisgarh. The BJP emerged as the single-largest party in Delhi with thirty-two of the seventy seats.[40] The Congress only won Mizoram. The results infused a fresh confidence in the BJP and validated the decision to hand the leadership of the party to Modi.

Ahead of the 2013 elections in Rajasthan, Vasundhara Raje launched a 14,500 km long Suraj Sankalp Yatra on 4 April that year. The yatra culminated with Raje covering 180 out of 200 assembly constituencies by addressing 135 public meetings and events which took place at 500 places.[41]

Narendra Modi, who had focused his energies on winning over the state from the Congress, was present in Jaipur along with party president Rajnath Singh to mark the culmination of the yatra. Modi gave a rousing speech. When the results were announced, the BJP had won a historic three-fourth mandate winning 163 seats in the 200-member house.[42]

Modi's rallies became increasingly popular. In these rallies, he talked about implementing the Gujarat model of development on the national scale. He also launched sharp attacks on the misgovernance of the Congress party.

On 27 October 2013, during Narendra Modi's Hunkar rally at Patna's Gandhi Maidan, a series of bomb blasts killed six people and injured about eighty.[43] An estimated three lakh people were at the venue for the rally and there was a fear of stampede and panic. Modi took the stage appealing for calm and remained undeterred. He went on to speak for about forty minutes.

During his public addresses, he gave a call for Congress-mukt Bharat, meaning to rid the country of a culture and a way of thinking which was imbued in dynasty politics, red tape and corruption. People had tried to change this Congress model of governance in 1967 by voting in large numbers for the Samyukta Vidhayak Dal (SVD), in 1977 by voting in the Janata Party government, in 1987 by installing a National Front government under V.P. Singh and in 1996, by voting for the BJP under Vajpayee. In Modi, people now had another opportunity to change the way the country was being governed.

Just days after being appointed the BJP's PM candidate, Modi addressed his first big rally in Haryana's Rewari, which is home to many ex-servicemen. This section of society was angry with the Congress for not delivering on the 'one-rank, one-pension' promise. There was also a sentiment that the Congress had been soft in its handling of Pakistan. The Rewari rally turned out to be a huge success.

Rattled by the acceptance Modi was getting, the Congress began to use unparliamentary language for him and in a show of arrogance and elitism, tried to dismiss him as 'chaiwala' (tea seller). Narendra Modi, who had never shied from accepting his humble beginnings, started a 'Chai pe Charcha' (discussion over tea) campaign. It was received well by the masses and turned out to be a successful way of meeting people and connecting with them. The first *Chai pe Charcha* was held on 12 February 2014 with good governance being chosen as the topic for discussion. The second such charcha was held on

International Women's Day that year on the topic of women's safety. Narendra Modi sat at a tea stall in Delhi for discussions, which drew an encouraging response, with the 16 December 2012 gang rape and murder case in Delhi still fresh in people's minds. The third, and last, phase of the campaign was held in Maharashtra's Vidarbha, and the topic of discussion was farmers' suicides and agrarian distress.

Modi's popularity and Congress's failures together created a buzz for him. To ensure his presence at multiple locations at the same time, Narendra Modi launched a 3D hologram campaign. This campaign strategy had been deployed by Modi in 2012 Gujarat assembly election as well and now the strategy was being scaled up during 2014 Lok Sabha elections. As a part of election campaigning for the upcoming polls, a ten-feet-tall 3D hologram of Modi was broadcast simultaneously in 200 cities across the country.[44][45][46]

With a ten-feet-tall 3D hologram of himself, Modi could reach out to a vast number of people at the same time. The BJP used social media widely and effectively to ensure a wider reach. A Stanford University study later said that the BJP was way ahead of all other parties in the use of social media, the number of political tweets by followers, retweets and positive posts. It said the gap widened towards the end of the elections from 7 April to 12 May in 2014.[47]

The BJP chose its main election planks in the 2014 elections as the UPA 2's corruption, policy paralysis, indecisive leadership, dynastic politics and other anti-incumbency issues. When the elections approached the BJP did give tickets to family members of the BJP leaders if it felt they could win, while at the same time it criticized the Congress as a dynastic party. To some commentators this was a contradiction. The BJP, however, was not a 'dynastic party' in the sense that the post of the top leader of the party was not reserved for any particular family. The campaign against the Gandhi family, and the frequent use of the term *shahzada* (prince) for Rahul Gandhi by Modi highlighted this difference between the Congress and the BJP.

Identity politics, whether it is about place, caste, class, language or religion, plays a critical role in political movements in India, where many voters can be galvanized into voting and passionate commitment to a particular party through the language of grievance. But apart from the BJP and the CPI(M), all parties after briefly stirring public sentiments, have degenerated into family-dominated political entities. For example, the socialist movement started by Ram Manohar Lohia was identified with the participation of the marginalized sections of society. Over the years this movement deteriorated into family-based parties. Wherever leaders became entrenched, they also ended the internal democratic systems and became dynastic. The position of party chief was reserved for family members of the party as happened with Lalu Prasad, Mulayam Singh Yadav, DMK, BJD, NRT, Akali Dal and Shiv Sena.

The BJP's campaign around dynastic politics was meant to appeal to voters in the context of a changing political environment, of the decline of many small parties into family businesses and of public disgust with corruption and the dominance of caste and entitlement politics. In this changing political narrative, the BJP sensed the importance of emphasizing that it was a unique party that was an institution and not a family business. While being from famous families like the Gandhi family was earlier expected to attract votes, by 2014 the mood of the voter seemed to have changed. The BJP appealed to the new median voter, the young voter who did not have a fascination with royalty and powerful families but wanted a party that could connect with his aspirations.

This approach helped the BJP simultaneously undermine the Congress, in the eyes of voters, and also the regional parties which were entirely family organizations. This fit with the new strength of the BJP in many states which had previously had strong local parties. The BJP had already started doing well in state elections such as Haryana, Delhi, UP, Himachal, Uttarakhand, Jharkhand, Bihar, Madhya Pradesh, Chhattisgarh, Gujarat and Maharashtra.

'They are *namdaar* (big names), I am *kaamdar* (worker). You have to decide who you want,' said Modi in April 2014 at a rally in Maharashtra. He was emphasizing that he was a 'kaamdar', someone who worked, he was not entitled, not a 'naamdar', someone famous or from a rich or powerful family, and appealed to the common voter to identify with him. This also helped the BJP position itself well with the underclass voters who Vajpayee's BJP had struggled to connect with.

'UP Mission Plan' for 2014

Uttar Pradesh had been a difficult challenge for the BJP for close to twenty years. After creating history in the 1991 UP assembly elections by winning 221 seats, the BJP saw its tally plunge in the subsequent elections, reduced to an all-time low of forty-seven seats in 2012. Even in the 2004 and 2009 Lok Sabha elections, the party got only ten seats out of eighty.[48] Amit Shah was the chief architect for the BJP's election strategy in 2014. He got involved in BJP activities in the 1980s. He came to prominence in Gujarat's cooperative sector. In 2000, when the Ahmedabad District Cooperative bank was on shaky ground and declared a weak bank, Shah was brought in as the chairman. Within a year of Shah's taking charge, the bank improved its position and declared a 10 per cent dividend.[49] He was elected as a Gujarat MLA in 1997, 1998, 2002, and 2007, and had worked as minister of state in Gujarat.

His distinctive approach to politics was the idea of endlessly refining the political party as a competent organization that could focus on winning one election after another. His task was to win UP or the 'UP Mission Plan' in the 2014 Lok Sabha elections, as a part of which he adopted a four-pronged strategy.[50]

The first step was to identify the seats which were not winnable, where contesting would be a waste of effort. The second step involved building a cadre of booth level workers and recruiting about 4,00,000 full time workers who kept a tab on ground realities and reported

to the core team in Lucknow on a daily basis. The third and the
biggest challenge was the 'social engineering' required to navigate
the caste politics of UP. Here, Shah focused his attention on 30 per
cent of the backward castes' voters, excluding the Yadavs, Jatavs and
the Muslims, who had no political representation at the state and
national levels. Finally, Shah devised various strategies to reach out
to the voters. He organized election campaigns banking on Modi's
popularity and his OBC status, a fact popularized by the Congress
and the BSP. The Modi rath and audio video messages with slogans
like 'Har har modi, ghar ghar modi' and 'Abki baar modi sarkar'
(vote for Modi government this time), are some examples. Shah and
Modi planned that the latter would contest the Lok Sabha elections
from Varanasi, India's spiritual capital. In order to reach out to the
OBC voters, Shah entered into an alliance with a small party called
the Apna Dal.

These strategies worked. Between 7 April and 12 May 2014, India
voted to elect the fifteenth Lok Sabha in nine phases. When the results
were announced on 16 May, the BJP had won a majority, a total of 282
seats on its own. The NDA as a coalition of parties won 336 seats. The
Congress won only forty-four seats and together with its allies, the UPA,
was limited to sixty seats.[51] In UP, the BJP exceeded expectations by
winning seventy-one out of eighty seats. There were 189 constituencies
in which there was a direct contest between the BJP and the Congress.
The BJP won 166 out of these, while the Congress won twenty-three.[52]

Table 2: Lok Sabha Elections of 2014[53]

Political Party	LS 2009		LS 2014	
	Vote Share	Seats Won	Vote Share	Seats Won
Bharatiya Janata Party	18.80%	116	31.34%	282
Indian National Congress	28.55%	206	19.52%	44
Communist Party of India (Marxist)	5.33%	16	3.28%	9

Modi contested from both Varanasi and Vadodara and decided to keep the Varanasi Lok Sabha seat. He won both seats with large margins. During the entire 2014 campaign, Modi addressed about 437 big rallies and 5,827 smaller ones.[54] With each rally, Modi's popularity had breached new limits. The seats won by Congress were not large enough to ensure that any Congress leader could become the Leader of Opposition. On 26 May 2014, Narendra Modi took the oath as India's Prime Minister.

* * *

On the surface, the UPA ruled the roost from 2004 to 2014. Under the surface, however, the Congress as an institution was breaking down. Too many Congress politicians were focused on the fruits of office, and were not nurturing the foundations of the party, party workers and loyal voters. The Congress was losing organizational capital.

The Indian economy faced difficulties in 2008. These difficulties were not handled efficiently by the UPA. As a consequence, by 2014, household prosperity was also under stress across India. After ten years, anti-incumbency had started to set in.

An array of scandals had arisen. Opposition parties were able to bring these to prominence, including through the non-partisan India Against Corruption movement which galvanized opposition to the UPA.

In this environment, the BJP brought two key strengths to the table. The first was the reputation and popularity of Narendra Modi. A tired Indian public wanted a decisive leader and Modi offered that. The 'Gujarat model' was an important aspect of the campaign, arguing that the model of prosperity of Gujarat led by Modi, and that such leadership in economic policy would now be implemented all across India by Modi as PM. The second was the organizational capability of the BJP.

Many political parties wilt when in the Opposition. Volunteers and funding tend to dry up when the attractions of power are absent. Control of the levers of government is always an advantage at a practical level when fighting elections. The BJP's achievement lay in preserving and strengthening the sinews of the organization through the ten-year dry period and eventually coming out more determined. Not only did the party survive, the organization that went into action in 2014 was stronger than the one employed in 2004.

9

Working in Unison: Party and Government (2014)

20 May 2014 was a historic moment for the BJP. The party, on its own, won 282 seats, safely past the half-way point of 273 seats that was required to form a government. The Prime Minister was a first-time member of Parliament who had risen from the ranks of the party.

As Narendra Modi entered the Central Hall of the Parliament, he said, 'I visited the Gujarat chief minister's chamber for the first time when I became the chief minister. I entered the Gujarat Assembly for the first time after I became the chief minister. I have come here also for the first time.'[1]

The election results of 2014 brought a break from the long period of coalition governments, where no party had crossed 273 seats. However, the party shared power with all its pre-poll coalition partners and nurtured relations between ideologically aligned parties. This was consistent with the behaviour of the Jana Sangh in its participation in the *Samyukta Vidhayak Dal* in 1967, the decision to merge into the Janata Party in 1977, and Vajpayee's 'coalition dharma' which created a stable administration in the 1999–2004 period while the BJP had a minority.

Even as the BJP expressed its willingness to share power with allies in 2014, the party's assessment of the results threw up some interesting findings. Assessing the results at its National Council on 9 August 2014, the BJP passed a resolution saying, 'BJP got huge support on seats reserved for SC/STs in these elections as a result of which the maximum number of SC/ST MPs got elected on BJP tickets. Three SC candidates of BJP, won on general seats. Moreover, BJP is honoured to have maximum representation of women MPs in Parliament today.'[2] The party also acknowledged that the 2014 elections were the biggest ever in the world with about 550 million voters exercising their right to vote.

Strengthening the Party

The key plan of the BJP in 2014 was to not be complacent after its victory, but to commit to building the party as an organization. The BJP assessed its growth prospects, acceptability and representation and began building upon them.

During the Congress regime, constitutional institutions were actively misused to target BJP leaders. Fabricated cases were filed against the BJP's topmost leaders including Narendra Modi and Amit Shah. In the wake of the Samjhauta Express blasts, Congress leader P. Chidambaram raised the bogey of 'Hindu terror'. The party tried to attack the Sangh Parivar and the BJP by branding them communal and projecting Hindutva as a divisive strategy. The Sangh and the BJP both felt that it was imperative to counter Congress's misinformation and smear campaign. At this point Suresh Soni was the joint general secretary of the RSS and coordinated with the BJP on behalf of the RSS. Soni worked closely with Modi, Shah, Arun Jaitely, Sushma Swaraj and other senior BJP leaders on key issues. RSS Sarsanghchalak Mohan Bhagwat had a modern outlook and a pragmatic and open approach. Suresh Soni as the RSS joint general secretary and Bhaiyyaji Joshi as general secretary worked in close coordination and had a moral influence on the BJP. This close coordination helped the BJP grow and increase its voter base by countering the Congress narrative on 'Hindu terror' and smear campaign against the BJP leaders.

The BJP, meanwhile, was moving towards a change of party president. The first cabinet featured Rajnath Singh as home minister. BJP rules forbid one person from holding two positions— one in the party and the other in the government. The principle is one of the Prime Minister who focuses on policy and the party president who focuses on the party as an organization. Hence, a new party president was needed. The natural choice was Amit Shah.

Amit Shah came to prominence in 2014, when under his charge the BJP won seventy-one seats in Uttar Pradesh, as compared with ten seats in 2009. This was arguably the greatest electoral triumph in the history of the BJP.[3] This achievement would have been remarkable if the election campaign was led by a person from UP; it was extraordinary considering that Amit Shah was from Gujarat. He took charge as party president on 9 July 2014. At age fifty, he was the youngest ever BJP President.[4]

It would have been easy to be triumphant in July 2014, it would have been natural to be complacent. However, there were important aspects about the BJP's achievements, which required a mature appreciation. The BJP's vote share in 2014 was 31.3 per cent.[5] In many ways, this was an election that the Congress had lost, through the combination of anti-incumbency, policy paralysis and corruption; such unusual moments would not always recur in the future. There were important parts of the country where the BJP had got less than 5 per cent votes. These included large states like Kerala, Tamil Nadu, Andhra Pradesh, Telangana, Odisha, West Bengal as well as the north-eastern states. Moreover, there were nearly 200 constituencies where the BJP did not have an effective presence.[6]

The National Council meeting of 2014, held in New Delhi, said, 'There is a lesson for the organization in these elections. The wave of popular leader and sentiment gets converted into votes where the organization is strong, and the local leadership is established. That is why it is essential to strengthen the organization in all the states of the country and that is our responsibility.'[7]

Shah looked into the future and set out to build the BJP into a new level of organizational capability, one that would achieve a higher vote share even when faced with anti-incumbency, one that would win on its own merits without a particularly weak Opposition, one which would expand geographically and be embraced by a much wider swathe of the population. Such strategic thinking was part of the BJP culture. As an example, in 1957, Deen Dayal Upadhyaya had said, 'Today's opponent should be our voter tomorrow. Tomorrow's voter, on the day after, should become our member and our member should later transform into our active worker.'[8]

While the party president has an important role, there is an ethos of avoiding top-down control, and the core team has other constituents too. Traditionally, organizational secretaries have played a very important role in the growth of the party organization and its ideological anchoring.

In the initial years of the party, Sunder Singh Bhandari was the organizational secretary who hailed from Rajasthan and introduced the culture of *pravas* (organizational tour) within the BJP. He strengthened the party in Rajasthan and a large part of north India. Kushabhau Thakre strengthened the party in central Indian states like Madhya Pradesh. Thakre did significant work in the Adivasi areas of the state. Even though he was not an exceptional public speaker, his transparent decency inspired the ground level worker. K.N. Govindacharya brought a new dimension to the BJP, increasing the acceptance of the BJP by widening its social base. During his tenure as the organizing general secretary, Modi gave the BJP systematic internal processes a political sharpness that was brought to bear on every decision and led a large expansion of the party in north India. Ram Lal too did some very significant work in expanding the BJP by motivating the ground level workers with a methodical and systematic outreach. V. Satish, B.L. Santosh, Shiv Prakash and Saudan Singh as joint general secretaries similarly contributed to an efficient, capable and thinking organization. These layers of competence were built not just at the level of the national party. At the state level too, organizing secretaries ensured that the party cadre was motivated, deepening the connection with people on the ground.

The equation that the BJP shared with the RSS helped in its ideological expansion. The RSS helped in cadre feeding by way of ideological engagement with the BJP workers on the ground.

The modern BJP represented the culmination of decades of work, combining organization design, ideology, political strategy, social acceptability, election campaign methodology, mass membership, communication, fund-collection and population-scale outreach.

On 9 August 2014, Amit Shah addressed the BJP National Council meeting at Delhi's Jawaharlal Nehru Stadium. He focused on building the organizational capabilities of the BJP, of building the BJP as an impersonal institution. He said: 'I want to say a few things to party workers in the context of the near future. If we are to look at the working of booths on the national scale, we realise booths are weak. They need to be strengthened. Second, BJP workers should not leave any election right from Panchayat to Parliament. Every election is an opportunity for expansion, every election is an opportunity to connect with the masses, every election is a window to take party ideology to the people. The party must contest all elections no matter what the result. I want to tell all units from Bengal, Odisha, Seemandhra, Telangana, Tamil Nadu and Kerala that the people from these regions voted for us but we couldn't convert the votes into seats because our vote-catching machinery, our organization is weak in these states.'[9]

As part of this work programme on strengthening the party, he introduced two amendments to the party constitution. One was with regard to making the party membership an online, technology-driven exercise and the other dealt with responsibilities of party's primary and active members. He put into action one of the biggest expansion programmes that transformed the BJP into the country's largest mass party.

One of the major reasons for the BJP's loss in 2004 was that when the party was in power from 1998-99 to 2004 most big and experienced leaders became part of the government. The BJP had experience of remaining in opposition and strengthening the organization but the first opportunity to remain in power and manage the organization arrived in 1999. It was important to have a connect between the government's work and organizational campaigns. But the connect was unfortunately missing. In 2014, when the party came to power again, the BJP actively worked on the organizational front managing its campaigns and movements. The BJP ensured party workers stayed connected with party activities and campaigns 365 days. Amit Shah introduced the changes to the party that had become the need of the hour. One of the prime examples of this government-party connect was the Namami Gange programme. When the government announced the programme, the BJP workers were made to join the Namami Gange project. When the government started the *Swachhta Abhiyan* (Clean India Mission), party workers started a nationwide project for swachhta. When the Prime Minister gave the slogan of '*Beti Bachao, Beti Padhao*', the party ran campaigns related to the programme. This established a strong connect between the government's policy rollouts and the party's works and programmes.

Focus on Welfare

On 15 August 2014, PM Modi delivered his first speech from Red Fort. In this speech, he announced the Jan Dhan Yojana, a building block of the financial plumbing through which government subsidies could accurately reach households. It consisted of the idea that everyone in the country should have a bank account and that a database should exist with the government where each individual is identified (using an Aadhaar number which is a unique identity number to identify individual Indian citizens) and linked to information about the bank account.

According to Census 2011, only 59 per cent of households in the country had access to banking services, of which rural households were 55 per cent and urban households 68 per cent.[10] Through this, along with the *abhiyan* (mission) for bank account opening, there was a mission for providing unique IDs.[11]

For decades, policy makers had dreamt of a world where bank accounts would be ubiquitous, and there would be an effective mechanism to identify recipients of government benefits. The BJP had always held that for social upliftment of people, their economic upliftment was important. The Jan Dhan Yojana and the Antyodaya Yojana were part of the BJP government's efforts to uplift people economically and socially. From 2014 onwards, a big push was seen with the PSU banks being mandated to reach out to people in the country and open accounts for each person. This laid the foundation of one of the world's biggest direct benefit transfer programmes.

Given the large number of government schemes in India and the introduction of new schemes year after year with none of the schemes ever shutting down, it was clear that there were leakages in the system. Former Indian PM Rajiv Gandhi is known to have acknowledged that barely 15 per cent of expenditure on welfare schemes actually reached the poor.[12] Reasons for the leakages were identified to be incorrect identification of the poor, ghost beneficiaries, duplication of beneficiary names and demands for bribes by government officials responsible for disbursing money to the final beneficiary.

Swachh Bharat

In his first Independence Day speech from the ramparts of the Red Fort, Prime Minister Narendra Modi squarely confronted one of the biggest, but least talked about, problems in the country. He said, 'Brothers and Sisters, we are living in the 21st century. Has it ever pained us that our mothers and sisters have to defecate in the open? Whether dignity of women is not our collective responsibility? The poor womenfolk of the village wait for the night; until darkness descends, they can't go out to defecate. What bodily torture they must be feeling, how many diseases that act might engender. Can't we just make arrangements for toilets for the dignity of our mothers and sisters?'[13]

Until then the topic of open defecation had been taboo, eliciting shame, and had not been discussed openly in these terms by political leaders and heads of nations.[14] These words were to lay the foundations of one of the biggest schemes under the Modi government that reached rural India, rural women as well as the urban poor. The government announced that millions of toilets would be built across the country. Prime Minister Modi pledged to make India free of open defecation and promised to build better infrastructure for solid and liquid waste management in the next five years.

The Swachh Bharat (Clean India) campaign had been a part of the BJP's 2014 election manifesto. It had said, 'Poor Hygiene and Sanitation have a far reaching, cascading impact. We will ensure a Swachh Bharat by Gandhiji's 150th birth anniversary in 2019, taking it up in mission mode by converging resources and building around *jan bhagidari*. The BJP had pledged to create an open defecation free India by awareness campaigns and enabling people to build toilets in their home as well as in schools and public places.'[15] Another election promise that fitted with the Swachh Bharat Programme was to eliminate manual scavenging.

The toilet scheme was challenging for many reasons. There were issues of embezzlement, the usual bureaucratic delays, lack of water supply, and of the 'misuse' of toilets. The most important hurdle to the use of toilets was the slow change in habits.[16] [17] The campaign strategy aimed to trigger a behavioural change in people by carrying out nationwide awareness campaigns through radio talk shows, plays, music and educating people on the importance of a clean India. Further, monetary incentives of Rs 12,000 were given to SC/ST households that were below the poverty line and could not afford to build toilets.[18] This amount was to help them build a low-cost but good quality toilet.[19]

The Pradhan Mantri Awas Yojana was another such scheme focused on the standard of living. It addressed the 'quality of housing' aspect of the poor who had lived in kutcha mud houses with thatched roofs, and now got houses constructed under the interest subvention scheme for building houses.

The party had repeatedly recommended a wide network of roads to link each village with highways, markets and other villages. It also emphasized an arrangement in villages of minimum necessary civic amenities such as drinking water, road, education, means of transport, public health and hygiene and medical aid etc. It argued that a village should be treated as the basic unit for development. Therefore, all amenities in villages should be popularized along with provision of employment and social security.[20]

Welfare programmes run by the Indian state, implemented at varying levels of competence, are not new. What was novel were the improvements in operational efficiency of these programmes, drawing on the advances in identifying infrastructure and mobile phones, and the direct connections with the political activities of the BJP. The BJP reached out to welfare recipients and requested them to become members of the party. In the following six years, about 400 million people received money in their Jan Dhan accounts through a variety of subsidy programs: for scholarships, under Mahatma Gandhi Rural Employment Guarantee Scheme, old age pensions, cooking gas connections (Ujjwala Yojana), farmer income support (Kisan Samman Yojana), housing for the poor (Pradhan Mantri Aawas Yojana), toilet construction and so on.[21] These direct benefit transfers went everywhere in India.

Transforming the Party

While the government was working on providing social and economic justice to people, many changes were going on within the party. The analysis of the results for the 2014 general elections gave support to the idea that a new politics was now taking root. The

BJP had traditionally been seen as an urban upper-class party with a strength in the west and in the Hindi heartland. During the days of the Jana Sangh, the party's members were mostly from urban India. In the 2014 results, the party saw the beginnings of a wider appeal among the voters.

The BJP's New Delhi National Council said, 'BJP has increased the numbers of its voters by a whopping 10 crores as compared to that of 2009 general elections. Out of 282 parliamentary constituencies won by BJP, its candidates have won by more than 1 lakh votes in as many as 206 constituencies. It was such a historic election that Congress could not open its account in fourteen states. (Gujarat, Rajasthan, Delhi, Himachal, Uttarakhand, J&K, Goa, Nagaland, Odisha, Jharkhand, Sikkim, Tripura, Tamil Nadu, Andhra Pradesh). Congress could not register victory even on one seat in six out of seven union territories (Andaman, Chandigarh, Dadra Nagar Haveli, Daman & Diu, Puducherry, Lakshadweep).'[22]

One important factor underlying BJP's unprecedented electoral victory was its ability to reach out to first-time and young voters. The 2014 campaign had laid emphasis on tapping into the votes of this section of the population.

The young are disproportionately important in Indian politics, given the country's demographic structure. There was a great wave of first-time voters in 2014, and the BJP had generally fared well with them, partly owing to excellent outreach through social media. The National Council said, 'The first time voters in the age group of eighteen to twenty-eight years made clear that their first choice is Narendra Modi.'[23]

It was important to consolidate this support from India's young voters. Hence, the party launched a membership drive, calling it *Sadasyata Maha-Abhiyaan*, on 1 November 2014, to convert its voters into party members.[24]

On the ground, a five-member central team was set up to make the drive a success. Additionally, *vistaraks* (membership drive in-charges) were appointed in each state. They performed a variety of activities to expand the membership drive. About 5,000 of these vistaraks remained associated with the drive for about six months. The party set membership targets for each state based on two sets of data—the current number of BJP members in a state and the number of votes polled for the BJP in that state.[25]

Narendra Modi became the first BJP member to register online.[26] The mass membership drive ran till 31 March 2015. The timing for the membership drive was carefully chosen: Right after the 2014 election results, other parties were demoralized, there was euphoria about the BJP in the air, and many individuals were keen to join the BJP.

Coining the phrase 'Digital BJP' at the launch of the Sadasyata Maha-Abhiyaan, PM Modi spoke about the convenience with which any citizen could become a member by giving one missed call on a specific mobile number or by registering online through a dedicated website. Under the new system, a toll-free number was launched, and people were asked to give a missed call on it. The party organized call centres through which a call would be made to the person, personal details were taken, and membership was confirmed. Within one week of the launch of the drive, the BJP saw an addition of 6 million members.[27]

The party constitution was modified, through which every 'primary member' was automatically made an 'active member'. Active members were tasked with inducting 100 new members each. All members were asked to spend seven days a year towards strengthening the organization by contributing to party activities.[28]

Prior to 2014, the BJP was a party with a loyal cadre, which had mastered the methods of political mobilization through yatras, rallies and protests. But after 2014, the party was in power and expanding towards becoming a mass party. The processes used within the party needed to change and reflect this.

Protest as a means of mobilization did not work for the party as it was itself in power. The new members had to be brought into the party's activities. New concepts of mobilization were now required to harness the energy of the new members and give them a greater sense of belonging to the BJP. Activities were created around community issues like cleaning the river Ganga (Namami Gange), campaigns around the girl child (Beti Bachao Abhiyan), tree planting, alongside the traditional yatra method. Recognizing the new digital age, all members were encouraged to channel their enthusiasm into social media. The party was taking on the government's programmes and policies by actively tailoring its activities accordingly.

Earlier, the party was organized around 'cells'. A major organizational redesign was undertaken in 2015. The party was reorganised around nineteen 'departments' and nine 'projects'. Each of these had a set of conveners, co-conveners and other members to supervise the day-to-day functioning.[29]

The purpose of departments was to establish the administrative structures of the party for the long-term. Some of these departments were: good governance, policy research, media, training, political feedback, party journal and publications, coordination of disaster relief and media relations. Three departments came to get the major focus of the party—*Aajeevan Sahyog Nidhi* (Lifelong Assistance Grant), IT, Website and Social Media Activities, and Documentation and Library.[30]

Alongside this, 'projects' were intended to enable the establishment of a finitely lived team that would pursue a short-term objective. Some of these projects were office modernization, setting up libraries, e-libraries, Swachh Bharat Abhiyan, National Training Abhiyan, National Membership Abhiyan, National Maha Sampark Abhiyan, etc. Three of these were given special importance and were heavily advertised to the public. These were the Beti Bachao Beti Padhao, Swacch Bharat and Namami Gange projects.[31] The goal was to project the party not only as one that engages itself solely in elections, but also one that does good work. It was felt that these projects would attract a different kind of idealistic person to forge links with the party and ultimately bring more support to the party from a more diverse community.

The BJP established a principle of stepping aside from active operational roles at age 75. The rich experience of the senior politicians was placed into a structure called the *Margdarshak Mandal* (guidance team), and they were harnessed for mentorship, advice and wisdom. BJP leaders such as L.K. Advani and Murli Manohar Joshi, given their rich and varied experience in political life, fit into these roles.

Some leaders with experience and some new faces made it to the Cabinet. Rajnath Singh, Sushma Swaraj, Arun Jaitley, M. Venkaiah Naidu, Nitin Gadkari, D.V. Sadananda Gowda, V.K. Singh, Harsh Vardhan, Uma Bharti, Najma Heptullah, Gopinath Munde, Kalraj Mishra, Maneka Sanjay Gandhi, Ananth Kumar, Ravi Shankar Prasad, Anant Geete, Narendra Singh Tomar, Jual Oram, Radha Mohan Singh, Thawar Chand Gehlot and Smriti Irani were inducted into the Cabinet.

The BJP had not been in power for ten years at the Centre, but the Cabinet members of 2014 had both administrative and organizational experience behind them. These new Cabinet members were former chief ministers, ministers in various states and also Union ministers in the Vajpayee government or had worked at the organizational level in the BJP.

Those who were not in the government were tasked with building the party organizationally. This was not new. Younger people had come to prominence in the BJP when Nitin Gadkari and Rajnath Singh were party presidents. Shah carried this process forward, pushing for a younger team.[32] People who became part of the new team were Muralidhar Rao, Vijay Rahatkar, Anil Jain, Dinesh Sharma, Arun Singh, Ram Madhav, Saroj Pandey and several others, including one of the authors, Bhupender Yadav.

Many political parties in India, particularly those characterized by dynastic succession, have faced difficulties with an ageing leadership. In 2004, when Manmohan Singh became Prime Minister, he was seventy-two and in 1991, when P.V. Narasimha Rao became Prime Minister, he was seventy. A key strength of the BJP, being a non-dynastic party, lies in its ability to always manage these multiple layers of a leadership team, to combine the wisdom and strategic sense of the elderly, and the experienced leadership of the people running the government, with the energy of the young who cut their teeth in building the party and winning elections.

This approach helps reduce the problem of anti-incumbency, where voters do not associate the difficulties of their everyday life with a single legislator over long decades. Such an approach is particularly attractive for an ambitious young person, who can envision a career path for himself through party work in the early decades, followed by government roles for some decades, followed by the role of elder statesmen.

In this vein, the BJP also created an important distinction between leadership of the party as an organization as opposed to leadership of one election campaign. The two responsibilities were distributed between two separate individuals. Panels were formed to take collective decisions and not allow any monopoly in the decision-making process.

Another principle was for the leadership of the party to remain connected with all levels of party workers. The party leadership, including the president, stayed either at the Circuit House or party office, and not in any five-star hotel, during visits to states to oversee party work. Other leaders also followed this principle. This brought in a sense of discipline and equality in the organization. Party office-bearers would have food in Dalit bastis. They also interacted with local language media, interaction with whom helped spread the BJP's messages across India, beyond New Delhi.

When the Congress gained power, the focus shifted to the work of the government, and the party tended to atrophy. Indeed, many powerful politicians neglected even important meetings of the party. The BJP self-consciously built an internal culture where the party remained important even in the eyes of persons shouldering important portfolios in the government. The meetings of BJP's Central Election Committee and Parliamentary Board always took place in the party office and never at the Prime Minister's residence. PM Modi always attended these meetings at the party office. He made it a point to sit through the party's National Executive meetings. He incorporated the suggestions made in his own speeches at the events.

Sweeping the Assembly Elections in 2014

Alongside this internal re-engineering of the BJP, Maharashtra, Haryana, Jharkhand and Jammu and Kashmir were headed for Assembly elections. All four states had different socio-political realities and so the factors that were to determine the BJP's strategy were also different.

In Maharashtra, the BJP and Shiv Sena were in a three-decade old alliance. Pramod Mahajan and Gopinath Munde from the BJP, and Balasaheb Thackeray from the Shiv Sena had stitched together the alliance. The Shiv Sena had deep roots in Mumbai politics and (to a lesser extent) in Maharashtra's hinterland. Its main rival in Maharashtra was the Congress. The Shiv Sena had come to acquire the position of the 'senior partner' in the early conception of the partnership with the BJP.[33] When the pre-poll alliance was being worked out, the Shiv Sena contested from more seats. The human relationships between Pramod Mahajan, Gopinath Munde and Balasaheb Thackeray, which had built and nurtured the partnerships were disrupted in the 2009–2014 period. After the sudden demise of Pramod Mahajan in 2006, the responsibility of running the coalition from the BJP's side fell on Gopinath Munde.[34] Unfortunately, he too died in a car accident in 2014.[35] In 2012, Balasaheb Thackeray died, and the Shiv Sena's leadership was transferred to his son, Uddhav Thackeray.[36]

In the 2014 Lok Sabha elections, the BJP and the Shiv Sena together won forty-one of the forty-eight seats in Maharashtra.[37]

When the results were out, everyone was convinced that this alliance would sweep the upcoming state elections too. However, the relationship between the two parties soured over the issue of seat distribution.[38] The state was set to go to polls in October. But till September, the two parties did not announce their candidates. The BJP, which had been electorally the more successful of the two partners for many years, suggested an equal distribution of seats. The Shiv Sena demanded a larger share.

There were other changes taking place in the Shiv Sena as well. In the hands of senior Thackeray, the Shiv Sena viewed itself as wielding political power without narrowly focusing on electoral politics. The next generation saw this differently. Uddhav Thackeray said during an interview that if the party came to power, he was willing to be chief minister.[39]

Maharashtra evolved from a two-cornered contest into a four-cornered contest when the long-standing partnership between the BJP and the Shiv Sena broke up, and coincidentally the long-standing partnership between the Congress and the NCP also came to an end.[40][41]

Political experts believed the BJP had taken a risk. There were about 150 seats in the state where the BJP had never fielded a candidate. This shaped up, once again, as a unique battle for the election-winning capabilities of the BJP. One important element of this was bringing in the small vote shares of regional parties. The BJP formed alliances with various parties in the state: the Republican Party of India, the Swabhimani Paksha, the Rashtriya Samaj Paksha, etc.[42]

The results were surprisingly good for the BJP. It emerged as the single-largest party. Of the 288 seats, the BJP won 122, the Shiv Sena won sixty-three. The Congress got forty-two seats and the NCP bagged forty-one.[43] This was a new display of political salience for the BJP, an ability to win in non-traditional locations.

Similarly, the BJP vote share in Haryana had never gone past 10 per cent. The state, which had been carved out of East Punjab in 1966 on a linguistic basis, had a majority of farmers. In the 2014 Assembly elections the BJP was optimistic. What fuelled the party's hope was the 34.8 per cent vote share and seven seats it won in the 2014 Lok Sabha elections.[44]

However, its alliance partner, the Haryana Janhit Congress (HJC) still wanted the seat-sharing formula for the assembly election to be 50:50, i.e., forty-five seats each. Amit Shah was keenly watching the developments and was looking for a political equation that would pave the way for the BJP's expansion. Shah decided to dig deeper into the ground situation to understand why exactly the BJP had not been able to establish roots in Haryana. A team was sent from Delhi to hold discussions with the general public and party workers in the state to analyse the ground reality in the state and communicate it to the party leadership.

The team visited Rohtak, Bhiwani and Dadri and met party workers there and reported three key findings back to the headquarters. First, after the election of PM Modi at the Centre, voters were more supportive as PM Modi was very popular. Second, the HJC's organizational strength was not such that it would be able to contest forty-five seats. Third, people in Haryana wanted to see a non-corrupt government in the state. It appeared that if the BJP aggressively positioned itself as a corruption-free party then people would be willing to see the BJP as a viable opposition.

The team reported that the Haryana Janhit Congress was demanding more seats than it deserved. In the negotiations, the two parties could not arrive at a consensus and the coalition fell apart.[45] This situation was similar to that seen in Maharashtra, where the BJP decided to step away from a partner and go on its own into elections.

The state of Jharkhand had been carved out of Bihar with the dream that it would achieve development in a way that had eluded Bihar. However, this did not work out, in no small part owing to political instability in the sense that state level politics consisted of short-lived coalitions. The BJP campaigned on the themes of backwardness and political instability, using the slogan 'Sampurna Bahumat Poorna Vikas' (absolute majority, total development).[46] It argued that to have development, Jharkhand needed to have a single stable party ruling it. It campaigned on the ground that this single party should be the same party that is at the Centre so that it could be a double engine government. The BJP partnered with the All Jharkhand Students Union (AJSU), and gave it eight seats, while contesting itself on seventy-two seats. The BJP-AJSU alliance got a clear majority to form the government.[47] The combination of Modi's popularity, the BJP's appeal in Jharkhand and the AJSU's local knowledge and regional appeal had come together to ensure another electoral success.

In the assembly elections in Jammu and Kashmir held in December 2014, Mufti Mohammad Sayeed's People's Democratic Party (PDP) emerged as the single-largest party with twenty-eight seats but not enough to be able to form the government on its own. In the Jammu region, the BJP won twenty-five seats, but did not achieve any success in the Kashmir Valley.[48] These results made it clear to the BJP that under the prevailing circumstances it was impossible for the party to win a single seat in the Valley, and that it was impossible to form a government without it. The BJP decided to be a part of the government by aligning with the PDP.

National parties and the leadership at the Centre had been over the years perceived with wariness in the Valley. The BJP had a stated position on the abrogation of Article 370, and teaming up with a regional satrap that was perceived to be 'soft' on the secessionists was a decision that people on both sides of the Jawahar Tunnel found hard to reconcile with. This was especially pronounced as many had blamed Mufti for the violence that erupted in Anantnag in 1986, when Hindu temples were desecrated. There were questions put to the BJP on how it would cope with the PDP's position on continuing with the special status to J&K or removal of Armed Forces Special Powers Act (AFSPA).

The coming together of two divergent ideologies was, therefore, viewed with suspicion and scepticism. Even before the coalition government was sworn in on 1 March 2015, with Mufti Mohammad Sayeed as the chief minister, many had already predicted its premature end. A government that had the BJP, perceived as a Hindu party in the Valley, as a partner, was not expected to last.

The BJP chose to go with a coalition in Jharkhand, while in Maharashtra and Haryana it chose to fight the elections alone. This appeared to be contradictory to some. The key idea behind these decisions was to be pragmatic and focus on the ground realities at each booth, in each seat. In Jharkhand, the AJSU was a good partner, and was required in carrying the coalition across to victory. In Maharashtra and in Haryana, the relationship with the partner was more problematic, and the BJP was in a stronger place and could go it alone. As political scientist Zoya Hasan has observed, in places where the BJP was not a strong contender for power, regional parties did not feel threatened in aligning with the party. The Congress was a threat to a regional party in almost all states, but the BJP was small enough in many states to achieve good partnerships at a critical time in its journey.

There was a non-dogmatic approach to alliances: In each of the four states, the party chose a path that was most likely to obtain victory in elections. The party did not announce a chief ministerial face in any state, which helped accentuate the prominence of Modi, who had played a key part in winning the recent 2014 Lok Sabha elections. Modi addressed about twenty-four rallies in Maharashtra, eighteen rallies in Haryana and a few in Jharkhand and J&K.

After the victory of 2014, this was the first time PM Modi's popularity was being put to the test. The party by now had a new president in the form of Amit Shah and so it was also a test for the organizational strategy under him. Shah was known for his organizational capabilities in Gujarat and had proven them in the Lok Sabha elections of 2014 in Uttar Pradesh.

The government's work and party's strategy succeeded in Maharashtra, Jharkhand and Haryana. In Maharashtra, the party was a little short of the majority with 122 seats but emerged as the single-largest party. The Shiv Sena, the Congress and the NCP won sixty-three, forty-two and forty-one seats, respectively. The BJP's vote share in Maharashtra rose from 14 per cent to 27.8 per cent. In Haryana, from four seats in 2009, the party's seats tally rose to forty-seven seats. In Jharkhand, along with AJSU, the BJP coalition bagged forty-two seats.[49] In Jammu and Kashmir, the BJP formed a coalition in which party leader Nirmal Singh became the deputy CM.

Raghubar Das was appointed the chief minister of Jharkhand. Das, who was once an employee of Tata Steel, served as MLA for five times representing Jamshedpur East constituency from 1995 to 2019. Das had been president of the BJP's Jharkhand unit twice. Das also served as the deputy chief minister and the urban development minister during the BJP-led government in the state. Das's political engagements began during his college days and he went on to join the Jaiprakash Narayan-led 'Total Revolution' movement in Jharkhand.

In Haryana, Manohar Lal Khattar became the chief minister. Khattar had been an old RSS pracharak. From 2000–2014, Khattar was the BJP's organizational general secretary in Haryana. He had worked on building the party in Punjab and J&K too. He had been instrumental in implementing the Deen Dayal Antyodaya Yojana on the ground. In 2014, he was the chairman of the BJP's Haryana Election Campaign Committee for Lok Sabha elections. Khattar had then gone on to become a member of the BJP's National Executive Committee.

In Maharashtra, the BJP needed twenty-two seats to get through. The gap was filled with Shiv Sena announcing support to the BJP government and Devendra Fadnavis of the BJP became the chief minister. At forty-four, Fadnavis was a young leader who had begun his political career in the mid-1990s. As a college student, Fadnavis was an active member of the ABVP. He won his first municipal election from Ram Nagar ward in 1992. In 1997, Fadnavis became the youngest mayor of the Nagpur Municipal Corporation and the second youngest mayor in the history of India. He had also been an RSS member.

In J&K, even though the party went on to form a government based on a 'Common Minimum Agenda', the coalition was shaky and eventually broke.

After the Maharashtra and Haryana election victories, *India Today* on 22 October 2014, in an article titled, 'Modi, Amit Shah redefining BJP's language of business', wrote, 'The BJP sent out a clear message that Modi and Shah will try to sustain the current momentum as long as they can, striking it big as long as it lasts. This puts on notice all other allies and every other regional party in power.'[50][51]

The BJP in its National Executive held in April in Bengaluru passed a political resolution titled 'Panchayat to Parliament—Politics of Development, Prosperity and Progress'.[52]

The BJP had also achieved successes in Panchayat and urban local body elections across the states of Madhya Pradesh, Rajasthan, Punjab and Assam. The National Executive said that the victories are making the BJP 'a party with formidable presence from Panchayat to Parliament.'[53]

Expanding the Party

Even as the BJP was gaining electorally, it was focused on expanding the party at all levels, including the booth.

In India, the typical polling booth is a physical location where about 1,000 voters cast their votes, and there are about 1 million polling booths. Electoral politics at its elemental level is about establishing an organizational capability at each of these 1 million booths, spread all over India, which manages voter turnout and voter sentiment. The overall organization that fights a national election is extremely large, which requires commensurate inputs of resourcing, information and management, with incentive compatibility at each level of the organization diagram. While political parties have long thought about how to play electoral politics at the booth level, this was taken to the next level by the BJP and Shah. Shah often says, 'whoever wins the booth, wins the election'.

As part of the organizational transformation which began in 2014, this 'booth management strategy' classified booths based on the vote share obtained by the BJP into three bins: small, medium and high. In each election, the objective at each booth was to convert 'small' into 'medium' and 'medium' into 'high'.[54] After each election, a post-mortem was done, to analyse data at the booth level, to understand reasons for success and failure.

At the lowest level of this management was a page that contained the names of about twenty to thirty voters. Given the nature of first-past-the-post elections, generally a 40 per cent vote share suffices to win an election, so the target associated with each *panna* (page) was to get to about fifteen supporters. This page was given to a *panna pramukh* (page leader). This person was responsible for meeting each of these voters, face to face. On election date, the page leader called these voters to cast their vote, which is permissible under the Moral Code of Conduct of the Election Commission of India. The page leaders help in micro-management of elections by helping take the party's plans and programmes to each doorstep.

For a polling booth with 1,000 voters, about fifty individuals were required to work as page leaders. They reported to a 'booth-in-charge' who led the work on one booth. The next level of the management structure was the *shakti kendra* which has oversight of five polling booths (i.e., of about 250 page leaders). The local shakti kendra personnel reported to the BJP MLA (or candidate for the state legislature), who reported to the BJP state leader.[55]

The number of party workers involved in such an organization was extremely large, well beyond those ever mustered by the Congress in its heyday. The simple arithmetic shows that fifty page leaders for 1 million booths require fifty million party workers right there. This insight was critical for the massive expansion of BJP's membership.

The party needed to have millions of members in order to support this scale of work.

The BJP had by now added over 10 crore members, a first for any party anywhere in the world. With this achievement in the backdrop, the party was looking at another year with more elections and newer challenges in the offing.

10

Expansion and Outreach (2015)

After the Sadasyata Maha-Abhiyan, the party resolution passed at the Bengaluru National Executive said, 'The BJP will start its "Mahasampark Abhiyan" with positive methods to reach all its members. Our focus is not just on becoming the largest party in the world but in ensuring qualitative improvement in public life and instilling the right values in our workers. We will be organizing training and orientation sessions to develop and further propagate these democratic values in our workers across the country.'[1]

With this intensified membership drive, the Mahasampark Abhiyaan, the BJP began contacting the new members personally, going beyond the digital outreach. Parallelly, the BJP began the process of involving the vast new party membership into the organization's activities and introducing the new members to the party's ideology. The party held meetings at zonal levels to discuss organizational expansion and Amit Shah himself attended most of these meetings.

Electoral Setbacks in 2015

The BJP had won several states in 2014 and had also expanded significantly by ushering in changes at the organizational level.

Spirits were also high given the massive and decisive victory of 2014. The party was now, however, faced with new elections in crucial states.

In 2015, Delhi and Bihar were scheduled for elections. From 1993 to 1998, the BJP had been in power in Delhi, but after that the Congress ruled for over fifteen years, with Sheila Dikshit as the chief minister. This equation had, however, changed a bit after the Congress landed at the third spot in the 2013 elections with the entry of the Aam Aadmi Party (AAP).

There was an anti-incumbency wave against the Congress government on the issues of law and order and inflation. The AAP campaigned with populist promises. The party managed to win twenty-eight seats in the 2013 Delhi assembly elections.[2] The BJP emerged as the single-largest party with thirty-one seats, while the Congress was limited to just eight.[3] The AAP first formed a government with the support of the Congress and then resigned after forty-nine days. Arvind Kejriwal soon realized this resignation was a mistake, and went back to voters apologizing for it when the elections took place again in 2015.[4] Law and order became a key issue in these elections.[5]

The BJP felt that winning in Delhi required projecting clarity of leadership. This led to the choice of Kiran Bedi, a former Indian Police Service officer, who had been a part of the anti-corruption campaign, as its candidate for chief minister.[6] The BJP felt that the initiatives of the Central government, and the success of the BJP in Delhi in the 2014 elections, would help carry them through. It felt that the initial infatuation with AAP would have been dented by its impetuous resignation which conveyed its lack of experience with the long slog of politics.

The results were, however, contrary to these expectations. In an unprecedented victory, the AAP took its tally of twenty-eight in 2013 to sixty-seven seats in the 70-member assembly.[7] The Congress vote share fell by fifteen percentage points; these votes mostly switched to the AAP.[8] While the BJP mostly hung on to its vote share, it won just three seats and even BJP's CM face Kiran Bedi lost from the Krishna Nagar seat.[9]

Table 1: Delhi Assembly Elections of 2015[10]

Political Party	AE 2013		LS 2014		AE 2015	
	Vote Share	Seats Won	Vote Share	Seats Won	Vote Share	Seats Won
Bharatiya Janata Party	33.07%	31	46.63%	7	32.19%	3
Indian National Congress	24.55%	8	15.22%	0	9.65%	0
Aam Aadmi Party	29.49%	28	33.08%	0	54.34%	67

There was soul searching and analysis after this debacle. It was a reminder that no matter how a party had fared in the last election, there were no certainties of faring well in the current one. In this analysis, it was felt that Kiran Bedi's rapid induction into the party had not been adequately internalized by the long-standing party cadre. In addition, rural Delhi voters were potentially worried about the Land Acquisition Bill, about which there had been a false narrative that it would lead to expropriation of their land.[11] A significant factor revealed by the results was that the Congress had lost its voters in the state of Delhi.

After the Delhi elections, the next important battle for the BJP was the election in Bihar. In Indian politics, Bihar has historically been a significant state. All important political strategies have emanated from the state's politics. From Gandhi's Champaran Satyagrah, to Lohia's fight for social justice, to JP's struggle against the Congress government's dictatorial policies, the most defining political movements find their origin in Bihar. Till the 1970s, parties from across the ideological spectrum such as the Jana Sangh, Congress,

Socialist parties, Communist parties and Jharkhand Mukti Morcha contested for influence in the state. Later, the Socialists came to gain considerable authority.

The long-standing Congress rule ended in 1990, when the Janata Dal government came to power and Lalu Yadav became the chief minister. Till 2005, Lalu's party, the RJD remained in power in the state. In 1997, a special CBI court issued an arrest warrant against Lalu Yadav in the animal fodder scam. On 23 July 1997, Yadav resigned from his post, but to ensure his hold on power, he appointed his wife Rabri Devi to the chief minister's chair.[12]

This RJD rule continued in Bihar till 2005. While his skills in administration were limited, Lalu Yadav had a good understanding of the caste arithmetic and created a winning coalition of Yadav and Muslim voters. Traversing various ups and downs, the Rabri Devi government lasted till 2005. From Lalu to Rabri, the state's law and order was in a shambles.[13]

During the 2014 Lok Sabha elections, the coalition was disrupted by Nitish Kumar's disagreement with the BJP.[14] Nitish Kumar had objected to the BJP projecting Modi as its prime ministerial candidate. Consequently, in 2015, the BJP was alone in the run up to the Bihar elections of October 2015. On 14 April, in a meeting with special strategists, Shah said, 'Of the 62,779 booths in Bihar, the results for 9,302 in the Lok Sabha election were decided by a margin of merely fifty votes . . . We must think about increasing 100 votes per booth.'[15]

Shah pointed out that booths on which the BJP won had a lower voting percentage than those on which it lost. This overall led to a loss for the party. The party thus realized every booth was important, including those it could win. The party thus divided booths into A, B and C categories. The booths where the BJP won over 60 per cent votes in the previous two or three elections were placed in category A; those where it won between 30 per cent and 40 per cent votes were placed in category B and those where the party won less than

20-30 per cent votes were placed in the C category.[16] Plans for public outreach and booth management were devised according to the category a booth fit into.

This approach of winning the booth to win elections was not new for the BJP. When Narendra Modi was Gujarat chief minister and Rajnath Singh was party president, the latter visited Gujarat. Party workers apprised Singh of the booth level mobilization and handed over a list of booth *pramukhs* (chiefs) to him saying he could dial any number on the list to speak to the booth in-charge. When Singh dialled one of the numbers his call was answered by a man who identified himself as the BJP booth pramukh of his area. When Rajnath Singh asked him about his profession, the man replied that he was a rickshaw puller. This was the deep connect BJP formed with its ground level workers.

Now, the party identified dedicated party workers on a national scale who could be deployed to work at the booth level during polls. The identified persons were given training in electoral processes and encouraged to lodge protests in case irregularities were witnessed. The booth in-charges and workers were foot soldiers of the BJP who were told to meet voters of their respective booths and help resolve their problems by staying in regular contact.

Nitish Kumar, on the other hand, joined forces with his arch-rival Lalu Yadav and Congress.[17] While an RJD–Congress–NCP alliance had been formed in the Lok Sabha elections, it had proven ineffective ahead of the Modi wave. This time, Nitish Kumar was also part of the alliance. To take on the Grand Alliance, the BJP formed an alliance with Jitan Ram Manjhi's party, the Hindustani Awam Morcha, in an attempt to improve its appeal with Dalit voters.[18] PM Modi was scheduled to start the party's election campaign from 25 July and did thirty-one rallies in all.[19] The party prepared 160 GPS-enabled convertible raths to reach the nooks and corners of the state and encourage voters to cast their ballot in favour of the BJP.

Table 2: Bihar Assembly Elections of 2015[20]

Political Party	AE 2010		LS 2014		AE 2015	
	Vote Share	Seats Won	Vote Share	Seats Won	Vote Share	Seats Won
Bharatiya Janata Party	16.49%	91	29.86%	22	24.42%	53
Indian National Congress	8.37%	4	8.56%	2	6.66%	27
Rashtriya Janata Dal	18.84%	22	20.46%	4	18.35%	80
Janata Dal (United)	22.58%	115	16.04%	2	16.83%	71
Nationalist Congress Party	1.82%	0	1.22%	1	0.49%	0

The results were disappointing for the BJP. It had contested 157 seats and won just fifty-three. Its allies, the Lok Janshakti Party, the Rashtriya Lok Samta Party and the Hindustani Awam Morcha that together fought on eighty-six seats, won only on five.[21] As part of the Grand Alliance, Nitish Kumar's party suffered a considerable loss of seats, while Lalu Yadav's RJD gained.

A major reason for the BJP's loss was the performance of its allies. Even though the party had won 24.4 per cent votes, the coalition partners failed to perform well, resulting in the loss. The BJP won fifty-three of the 157 seats it contested, with a strike rate of 30 per cent, while the allies won just 4 per cent of the seats they contested. On the other hand, despite being unnatural allies, the JD(U) and the RJD were successful in transferring their votes. The same did not happen in the case of the BJP and its allies.

Cooperative Federalism

Alongside the electoral challenges and organizational work, the BJP government was working on ushering in the key reforms that had been long due in the country. One of the most important of those reforms concerned the Planning Commission.

The Constitution of India defines India as a union of states. Yet, many decades of central planning had taken power away from the states and made the Central government very powerful. The Planning Commission was set up by Nehru to develop and implement five-year plans following the approach of socialist countries such as the Soviet Union. Sixty-four years after its creation, the body was primarily running an endless number of welfare schemes announced by the Central government. The National Development Council (NDC), which was meant to promote the plans made by the Planning Commission, held meetings with chief ministers. The commission's manner of working was often criticized by the chief ministers who resented being called by the deputy chairman of the Planning Commission every year for approval of their state plans.

'We have come to Delhi just to be told by the Commission how we should spend our own money,' Tamil Nadu chief minister J. Jayalalithaa had said in 2012 after a meeting with the then Planning Commission deputy chairman Montek Singh Ahluwalia.[22]

Modi was chief minister of Gujarat from 2001 to 2014. At the fifty-eighth meeting of the NDC in 2012 he said that it was with a 'sense of great anguish and deep regret' that he was drawing attention of the NDC to 'attempts being made by the central government to tinker with federal structure mandated by the Constitution'. He added, 'The central government should exercise extreme vigilance and caution to ensure that all constitutional authorities are allowed to carry out their mandated functions and at all times observe the federal dharma.' Modi emphasized further, 'It is important to trust the states. All decisions regarding implementation of central schemes must be taken in the states by state-level committees and by state officials.'[23]

After forming a BJP government at the Centre in 2014, Prime Minister Narendra Modi said in his Independence Day address, 'Sometimes it costs more to repair an old house, but it gives us no satisfaction. We have a feeling that it would be better to construct a new house altogether. Therefore, within a short period, we will replace the Planning Commission with a new institution.'

On 1 January 2015, the sixty-five-year-old Planning Commission was abolished. It was replaced by a new body, 'NITI Aayog' or National Institution for Transforming India, which would serve as a policy think-tank for the Central and state governments. The idea of central planning had been opposed by the party from the days of the Jana Sangh. The theme of decentralization and a more powerful federal structure with reduced power to the Union government had been a recurrent theme with the BJP and earlier, the Jana Sangh.

Another important element of the BJP's decentralization theme and giving power to the states was acceptance of the recommendations of the fourteenth finance commission that recommended that a greater share of revenue be given to the states out of the share of taxes collected by the government. The underlying principle was that the Union collected revenues on behalf of states. This principle was also what lay behind the formation of the Goods and Services Tax (GST) council that comprised all finance ministers of all the states who would decide the GST rate for different items. The government introduced the goods and services tax where states had an equal share and set up the council where the Union government is but one participant in decision-making. This again emphasized the federal nature of India, as opposed to the previous system in which the Union Budget would propose duties such as excise duty and service taxes on different items that it chose on its own, while each of the states chose its rate of sales tax on different items. When GST was introduced, it brought a single national rate of tax for the whole country, removed frictions like octroi and created a single national market in India. The BJP had pushed on the theme of national integration and a single nation in many ways. A single national market was part of that theme as well, and with the GST it was one where state governments wielded equal power. Another element of a single nation was a unique national identity which helped create a more equal standard of living for all who lived in the country.

The Modi government focused on improving the standard of living of the poor through improvement on various social and economic parameters based on nutrition, child mortality, years of schooling, school attendance, cooking fuel, sanitation, drinking water, electricity, housing and household assets.[24] The government's focus was on providing assets directly to the poorest families. This was done in a manner that reduced corruption and leakages using a unique identity number and with cash transfers. Consequently, many more people could be reached with the same amount of public expenditure. Schemes were implemented by the Union government through Central ministries which were small and where accountability could be easily pinned. With the progress of schemes available on their websites, with online application mechanisms and use of individual unique identity numbers, the Modi government was not only able to reach out to millions of beneficiaries but also monitor the progress of the schemes.

Aadhaar became the foundation for rollout of almost all government schemes. It provided a unique biometric identity to every resident. The most important impact of Jan Dhan accounts was on reducing leakages in welfare programmes. Direct Benefit Transfer (DBT) schemes would link the Aadhaar number of the account holder to his or her bank account. By directly transferring subsidies to the beneficiary accounts, the DBT scheme hit out at the nexus of middlemen.[25] The government enrolled millions for Aadhaar and made it the platform for DBT payments.

The disbursement of provisions under central schemes by government officials was followed up by party workers contacting the beneficiaries directly. This paved the way for the government to improve the standard of living of the poor in a very tangible and direct way. At the same time the government was able to reach its goal without encountering the legendary leakages within the Indian system. As part of its programmes throughout the five years of the government as well as in election campaigns, BJP activists moved beyond their traditional voter base, and connected directly with their beneficiaries.

Adopting the Monetary Policy Framework

Many elections had been lost due to price rise. The price of onions was said to be responsible for the BJP government's loss in Delhi elections back in 1998. On average, India had witnessed inflation rates of about 7 per cent. In the short run, inflation fluctuates based on events like the monsoon. But in the long run, inflation is controlled by monetary policy. Numerous experts had recommended that India move to an inflation targeting monetary policy framework.[26] An inflation targeting framework helps people and businesses by providing predictability of inflation.[27] It helps create stability in the economy.

Reforms of the monetary policy framework by the Modi government were initiated with the signing of the Monetary Policy Framework Agreement between the RBI and the government of India in February 2015.[28] Later in 2016, India statutorily adopted inflation targeting as a major objective of monetary policy through the Reserve Bank of India Amendment Act, 2016. The amendment set up a Monetary Policy Committee to set the policy rate to pursue an inflation target.

The new framework helped by global price stability led India to witness low and stable inflation during the tenure of the government. For the elections held during this regime, *mahangai* or price rise no longer figured as an election issue.

Political Mobilization

The BJP had a remarkable phase, winning the Lok Sabha in 2014, as well as quite a few state elections. The victories were a result of the decline of the Congress, the popularity of Modi, and the remarkable organization-building initiatives which were in play. The vote share of the BJP had risen, but not to a point of invulnerability. The very strength of the BJP was helping to bring foes together, and first-past-the-post elections were then keenly contested. Not all state elections had worked out right.

During a press conference following the loss, Shah was asked what the impact of the results on the party would be. He said, 'You are asking this because BJP's organizational elections are approaching. Correct? If victory and defeat decided the BJP's presidency, it would be difficult for the BJP to ever elect a president.'[29]

In the meantime, the plan of expanding party membership was being rolled out with vigour. The BJP had a long tradition of training its workers and members. In 1982, Pramod Mahajan had established Rambhau Mhalgi Prabodhini whose aim was 'to work for building the capacities of the elected representatives, political party activists, and voluntary social workers while understanding the overall human resource development needs of these sectors.'[30]

The party was now moving towards a more institutionalized training programme. On 30 June 2015, the party launched its Maha Prashikshan Abhiyan, a mission to train the new members.[31][32] This mission was able to sift through the flood of new members, some of whom might have signed up in a mere burst of enthusiasm and optimism, and identify those who were willing to commit time for party work, and those who could graduate from sympathizers to members.

These workshops involved educating party members as well as MPs, MLAs, members at local units, about the history and ideology of the party, telling them about the BJP government's achievements at the centre and state levels, and customizing content in every state to discuss the existing socio-political situations.[33] The programme was organized in a phased manner over a period of four months.[34]

There are two scarce resources in every modern society: people who are willing to become volunteers for a political party, and voters' attention. Use of technology for political mobilization, a series of celebrations and social campaigns generated enthusiasm in party workers and in the minds of the voters. It helped create an energized band of party workers and a large base of public support.

Political mobilization on issues that touched on the life of the poor as well as the middle class were hugely popular. One such project was around subsidized LPG cylinders. In March 2015, PM Modi appealed to affluent households, requesting them to voluntarily give up their subsidies, promising that each subsidy slot that was freed up by a rich household would generate a subsidy for one poor household.[35] The BJP campaigned massively for this initiative. Going ahead, PM Modi coined a slogan for the campaign. He said, 'The "Give it up" campaign should be taken up on the lines of Swacch Bharat and Beti Bachao, Beti Padhao initiatives . . . I appeal to all MPs, MLAs, ministers, IAS and IPS officers, professors and professionals to forgo their LPG subsidy and derive happiness by doing so.'[36]

Until 2015, every buyer of an LPG cylinder received subsidies from the government. Making an argument in the spirit of sacrifice and helping the poor, PM Modi said, 'Gas cylinders surrendered by them would be transferred to the poor who use wood for cooking. If one crore people give up their LPG subsidy, one crore poor people will benefit as they will be given new LPG cylinders instead.'[37] As a result of this public appeal, nearly 1 crore LPG consumers gave up their subsidised gas connections.[38] It created a feel-good factor and connected them with Modi's scheme. With its huge outreach, millions of people attributed the free cylinder, received under the Ujjwala Yojana, to Prime Minister Modi and it created a direct connection between the party and the poor across the length and breadth of the country. A remarkable 10 million affluent households voluntarily gave up their subsidies. This helped increase their emotional connection with Modi and the BJP.[39]

Several such political mobilization projects were executed throughout the year.

The one year of the BJP rule was celebrated as *Jan Kalyan Parv* from 26 to 31 May 2015.[40] When Narendra Modi was chief minister of Gujarat, he started a unique model that saw governance with *jan bhagidari* (public participation). This involved taking public opinion both at the time of policy formulation and seeking feedback after the rollout of government schemes. When the BJP came to power on the national stage, the party ensured that a link was established between the government and people. The Sampark and Parikshan Abhiyan of the BJP had helped connect people to the party and train those involved in party activities. The Jan Kalyan Parv was the party's attempt to connect the government with the people. BJP leaders talked about the achievements of the Modi government at rallies and press conferences all over India as part of the programme.

Celebrations were held around 11 October 2015, the 113th birth anniversary of Jaiprakash Narayan, as 'Save Democracy Day' and used to criticize the Congress in the context of the fortieth anniversary of the Emergency announced by Indira Gandhi.[41] For this, PM Modi ran a show in Delhi, and Shah held an event in JP's native village of Sitabdiara in Bihar.

The BJP emphasized the contribution of Vallabhbhai Patel, who was part of the leadership during the independence movement. His birthday was celebrated as 'National Unity Day' on 31 October 2015.[42][43]

Organizationally, while the BJP expanded through the Sampark Abhiyan and other party activities, electorally, the year wasn't a satisfying one. Delhi and Bihar were significant states that the party had wanted to win, but lost.

11

Winning the States (2016–2018)

Putting behind the losses of 2015, the BJP was faced with elections in five states in 2016—Assam, Puducherry, West Bengal, Kerala and Tamil Nadu—and the BJP was organizationally weak in all of them. The Election Commission of India announced the poll schedule on 18 March and said that elections would be held between April and May. The political strategists in the BJP wondered how the newfound organizational capabilities and processes of the party could be applied in these settings.

The BJP chose to not have a uniform strategy on whether a person should be promised, prior to elections, the chief minister's position in the event of victory. This decision was taken one election at a time, based on a judgement about what worked best where.

While the BJP had not been in power in any of the states, its chances of a win looked brightest in Assam. The Congress was in power in Assam. In 2011, the BJP had contested 120 seats and won five. By 2014, the BJP was in better shape; in the Lok Sabha elections it added 20 percentage points to its vote share and won half of the fourteen seats.[1] In 2016, BJP started reaching out to regional politicians and parties. The BJP formed alliances with the Bodoland People's Front and Asom Gana Parishad (AGP). The

AGP is one of Assam's oldest parties and had been in power from 1985 to 1990. The Bodoland People's Front was also an important party that represented tribals. The BJP felt that this combination was within range of getting through. It was sensitive to the idea of development centred around regional aspiration and national ambition. Smaller parties may not have enough sway in a region to form governments, but they represent the aspirations of significant sections of the population and therefore the BJP valued alliances with them.

In addition, an important tactical development helped the BJP. Himanta Biswa Sarma's shift from the Congress to the BJP in 2015, along with the decision to project Sarbananda Sonowal as the party's chief ministerial candidate.[2] Himanta Biswa Sarma, who had a mass appeal in Assam, quit the Tarun Gogoi-led Congress government ahead of the 2014 Lok Sabha polls and quit the Congress party in 2015. Gogoi was growing old and Sarma's exit virtually made the Congress look leaderless in the state. Sonowal, on the other hand, was serving as the Union minister for sports and youth affairs since 2014. He had earlier served as the president of the BJP's Assam unit and was also a National Executive member of the party. From 1992–1999, Sonowal was the president of the All Assam Students Union (AASU) and was firmly rooted into the politics of the state. After the AASU, Sonowal joined the Asom Gana Parishad and became an MLA. Hailing from the Kachari tribe, he was known as a *jatiya nayak* (regional Assamese hero) during his days with the AASU. In 2004, he entered Lok Sabha after defeating Congress heavyweight Paban Singh Ghatowar from Dibrugarh. The BJP felt that projecting him as the prospective chief minister would help win votes.[3]

Opinion polls showed BJP's strength to be growing by March and April.[4][5] The results, which were released on 19 May, left the BJP with sixty out of 126 while the Congress got only twenty-six.[6] The BJP thus grew from five seats in 2011 to sixty in 2016.[7]

Table 1: Assam Assembly Elections of 2016[8]

Political Party	AE 2011		LS 2014		AE 2016	
	Vote Share	Seats Won	Vote Share	Seats Won	Vote Share	Seats Won
Bharatiya Janata Party	11.47%	5	36.86%	7	29.51%	60
Indian National Congress	39.39%	78	29.90%	3	30.96%	26
Asom Gana Parishad	16.29%	10	3.87%	0	8.14%	14
Bodoland People's Front	6.13%	12	2.21%	0	3.94%	12

Elections in West Bengal, Tamil Nadu, Kerala and Puducherry were next. All these states fell in a pattern. The BJP had not done well in the previous assembly elections, had not won a significant number of seats in the Lok Sabha elections of 2014 (Bengal-two, Tamil Nadu-two, Kerala-zero), but had gained vote share in 2014 suggesting the beginning of mind share with voters. While a significant effort was put into each of these elections in 2016, the gains were modest.[9] [10]

To summarize the state elections from 2014–2016, the BJP expanded its strength significantly in four large states: Maharashtra, Haryana, Jharkhand and Assam while not losing vote share anywhere.

At the end of 2016, the BJP became the ruling party of one more state: Arunachal Pradesh. In the assembly elections held along with the Lok Sabha election of 2014, the Congress had won forty-two of the sixty seats, and the BJP eleven seats.[11] But towards the end of 2016, Congress MLAs began joining the BJP. On 31 December, Pema Khandu joined the BJP along with thirty-three MLAs of the People's Party.[12]

With the BJP forming a government in Assam and Arunachal Pradesh, the party gained a foothold in the northeast for the first time.

Outlook on Nationalism

In 2014, when the BJP came to power, a narrative was created to paint the party as authoritarian, orthodox and one with a very narrow vision. This was part of a sustained and motivated campaign. The Opposition tried to create a narrative that the BJP was working towards taking away from India's people their freedom of expression.

The BJP conveyed to people that it did not have an exclusivist or sectarian ideology. For instance, right ahead of the Bihar elections, some writers and filmmakers started a planned campaign of 'Award *wapasi*' (returning awards). Going ahead it became clear that the development was part of an agenda being run by intellectuals of the Left wing.[13] An interview by Vishwanath Prasad Tiwari, president of the Sahitya Akademi at that time, made it clear that Award wapasi was part of an agenda.[14] He said, 'I have evidence to prove award wapasi was not spontaneous but an organised effort led by five writers, many of whom were holding anti-Modi sabhas even before he came to power.'

The BJP believed some universities in the country were in the grip of a separatist mindset. On 9 February 2016, some students of Jawaharlal Nehru University (JNU) held a protest on the university's campus against capital punishment meted out to the 2001 Indian Parliament attack convict Afzal Guru and Kashmiri separatist Maqbool Bhat. Anti-national slogans in favour of separation of Kashmir from the Indian Union were raised during the event.

The BJP had held nationalism as the basic tenet of its politics. Nationalism was the founding principle of the Jana Sangh. The party launched a campaign in the face of the JNU incident calling it the Jan Swabhiman Abhiyan from 18–20 February. A party release explained the purpose of the campaign thus: 'The campaign is against attempts by some political parties to mislead the country by linking separatist voices with freedom of expression over incidents at the prestigious Jawaharlal Nehru University.'[15] The programme was carried out from the zonal and district levels to the state level.

BJP members, supporters and sympathizers organized sit-ins and signature campaigns in support of India's unity and integrity.

The party's National Executive meeting was held on 19–20 March 2016 in Delhi. At this meeting, Shah said, 'Sedition is being camouflaged as freedom of expression. In the name of expression of freedom, the debate on anti-national slogans is being turned in another direction . . . Blatant anti-national activities are taking place on the pretext of freedom of expression. While criticism of the BJP, the government and its leadership was permissible, no criticism of the nation will be tolerated.'[16] The party resolution at the end of this National Executive meeting said, 'Our Constitution describes India as Bharat also and refusal to chant victory to Bharat is tantamount to disrespect to our Constitution itself. "Bharat Mata Ki Jai" is not merely a slogan. It was a mantra of inspiration to countless freedom fighters during the independence struggle.'[17]

Thus, on 9 August 2016, the BJP launched the Tiranga Yatra with the aim of inspiring patriotism and nationalism among the citizens. A week-long campaign was undertaken until 15 August on the occasion of Independence Day. By issuing a slogan *70 saal azadi zara yaad karo qurbani* (70 years of Independence, let's recall the sacrifices) during the campaign, the BJP wanted to familiarize the citizens, especially the youth, with the sacrifices made by freedom fighters during India's independence struggle. Union ministers were asked to take a tour of sites across the country that held importance during the independence struggle and foster patriotism. At the same time, MPs and MLAs were asked to visit their respective constituencies and remind people about how India won its freedom struggle. On 25 September 2016, the BJP organized its National Executive meeting in Kozhikode. Deen Dayal Upadhyaya's birth centenary was on 25 September. The choice of Kozhikode had been made because Upadhyaya had become the president of the Jana Sangh in Kozhikode in 1967. Though Deen Dayal presented some revolutionary ideas such as Integral Humanism and Antyodaya, not many in India were aware

of his ideological contributions. Now in power, the BJP had to give
shape to his ideas.

Right before the Kozhikode National Executive, on 18 September
the army base in Uri in Kashmir had faced a terrorist attack and
eighteen soldiers had lost their lives.[18] PM Modi said, at the meeting,
'Hindustan has never bent, nor will it ever bend. Terrorists will be
defeated. Terrorists, open your ears wide and listen, this country will
never forget this issue . . . I wish to tell the people of Pakistan that
your rulers warned us of a thousand-year war to deceive you. I'm
ready for the challenge. Our government in Delhi is ready to accept
your challenge. Pakistan's people, India is ready to fight with you.
Come forward, if you have the courage.'[19]

On 28 September 2016, the Indian army mobilized nearly 100
of its specially trained operators to attack terror launchpads and on
29 September the army launched a strike on terrorist bases across
the Line of Control.[20] From the attack (18 September) to the speech
(25 September) to the reprisal (28 September), the electronic and
social media was dominated by these themes, and the commitment
to nationalism encouraged many more people to associate with
the BJP.

Other Elements of Political Mobilization

To maintain the energy and morale of loyal party workers and
supporters, the BJP organized a continuous stream of slogans,
campaigns and creatively designed political activities. While some
were more important than others—and each one of them might not
appear important in and of itself—they should be seen as part of the
larger calendar where the life of a party worker or a strong supporter
was made up of an intermittent mix of such activities, visits from
seniors, and elections at various levels.

In that spirit, the union government launched the Gram Uday se
Bharat Uday Abhiyan (rise of village to rise of India Mission) or the
Village Self Governance campaign in association with all states and

panchayats in the country.[21] This campaign ran from 14 to 24 April 2016. As 14 April was the 125th birth anniversary of Babasaheb Ambedkar, the campaign began from his birthplace—Mhow in Madhya Pradesh. The campaign also appealed to Dalit voters, a community where the BJP was relatively weak. It culminated in Modi addressing a rally in Jamshedpur.

On 20 October 2016, the BJP launched a dedicated outreach programme under which it asked party members to leave their homes and work for the party for as many days as they could. The time period could be anywhere from fifteen days to three years. Those who volunteered were assigned places they could go to, where they would meet people and introduce them to the BJP's ideology.

India's most populous state, Uttar Pradesh, was also headed for elections in 2017 and the BJP was looking to consolidate the gains made in the 2014 Lok Sabha elections. The 2017 elections were to be held against the backdrop of the BJP government's decision to outlaw Rs 500 and Rs 1,000 notes to fight corruption and terrorism. In a certain sense, these elections were seen as a referendum on demonetization.

Demonetization

On 8 November 2016, in an unexpected and unprecedented decision, PM Modi addressed the nation at 8 pm and announced that legal tender status of higher denomination notes (Rs 500 and Rs 1000) would be discontinued from midnight. At the time when this decision was announced a total of Rs 17.9 lakh crore was being held as cash with the public. The decision to demonetize 86 per cent of India's currency meant that after four hours people could no longer use most of the cash they had, for buying goods or services. The total value of these notes added up to Rs 15.44 lakh crore. The government exempted a handful of establishments like petrol pumps, hospitals, crematoriums, from the notification. They were allowed to accept the old Rs 500 and Rs 1000 notes for a few days more.[22]

This decision was expected to resolve three sets of problems. The first was to control black money, a term typically used for unaccounted wealth, which has been accumulated illegally. Black money can be created either through the non-payment of tax on an income earned from a legal activity, or through income from an illegal activity (e.g., smuggling).[23] This is wealth earned in the 'shadow economy'. Published World Bank estimates of the size of the shadow economy in India range from 20.7 per cent to 62.02 per cent.[24 25]

PM Modi, in his speech announcing the demonetization decision, highlighted several actions taken earlier to address the black money problem. He said, 'We began our battle against corruption by setting up an SIT headed by a retired Supreme Court judge, immediately upon taking office. Since then a law was passed in 2015 for disclosure of foreign black money; agreements with many countries, including the USA, have been made to add provisions for sharing banking information; a strict law has come into force from August 2016 to curb benami transactions, which are used to deploy black money earned through corruption; a scheme was introduced for declaring black money after paying a stiff penalty.'[26]

Another reason for implementing the demonetization decision was the widespread circulation of fake currency in India, which is produced without legal sanction of the state. One estimate of the total fake currency in the Indian economy placed its face value at Rs 400 crore.[27]

The third objective of the demonetization exercise was to push the country towards a cashless economy. Cash is often used for bribes. Further, terrorists also use cash to plan and conduct their operations, as use of electronic money leaves a trail.

The scale and complexity of the decision made it difficult to predict all the eventualities. Responding to the evolving situation, the government and RBI had to make several changes to the original plan. The expected timeline for sending new notes into the economy was a few weeks, and the exercise was expected to be completed by

December-end. However, it took longer. Many changes were made to the rules to respond to the demands from the ground.[28]

Six states were going to polls in 2017 apart from Uttar Pradesh: Punjab, Goa, Gujarat, Uttarakhand, Himachal Pradesh and Manipur. Of these, Gujarat and Goa had a strong and successful BJP government. In Punjab, the BJP was in power with a partner, the Akali Dal.

The biggest of these was, of course, Uttar Pradesh, with a population of nearly 204 million, 403 seats in the Legislative Assembly, and eighty seats in Parliament. UP was in relatively good shape until the 1950s but had fallen into great difficulties after that. Over the years, Congress domination declined with the rise of the BJP, the Samajwadi Party (Mulayam Singh Yadav and his son Akhilesh Yadav) and the Bahujan Samaj Party (Mayawati). The traditional winning Congress combination of upper castes and Dalits was disrupted when the upper castes went to the BJP and the Dalits went to the BSP. The BJP last had a chief ministership under Rajnath Singh, which ended in 2002, after which the ruling position stayed within the SP and the BSP.

The BJP's revival in UP began with the planning for the 2014 Lok Sabha elections, where it was understood that the path to 273 seats required a transformative change for the party in UP.

The new BJP has built a rather different strategy of bringing in expertise from outside the state to participate in electoral politics of a particular state. A key principle was that the experience of a party worker, measured not in years but in the number of election campaigns that she has worked on, matters.

Preparing for UP Elections

The BJP had set the stage for the 2017 Uttar Pradesh elections in November 2016. The party launched a four-legged 54-day Parivartan Yatra (march for change) in the state. On 4 November, the first was launched from Saharanpur; the second on 6 November left from Jhansi; the third on 8 November from Robertsganj; the fourth on 9 November from Ballia. The Parivartan Yatra covered 17,000 km and passed through 403 assembly seats. The party organized twenty-six big rallies of its senior leaders across the state.[29] Six of these were addressed by Prime Minister Modi. Rajnath Singh, Uma Bharti, Keshav Prasad Maurya and other Union ministers and leaders also addressed rallies in different parts of the state. Parivartan Yatra meetings were held across all district headquarters. Issues such as deteriorating law and order, lack of development and Akhilesh Yadav's unkept promises were raised before the public. Forty-nine days later, on 24 December the Parivartan Yatra culminated in Lucknow. It helped to establish a connection between the people of UP and the BJP's top leadership in 2016, long before the elections.

Applying the methods that had worked well for the BJP elsewhere, the BJP decided that it would not just contest Lok Sabha and assembly elections, but every election from the panchayat to Parliament. Fighting elections requires experienced individuals. A party that is idle for long periods of time loses the ability to fight elections. The membership drive had obtained 18 million new members for the BJP in UP. These persons were harnessed to set up the usual BJP organization with inculcation of nationalism, a steady procession of political mobilization projects, leading up to booth-level management.

UP was witnessing a four-cornered fight between the BJP, the SP, the BSP and the Congress. In UP, marginalized communities (especially the OBC groups) have witnessed a rise in political consciousness. The party appointed Keshav Prasad Maurya, an OBC leader, as party chief with the objective of social engineering. To ensure a socially inclusive campaign, the BJP shared the election stage with leaders from all sections of the society and formed alliances with some regional parties.

These developments were watched by all political parties in UP that by now knew that the BJP management techniques generated a formidable election-winning force. The BSP was conscious about the extent to which welfare programmes of the BJP government at the union level, such as Ujjwala Yojana (a Central government scheme to give LPG connections to women of families below the poverty line), were well liked among its Dalit constituency. The Samajwadi Party was caught in an intra-family conflict. The Congress was very weak in the state. It tried its first campaign on its own, with Rahul Gandhi attacking the SP with the slogan, @*Satais saal, UP behaal* (twenty-seven years, UP suffering). Then it decided to partner with the SP, with the new slogan just before the election: *UP ko yeh saath pasand hai* (UP likes this alliance).

Alongside the strategy of pre-electoral alliances, was the ground game, the management system going all the way to the booth level. A 'booth committee' of about ten–twenty people was set up for each of the 1,40,000 booths. There were 1.35 million party workers at the booth level. Street plays and motorcycle rallies were organized in each constituency, to generate political mobilization.

The party invited suggestions for what the manifesto should include from the people. The *Jan Akanksha Petis* (suggestion boxes) followed the BJP rallies across UP with people being asked to share their ideas, aspirations and demands with the BJP. The *petis* were placed at local grocery shops and *paan* stalls in the state for easy access. The manifesto for the elections was drafted after incorporating these points. The party's manifesto, *Lok Kalyan Sankalp Patra*, promised Internet and LPG connection, and strong action against crime, corruption and land mafia. The manifesto also touched upon issues of triple talaq and Ram temple.

The Election Commission had announced a seven-phase election for the state. The BJP made zones on the basis of the phases and set up media cells accordingly. The zones corresponded with geographical regions of UP such as *poorvanchal*. The party ran a concerted media strategy in the state. The state had been witness to caste-based politics for long and so the BJP decided to make it an issue-based election. It started a 'daily question' programme where each day, the BJP posed one question for the SP–Congress alliance. The questions were centred around development and governance issues. This campaign was called *Aaj Ka Sawaal* (the question of the day).

In the seventh and last phase of polling set for 8 March on forty seats, the Prime Minister held a roadshow in his parliamentary constituency of Varanasi. Varanasi is considered not only the cultural epicentre of the poorvanchal region but also the political nerve centre of eastern UP. The roadshow helped create support for the BJP in the whole of poorvanchal.

On 11 March, when the results were declared it was a surprise for everyone. The BJP won 312 seats, while SP had forty-seven, BSP had nineteen and Congress seven.[30] The BJP's vote share had risen by 24.7 percentage points over the previous elections. This indicated that the plan of winning votes beyond the traditional voters of the OBC community had proven effective.

Table 2: Uttar Pradesh Assembly Elections of 2017[31]

Political Party	AE 2012		LS 2014		AE 2017	
	Vote Share	Seats Won	Vote Share	Seats Won	Vote Share	Seats Won
Bharatiya Janata Party	15.00%	47	42.63%	71	39.67%	312
Indian National Congress	11.65%	28	7.53%	2	6.25%	7
Bahujan Samaj Party	25.91%	80	19.77%	0	22.23%	19
Samajwadi Party	29.13%	224	22.35%	5	21.82%	47

The BJP leadership debated the best path for a new leadership team for the state. The party had not fought the elections with any one face projected as chief minister. Rajnath Singh, Yogi Adityanath, Uma Bharti, Keshav Prasad Maurya and Kalraj Mishra had all participated in the Parivartan Yatra and the party had come to power in the electorally critical state after a long time. The Congress first, and later the SP and the BSP, had all worked towards dividing UP along caste and religious lines.

The parliamentary board of the party zeroed in on Yogi Adityanath. Adityanath had become a disciple of Mahant Avaidyanath, then the head priest of Gorakhnath *Math*, at the age of twenty-one. He grew to head the Gorakhnath *Math*. The *math* represented the Nath community which was known for its history of fighting social evils. The Nath community had launched campaigns against untouchability, discrimination and for preservation of moral values. People from all sections of society are sadhus in Nath *maths*. As the successor of Guru Gorakhnath temple, Adityanath ran schools, colleges and even a hospital.

Venkaiah Naidu and the Bhupender Yadav flew from Delhi to Lucknow to convey the decision of the parliamentary board to Yogi Adityanath. The two met Yogi at the party's guest house and told him that he would be UP's next chief minister. Yogi Adityanath was caught by surprise at the decision. Given the size of Uttar Pradesh, the party felt that it was imperative that two deputy chief ministers work along with Yogi Adityanath to ensure effective governance of the state and Keshav Prasad Maurya and Dinesh Sharma were chosen for the job.

State Elections in 2017

Of the other four states—Punjab, Goa, Uttarakhand and Manipur—the BJP lost one, saved another and won in the other two. In Punjab, public anger towards the Akalis was palpable, but the BJP chose to stand with its ally, and the coalition lost.[32]

Ahead of the election in 2016, the ground for the Harish Rawat-led Congress government had begun to shake. Uttarakhand had not seen much political stability since it was carved out of Uttar Pradesh in 2000. The BJP had a dedicated voter base in the state, as well as leaders with a lot of experience. The challenge had been to

accommodate personal ambitions and stay united. The troubles for
the Harish Rawat government had eased the ground for BJP but the
party showed no complacency and prepared a detailed plan to win
booths and engaged the new and enthusiastic BJP members to win
them. The experience of old members was also tapped to prepare
a winning strategy. As a result of this fine planning, the BJP won
over two-thirds of the seats in Uttarakhand. In the 70-member
Uttarakhand assembly, the BJP got fifty-six seats.[33][34]

In Goa, the absence of Manohar Parrikar, who was now a
minister in the Centre, cost the party dearly and the BJP suffered
a loss of eight seats. The BJP won thirteen seats, and the Congress
won seventeen.[35] In the 40-member assembly, the Congress needed
twenty-one seats to form the government. It was slow in locking
down this coalition. By evening, the BJP reached the Governor and
staked its claim to form the next state government with the support
of the Goa Forward Party, the Maharashtrawadi Gomantak Party
and independents.[36] This coalition was formed on the condition that
it be led by Manohar Parrikar. As a result, Parrikar returned from his
position as minister of defence in the Union government, to become
Goa chief minister.

After Assam and Arunachal Pradesh, Manipur was the third
North-eastern state where the BJP gained ground. On 24 May 2016,
the BJP formed the Northeast Democratic Alliance (NEDA) with
regional parties who were not part of the National Democratic
Alliance, aiming to grow roots in the North-eastern states.[37] North-
eartern states have their individual identities apart from having
national concerns such as security, growth and employment. To
address these aspirations a regional organization was needed and
NEDA was born.

These new capabilities showed up strongly in Manipur, where
the BJP went from 2.2 per cent votes in 2012 to 36.3 per cent in 2017
which gave it twenty-one seats of the 60-member house. The BJP
had never had a single MLA in the state. With twenty-eight seats,
the Congress emerged as the single-largest party but was not yet at

the required thirty-one seats.[38] The BJP managed to obtain support from a few MLAs and get to the mark. N. Biren Singh was made chief minister.

Overall, the BJP gained significantly in the elections in these five states. It had only lost in one state, which was being run as part of a coalition, while it had won in three new states. The BJP now firmly established its identity as a pan-India party with various regions, religions, castes, languages, professionals, intellectuals, rural and urban populace joining the party-fold either as members or voters.

Alongside these elections, there was one important development in 2017. There were fissures in the JD(U)–RJD alliance that began coming to the fore. Social politics had basically progressed in Bihar along two strands since the early 1990s. One was led by Nitish Kumar's JD(U) that focused on governance and the other by Lalu Yadav that was a family-based system rooted in corruption and misrule. After ten years of alliance with the BJP, the JD(U) decided to part ways with it on unfounded grounds. After the 2014 Lok Sabha elections, seeing the BJP's ground support, the JD(U) realized it couldn't come to power alone. The RJD, on the other hand, sensed that if it did not forge an alliance and come to power, it would become irrelevant to Bihar's political landscape. Once, however, the two had been in government, Nitish Kumar realized that the RJD was corrupt and providing good governance to the people of Bihar wasn't possible by being in alliance with the party.

When the JD(U)-RJD alliance broke in July 2017, expressing his inability to 'work under current circumstances', Nitish Kumar resigned as state chief minister.[39] Modi signalled his willingness to let bygones be bygones, and tweeted, 'For a bright future, India, especially Bihar, needs to rise above political disagreements to fight corruption; this is the need of the hour'.[40] Soon, a new BJP–JD(U) government came together.

The JD(U) also realized that PM Modi's vision of India was an inclusive idea and that the BJP government at the Centre was actually implementing programmes that worked for all sections of the society, especially the most downtrodden. It was Lohia who had in the mid-1960s spoken about the need for *Har Ghar Shauchalaya* (toilet in every house), a programme that the BJP government took up in the very first year of its formation.

There were two more state assembly elections in 2017: Gujarat and Himachal Pradesh.

The long period of Modi's rule in Gujarat had left the BJP as a strong organization and had decimated opposition parties. But he was now Prime Minister. After his departure, Gujarat had seen a bit of political uncertainty.

The Gujarat elections were important from the BJP's point of view because after a long time the state was going into polls without Narendra Modi as the chief ministerial candidate. Modi had served as the Gujarat Chief Minister for close to 13 years.

With Modi taking over as Prime Minister, the state saw a quick change of leadership from Anandiben Patel to Vijay Rupani.

The 2017 election was also an election in which the traditional bipolar politics of Gujarat had now opened up with the emergence of young politicians like Hardik Patel, Jignesh Mevani and Alpesh Thakor who were playing caste-based politics. The leaders were supported by the Congress.

Shankersinh Vaghela, who had been a BJP member at one point, jumped into the fray with his party, the Jan Vikalp Morcha. While the BJP had ruled Gujarat for a long time, the Congress also had a loyal vote base. As an example, in the 2012 elections, the BJP won 47.85 per cent votes and the Congress 38.93 per cent.[41] The Congress fared well by pulling together the charisma of new faces. Rahul Gandhi felt that projecting a more religious image, would help reassure certain voters who saw the secular image of Nehru, Indira Gandhi and Rajiv Gandhi as anti-Hindu. He visited twenty-seven temples in Gujarat, and party leaders declared him a *janeudhari* (wearing the sacred thread worn exclusively by high caste Hindus).[42] From pseudo-secularism, the Congress moved on to pseudo-Hinduism.

The BJP established a detailed plan for connecting with the public and its cadre. The party reached out to young men and women through Town Hall programmes. Through the day, senior party leaders remained engaged in reaching out and connecting with the people on the ground. Through the night, meetings were held and political outreach activities for the next day were planned out. Arun Jaitley, who was the election in-charge, oversaw the preparations and strategies. The party organized many Town Halls for public connect. There was a Yuva Town Hall (addressed by Amit Shah), a Women Town Hall (addressed by Sushma Swaraj). The party launched a march across 149 out of 182 constituencies in the state to highlight the government's achievements.[43] In retaliation, the Congress ran a campaign critical of the government's policies which said *vikas pagal ho gaya hai* (development has gone mad).

Elections in Gujarat were being held simultaneously with those in Himachal Pradesh where Virbhadra Singh of the Congress was in power. The BJP fielded former chief minister Prem Kumar Dhumal as its chief ministerial candidate. There was widespread disaffection with the Congress, and the BJP felt it had an opportunity to win.

On 18 December 2017, results for both the elections were announced. In Himachal Pradesh, the BJP succeeded in wrestling power from the hands of the Congress. It got forty-four out of sixty-eight seats with a 48.8 per cent vote share.[44] The CM candidate, P.K. Dhumal lost in his constituency. As a result, the BJP decided to make Jairam Thakur, who had won from Siraj for the fifth time, the CM. Since 1998, Thakur had served as Cabinet minister in previous Himachal govenments. During his college days, Thakur was associated with the ABVP and went on to serve the organization in various capacities.

In the 2017, Gujarat assembly results the BJP's seat count declined by sixteen seats, but the party obtained a majority with ninety-nine seats.[45] The party once again made Vijay Rupani the state chief minister.

Table 3: Gujarat Assembly Elections of 2017[46]

Political Party	AE 2012		LS 2014		AE 2017	
	Vote Share	Seats Won	Vote Share	Seats Won	Vote Share	Seats Won
Bharatiya Janata Party	47.85%	115	60.11%	26	49.05%	99
Indian National Congress	38.93%	61	33.45%	0	41.44%	77

Building Party Offices

Even as electoral victories continued, the BJP was parallelly focused on party work.

In 2016, the party had begun to build physical structures in the form of a modern party office in each district of India. In many districts, the BJP was already present, and there was just incremental improvement compared to previous arrangements, but in many districts, the BJP was a new political party, getting introduced to voters for the first time.[47]

It was felt that the existing party headquarters, at 11 Ashoka Road in the environs of Lutyens Delhi, was not adequate or digitally equipped. It was decided that a new headquarters would be constructed. The foundation stone was laid for the new building on 80,000 square metres of land at Deen Dayal Upadhyaya Marg in New Delhi, in August 2016.[48] Now the BJP as an organization had office infrastructure in the headquarters and in every district.

In 2017, the party embarked on another tool for political mobilization: a *pravas* (tour). The party president, Amit Shah, embarked on a 95-day nationwide tour in April 2017. It was at the party's National Executive held in Bhubaneswar from 15–16 April that Shah announced his Rashtriya Pravas plan.[49] With an eye on the 2019 Lok Sabha elections, this tour was aimed at examining and pushing organizational capability.[50] A team of twelve office bearers was assembled and given the task of visiting three states every four months, thereby ensuring that every state was visited by a minimum of three different office bearers during the year.[51] Every district or constituency where the BJP's reach and influence wasn't very significant; for example, each of the 120 seats which the BJP contested and lost in 2014 was visited.[52] Apart from visiting every state for a period of three days, multiple visits were arranged in the states where the BJP was weak. For instance, Telangana and West Bengal were visited twice during the campaign. States like Maharashtra and Haryana were visited as well, to rekindle the spirits of party workers who were dissatisfied at the time with respect to certain issues.[53]

These visits helped address agency problems in the party as an organization. The senior leadership of every large organization needs to regularly inspect the working of its organization in a practical way, to overcome the difficulties that emerge in achieving its aims on the ground. Shah's emphasis on running hard in *every* election is generally seen as a learning from experience. People who run many campaigns get good at it. But it also helps reveal the actual ground reality and exposes the pockets of the organization where development or effort is lacking.

Aspirational Districts Programme (ADP)

In 2017, there was a prolonged farm crisis in western and central India. The Mood of the Nation Survey conducted in January 2018 by the Lokniti research programme at the Centre for the Study of Developing Societies (CSDS) indicated a decline in support for the BJP among the farming community compared to the previous year's survey results.[54]

These developments suggested to the party that the government might not be able to reach the poor and underdeveloped parts of India as desired. It was a little over one and a half years before the Lok Sabha elections. The BJP Manifesto in 2014 had said, 'We will identify 100 most backward districts of the country to bring them at par with other districts through prioritized and integrated development.'[55] This election promise was now sought to be fulfilled.

In January 2018, the government chose 115 districts to be 'aspirational districts'. At least one district was chosen from each of the twenty-eight states. A composite index was developed to assess the performance of these districts and improve their socio-economic status. There were five distinct themes, namely, health and nutrition, education, agriculture, financial inclusion, skill development and basic infrastructure. These were assigned a different weightage and were central to the composition of the index. The index identified forty-nine key performance indicators across the five themes along with eighty-one data points that were collected to track the progress of every district. For each of the themes or indicators, a monthly ranking was made publicly available on the official website.

The operational framework for ADP involved NITI Aayog leading the initiative in thirty districts, followed by individual ministries being given responsibility to oversee the implementation process in another fifty districts. Additionally, the ministry of home affairs focused on about thirty-five left wing extremism-affected districts.

Election Preparation for 2019

The year prior to the Lok Sabha elections tends to be important for all political parties. For conventional parties, this was the time to gear up to fight the 2019 elections. For a party like the BJP, the question was: How well will the election-winning machine that was built over 2014–2018 now perform, given that opposition parties were joining forces against the BJP?

On 14 April 2018, Ambedkar Jayanti, the day B.R. Ambedkar's birthday is celebrated, the BJP government embarked upon a massive outreach to cover the marginalized sections of society under the key welfare schemes of the BJP government. It was called the Gram Swaraj Abhiyan (Village Self-Rule Mission). The BJP identified 21,058 villages where scheduled castes and scheduled tribes constitute more than 50 per cent of the population.[56] BJP MPs, including Union ministers, were asked to ensure that everyone in these villages was covered under the schemes aimed at providing LPG connection, vaccination for children, Jan Dhan accounts and electricity for households. While MPs spent at least a night in one such village under the campaign, Union ministers spent two nights in different parts of the country. The BJP had traditionally been considered a party of upper castes. This campaign helped to increase the BJP's connection with economically weaker voters belonging to other castes.

The party, meanwhile, was also taking stock of the government's performance in order to chalk out its future course of action. In May 2018, the BJP organized a meeting of its state unit chiefs and organizational heads. The agenda of the meeting was to assess the efficacy of government schemes on the ground and the party's own organizational work. Under the Sabka Saath, Sabka Vikas Yojana (*Everyone's support, everyone's development*), party MPs were asked to undertake night stays in villages that had a population of over 1,000. MPs were to do this in collaboration with the local MLAs, other public representatives and office-bearers. The party also held conferences with beneficiaries of central and state government schemes. There was a special *samrasta sampark* (contact for harmony) in scheduled caste clusters. A Booth Sampark Abhiyaan (booth contact mission) was launched where the booth in-charge met over fifty voters and shared documents detailing the government's achievements and pasted stickers outside people's homes. The idea was to collect feedback from the ground about government subsidy programmes which actually worked as opposed to those that did not. The party and government were working parallelly to ensure that benefits of schemes and government efforts reached the intended people.

On the electoral front in June 2018, the central leadership took the call to pull out of the coalition with the PDP in J&K, ending a long moral dilemma. The BJP decided to end the alliance as schisms existed over a host of issues such as talks with the pro-secession Hurriyat; the PDP's policy towards separatism; the politics that played out over the rape of a minor in Jammu's Kathua; the PDP's response to the killing of Hizbul Mujahideen commander Burhan Wani whose death led to violent protests across the Valley and the Centre's decision to call off the Ramzan ceasefire.

Meanwhile, in early 2018, elections in Tripura were held. As with the other North-eastern states, the BJP was traditionally weak, but had embarked on building an organization in the 2013–2018 period. From 1993 onwards Tripura had been under Communist rule and the Congress had been in decline. When the BJP membership drive started, the party had only 10,000 members in the state. By 2015, 175,000 people had joined the party. In the elections anti-incumbency against the Communist government that had been ruling for over two-and-a-half decades helped the BJP.[57]

The new BJP organization contested the elections in February 2018 and won. In the 60-member Assembly, the BJP won thirty-five seats. Its vote share went up sharply from 1.5 per cent to 43 per cent.[58] Most of the winning candidates were young and below the age of thirty-five.[59] Biplab Kumar Dev, who was BJP state president, was chosen to lead the state.

During this period when the BJP's journey continued with electoral wins and setbacks and organizational strengthening, Vajpayee's health became critical. He had been ill for a while and had remained away from any political activities since 2004. On 16 August 2018, he passed away. In Vajpayee, the BJP lost its founder and mentor. The party paid him the highest respect. On the hot and humid day of 17 August, PM Modi, then BJP president Amit Shah, Union ministers and BJP chief ministers marched behind Vajpayee's hearse from the BJP headquarters on Deen Dayal Upadhyaya Marg to Rashtriya Smriti Sthal, a distance of over five km. Vajpayee's contribution in the journey from Jana Sangh to the BJP, which also gave the country its first full term non-Congress government, was no ordinary leadership.

With the loss of Vajpayee in the backdrop, the BJP government continued the work it had committed to complete.

Granting of constitutional status to the National Commission for Backward Classes had been a long-pending demand. Adhering to Article 340 of the Constitution of India, the First Backward Classes Commission was set up by a presidential order on 29 January 1953 under the chairmanship of Kaka Kalelkar. The commission submitted its report on 30 March 1955, but the recommendations were not implemented till the Janata Party government came to power in 1977. The second Backward Classes Commission was set up in 1978 under the chairmanship of Bindeshwari Prasad Mandal. The report was submitted in December 1980. The commission laid out eleven criteria for determining social and educational backwardness among people. This report too had been put in cold storage by the Congress government and pulled out by V.P. Singh in 1990.

The V.P. Singh government accepted major recommendations of the Mandal Commission and issued orders in August 1990 providing 27 per cent reservation for Other Backward Classes in Central civil posts.

The order of merit providing 27 per cent reservation to OBCs in Central government posts had been challenged in the Indra Sawhney case. In 1992, the Supreme Court of India in the matter of Indra Sawhney and others V/s. Union of India and others (AIR 1993, SC 477) had observed the following: 'The Government of India, each of the State Governments and the Administration of Union Territories shall, within four months from today, constitute a permanent body for entertaining, examining and recommending upon requests for inclusion and complaints of over-inclusion and under-inclusion in the list of other backward classes of citizens. The advice tendered by such a body shall ordinarily be binding upon the Government.'

In accordance with the judgment, the National Commission for Backward Classes Act was enacted in April 1993 and the National

Commission for Backward Classes was constituted on the 14 August 1993 under the said Act. But the law needed amendments because under the NCBC Act, the commission merely had the power to recommend inclusion or exclusion of communities in the OBC list.

The backward communities had long demanded a body with wider powers to allow it to look into all matters regarding the welfare and development of backward classes. The demand was to extend the right to adjudicate matters to the commission. Until then the Scheduled Castes Commission, which looks into cases of atrocities against Dalits, was also responsible for hearing grievances from OBCs. These complaints were limited in nature and extended only to matters such as the non-implementation of reservations in jobs and educational institutes. The amended law gave the Commission powers equivalent to that of a civil court.

It allowed the Commission to summon any person, ask for a document or public record, and receive evidence on affidavits. It also made it binding for Union and state governments to consult the Commission on all policy matters affecting socially and educationally backward classes. The Commission now regulates its own proceedings.

When the Bill was placed before the Rajya Sabha in 2017, several members said such an important constitutional amendment needed a more detailed study. Going by the demand of Parliament, the Bill was referred to a select committee.

The BJP's attempt to pass the law in 2017 failed because the party did not have sufficient numbers to pass it. On 6 August 2018, the government finally managed to successfully get the laws passed. The President's assent gave the National Commission for Backward Classes constitutional status.

As the government granted constitutional status to the NCBC by moving a Bill through Parliament, the party decided to organize a *Samajik Nyay Parv* (Social Justice Festival) between 15 and 30 August 2018 to take its message to the people.

All party workers along with public representatives were asked to attend *chaupals* among poor and backward classes and the district units were asked to organize them. *Samrasta Bhoj* (community dining) was organized as part of the Samajik Nyay Parv and required the presence of all important party leaders. The party also organized the screening of *Chalo Jeete Hain*, a film based on Modi's childhood to gain the voter mindshare of Modi.

In 2018, BJP MPs were asked to walk 150 km in their respective constituencies to mark the 150th anniversary of Mahatma Gandhi's and 144th anniversary of Sardar Patel's birth. It was decided that every MP should walk from 2 October, the birth anniversary of Mahatma Gandhi, till 31 October, the birth anniversary of Sardar Patel. The idea was that during the course of the padyatra, MPs would reach out to people in villages and make them aware of government schemes and establish a direct connection with them.

Between November and December 2018, Madhya Pradesh, Chhattisgarh, Rajasthan and Mizoram went to polls. The BJP suffered a setback. Although Chhattisgarh had been a BJP stronghold for fifteen years before that, the party did not win owing to the inherent anti-incumbency fervour that had been building up. The BJP was limited to just fifteen seats in a 90-member Chhattisgarh Assembly after losing its OBC voters in the state. In Madhya Pradesh, however, the BJP had a close call winning 108 seats of the total 230. In Rajasthan, the election outcome of 2018 was in line with the state's peculiar electoral tradition of voting out the incumbent government after one term.

The election outcome in Chhattisgarh and Rajasthan was a morale booster for the Congress, which had not tasted such electoral success in a long time. In the Lok Sabha elections of 2014, the BJP had done well in all three states. The party won nine of the eleven Lok Sabha seats in Chhattisgarh, twenty-seven of the twenty-nine seats in Madhya Pradesh and all twenty-five seats in Rajasthan.[60] The results of the assembly elections once again proved that the mature Indian voter votes differently in state and national elections.

The defeat in elections in three states, at the end of 2018, had
led many to raise questions on the BJP's prospects in the upcoming
elections in 2019. The Opposition tried to project the results as a
verdict on the popularity of PM Modi and organizational abilities
of BJP president Amit Shah. Every Lok Sabha constituency maps
a clearly defined set of assembly constituencies, so it was easy for
analysts to use those numbers and make predictions for what would
happen in Lok Sabha elections if voting took place exactly as it did
in the recently concluded assembly elections. These calculations
generated predictions of a sharp reversal for the BJP.

The BJP also examined the results carefully. The National
Executive of the party was held on 11 January at Ramlila Maidan in
Delhi. Addressing the National Executive, Shah said, 'We have lost
elections in three states, but the BJP has not lost its ground in any
of the states. The BJP workers need to keep up their morale and not
lose it. We have an opportunity to ensure that in the 2019 Lok Sabha
elections in all these three states become the foundations for forming
the Narendra Modi government. We have to work towards it.'

A careful reading of the election results was a reminder that
small shifts in votes can generate a large impact upon the number of
wins in the first-past-the-post system. In Madhya Pradesh, the BJP
got 41 per cent votes and 109 seats, while the Congress won 40 per
cent votes and 114 seats. In Rajasthan, the BJP won seventy-three
seats with 38.80 per cent votes, while the Congress got 100 seats with
38.85 per cent of the votes.[61] In these two states, it was apparent that
while the Congress was a formidable force, winning more seats was
a quirk of the first-past-the-post system. It was only in Chhattisgarh
that the BJP was weakened: the vote share declined by 8.4 per cent in
comparison to what it got in 2013.[62]

Narendra Modi's popularity remained high on the national
stage but in these three states anti-incumbency cost the BJP dear.
The BJP had built up a powerful election-winning organization—the
likes of which had never before been seen in India—that was more
capable than the Congress in its heyday. And while this organization

had delivered innumerable victories, it had suddenly suffered from three important defeats to the Congress that was considered to be in terminal decline. This was the framing of the year 2019, when Lok Sabha elections would take place. The media and Opposition began saying the BJP had lost the semi-final and that it had little to no hope of a full majority in the Lok Sabha elections just months away.

The party, however, understood that the verdict of assembly elections would have no bearing on the national elections as the voters knew how to differentiate between national ambitions and regional aspirations and so the BJP continued preparing for the national elections alongside.

12

The Campaign for Lok Sabha 2019

The BJP entered 2019 against the backdrop of electoral defeats in three crucial states—Madhya Pradesh, Rajasthan and Chhattisgarh—and the challenge of winning a second term at the Centre, a feat no non-Congress party had ever achieved in India. The BJP had governed the country for five years as a full majority government, and anti-incumbency was seen as a natural challenge.

Communication since 2014

Since the government came to power in 2014, it began work on reversing the policy paralysis that had set in during the times of the UPA government. The BJP government of 1998 had also set into motion many reforms but had failed to communicate its work properly to the voters. The BJP post 2014, under PM Modi and party president Amit Shah, did not make the same mistake.

PM Modi had committed in 2014 that the BJP government would provide a pro-poor government. Subsequent government schemes were planned in a way to ensure the economic and social upliftment of the marginalized. Be it the Ujjwala Yojana, the Jan Dhan Yojana, Mudra Yojana, PM Awaas Yojana, Soil Health Card or PM Fasal Bima Yojana, all schemes targeted the poor.

The party ensured its communication engines worked round the-clock to keep voters abreast of party plans, programmes and achievements. It also ensured people's participation by making communication channels two-way systems. BJP's biggest asset remained PM Modi's popularity among the people. His direct communication with the people came not only through his rallies and public appearances but also through new means of communication.

The party realized that while TV and social media had achieved huge penetration in India, radio remained important. Radio is more relevant for a new kind of urban consumer who listens to audio content in homes and also on the move. It also reaches remote communities in India where broadcast TV or internet connectivity may have spotty coverage.

In October 2014, PM Modi launched a monthly programme on state radio called 'Mann Ki Baat' (What's on my mind). Some television channels started broadcasting these talks. PM Modi's gift as a leader lies in his understanding of issues of the common man. His programme addressed everyday issues that mattered to ordinary people. He spoke about the need for toilets, the importance of cleanliness, empowerment of women, women's safety, exam stress, freedom fighters, sacrifices of Indian armed forces, among others. In a similar way, a mobile app named the 'Narendra Modi Mobile App' (popularly referred to as NaMo App) was launched in 2015. This gave a feed to users about the activities of the prime minister and of the Union government, and a channel through which individuals could send messages to the PM, give feedback on government schemes, and volunteer for party activities. Leveraging the potential of the communication channels at his disposal, PM Modi invited suggestions and ideas from the people on a host of issues including his own Mann Ki Baat. This model of participative democracy ensured people were not just aware of what the government was doing but were also offering their inputs on how they wanted things to be. The BJP also ensured that people actively participated in such communication exercises and thus tried to understand the pulse of the voter. By way of this engagement the BJP successfully turned what could have been anti-incumbency into pro-incumbency.

Thus, during these five years, the government and party introduced new modes of communication including radio programmes and apps. The government created means through which people participated in the process of governance. This transparent and participative approach helped create a pro-government, rather than an anti-incumbency mood.

Focus on Governance

The BJP focused on politics of governance. From the very beginning, improving governance was at the top of the government's agenda. The government launched an ambitious series of projects of digitization to cut red tape and weed out corruption from governance. The Direct Benefit Transfer under various schemes was part of this project. The government launched the 'Transformation of Aspirational Districts' programme with an aim to develop world-class districts with public participation. The BJP government had introduced key reforms that had been long-pending in the country. Pradhan Mantri Ujjwala Yojana, Jan Dhan accounts, Pradhan Mantri Awas Yojana, Goods and Services Tax, Swachh Bharat Mission and electricity for all were among the pioneering schemes of the government that people had benefited from. For the first time in India benefits of government schemes were reaching the intended beneficiaries without delay and without the involvement of middlemen. With the government making women the primary beneficiaries of most of its schemes, and with schemes like Ujjwala being tailor-made for women of the country, a social churning was set into motion by the Modi government. By making women the focus of policy reforms, the BJP government had earned itself a dedicated voter base.

Global Soft Power

Even as the government worked for the poor and improved the ease of living for all, it simultaneously worked on building India's soft power globally.

Decades of poverty had made many voters in India insecure about India's place on the global stage. For this reason, foreign policy was unusually important in Indian domestic politics. When India appears to command respect on the global stage, national pride matters to many voters. High GDP growth from 1979 onwards has made India more important, and this creates new opportunities for elements of international relations which impact domestic voters.

This process began with PM Modi's decision to invite SAARC leaders to his swearing-in ceremony on 26 May 2014. In January 2016, Narendra Modi and François Hollande jointly laid the foundation stone of the International Solar Alliance (ISA) headquarters in Gurugram. The ISA alliance was initiated by India and brought together 121 sunshine countries, which lie either completely or partly between the Tropic of Cancer and the Tropic of Capricorn, with an objective to work for efficient consumption of solar energy to reduce dependence on fossil fuels. This was a novel situation, where India was playing a leadership role in an international organization.

India increased its global leadership in climate and disaster resilience not only when it initiated the International Solar Alliance, but also when PM Modi initiated the Coalition for Disaster Resilient Infrastructure at the Asian Ministerial in 2016, a coalition which has twenty-nine members today.

Yoga is a centuries-old Indian tradition and the science of wellness. It exemplifies India's soft power to the world and interconnects cultures. The Modi government proposed to the United Nations General Assembly to designate 21 June as 'International Day of Yoga'. Modi led 35,000 people in Delhi in performing yoga on 21 June 2015. Satellite events were organized by the BJP all over India and helped the party popularize the theme of Indian pride and respect for an Indian tradition on a world scale. There was a blizzard of social media activity, and there was pride in the fact that an element of traditional Indian culture was finding its place under the sun owing to the leadership of Modi. As with many other elements of the BJP strategy, a long ignored Indian tradition that offered an opportunity in the global mind space was harnessed for positive messaging and political mobilisation.

All politicians face the twin problems of achieving mind share in the eyes of voters, and in getting their message through to the desired audience without distortions introduced by information intermediaries. With the radio show and the app transmitting the government's messages to people, including updates on yoga functions and India's rising global stature, PM Modi and the BJP achieved more direct channels through which they got unfiltered access to the people.

The Mahagathbandhan against BJP

The BJP's victory of 2014 had rattled the Opposition. By 2019, through Modi government's work on the ground and connection with people, a bigger win was imminent. This unsettled opposition parties further. Prior to the election, many alliances were made, based on the belief that if the votes of certain non-BJP parties were added up, there was the possibility of winning. The 2017 Bihar elections had induced some optimism about such calculations.

For all such parties the BJP was a natural adversary and aversion to BJP and PM Modi the sole glue. These ideologically opposed parties that had in the past bitterly fought each other decided to form a joint front against the BJP.

In January 2019, a 'United India' rally was organized at Kolkata's Brigade Ground that saw the participation of twenty-three parties, including the Congress, Trinamool Congress, Samajwadi Party, Nationalist Congress Party, Bahujan Samaj Party, Rashtriya Janata Dal, DMK and Aam Aadmi Party.[1] The parties had no clear agenda or plan for India. What was clearly visible was that leaders who participated in the 'United India' rally were divided over their prime ministerial ambitions. Each leader present at the rally nurtured his/her own prime ministerial ambitions.

More such rallies followed across the country with different leaders in different states playing host. In Delhi, an opposition rally was held at Jantar Mantar in February. All such rallies demanded the removal of the BJP government from the Centre without presenting any alternative to the country. The Opposition could not agree on a face to present as an alternative to PM Modi. The only strategy was to target the PM relentlessly at all public meetings.

Seeing their political ground erode in Uttar Pradesh, Mayawati, Mulayam Singh Yadav and Akhilesh Yadav came together to share the dais in Uttar Pradesh's Mainpuri after twenty-four years of bitter rivalry. Mulayam and Mayawati have been political rivals since 1995 when the Bahujan Samaj Party chief withdrew support from the SP. This was followed by SP workers attacking Mayawati and her supporters, who were camping at the UP state guest house. As a compromise to the alliance, Mayawati withdrew the case filed against Mulayam Singh in the guest house incident.

What made the SP–BSP alliance hopeful of brighter prospects in Uttar Pradesh were the by-poll results of 2018. The by-elections were necessitated after UP Chief Minister Yogi Adityanath and deputy CM Keshav Prasad Maurya vacated their Lok Sabha seats in Gorakhpur and Phulpur, respectively, on taking office. The BSP and the SP set aside their rivalry to join forces for the by-elections. SP candidates won seats from the BJP with BSP campaigning for them. Both parties made the mistake of thinking the by-poll results were a reflection of the mood before the Lok Sabha elections of 2019. The media too said that the SP–BSP alliance was set to upset BJP's apple cart in UP. The SP–BSP thus entered the Lok Sabha election arena together.

While the Opposition tried to put up a united front ahead of the country, personal ambitions had riven the grouping with inherent contradictions. Each leader of the Mahagathbandhan wanted to use the alliance as a stepping stone to the PM's chair.

BJP's Alliances

As opposed to the Mahagathbandhan, which followed a negative agenda based on creating anti-Modi and anti-BJP sentiments, the BJP was working to forge natural alliances that would help the party both at the regional and national levels. One important story that unfolded in the year prior to each Lok Sabha election is the negotiation with allies. Of the twenty-nine states and seven union territories, the BJP fought the election in alliance with regional political parties in eleven states: Assam, Bihar, Jharkhand, Karnataka, Kerala, Maharashtra, Nagaland, Punjab, Rajasthan, Tamil Nadu and Uttar Pradesh and the Union Territory of Puducherry.

In UP, it tied up with Apna Dal; in Bihar, with LJP and JD(U); in Punjab, with the SAD; in Rajasthan, with the Rashtriya Loktantrik Party; in Maharashtra, with the Shiv Sena; in Tamil Nadu, with AIADMK, PMK, DMDK, Puthiya Tamilagam, Puthiya Needhi Katchi and Tamil Maanila Congress; in Kerala, with Bharath Dharma Jana Sena and Kerala Congress (Thomas); in Assam, with Asom Gana Parishad and Bodoland People's Front; in Jharkhand, with All Jharkhand Students Union; in Nagaland, with the Nationalist Democratic Progressive Party; in Puducherry, with All India NR Congress; and in Karnataka, the BJP supported Sumalatha as an independent candidate.

This wide network of alliances showed that the BJP had left days of political isolation far behind. Indeed, in many situations, it was the BJP which had the upper hand, and could choose its allies.

The BJP not only succeeded in stitching alliances but did it well before its political rivals. In the states of Bihar, Maharashtra and Tamil Nadu, BJP-led alliances were already in place at a time the Congress was still working out finer deals with its partners.

The party formed Lok Sabha Sanchalan Samitis (Lok Sabha level steering committees) for all seats and appointed senior leaders to be in-charge of the committees. The committees were formed to monitor BJP's election preparedness in each Lok Sabha constituency. These committees saw national BJP leaders hold meetings at the state level and state leaders hold meetings at the national level to ensure proper connect, communication, identification of key issues and devising foolproof strategies. The committees discussed the work being done at the booth level. It was decided the party would have fifty new members on each booth and these new members would come from all sections of society—twenty from SC/ST/EBC, twenty from OBC and ten from any other section.[2]

Apart from booth management, the samitis took up many other tasks which included ensuring NaMo app reached more people so that the BJP government's work could find deeper penetration. The samitis also appointed in-charges for voter lists of their constituencies to try and establish connect with voters in their respective areas.

To ensure members at the booth level stay motivated and feel meaningfully engaged in party activities, the BJP marked certain days of the year on which booth-level workers could connect the masses with BJP's ideas and ideology. 6 April was marked as Foundation Day since the BJP was established on this day in 1980. 14 April, Dr B.R. Ambedkar's birth anniversary, was celebrated as *Samrasta Divas* (Social Harmony Day). 11 February was commemorated as *Samarpan Diwas* because it was Deen Dayal Upadhyaya's death anniversary and Upadhyaya had dedicated his life to the Sangh's ideology and spoken of the upliftment of the downtrodden by talking about Antyodaya. 23 June was marked as *Balidan Diwas* in memory of Dr Syama Prasad Mookerjee, who on this day laid down his life fighting for India's unity and integrity in Jammu and Kashmir. 25 December was marked as *Sushashan Diwas* (Good Governance Day) since it was Atal Bihari Vajpayee's birth anniversary and Vajpayee had presented the good governance model to the country.

Political Mobilization

Mahatma Gandhi had organized the Congress as a political and social party that engaged with the people and continuously renewed itself. The fact that the Congress did not wield power in the government at that time helped ensure that a certain kind of person did not bother taking up political activism, and the full energy of the Congress leadership was devoted to the party and to the people of India. As an example, before Independence, the Congress organized mechanisms, with thousands of foot soldiers, to carry the resolutions it passed as a party to every person across the country. It seems hard to envision an age, when party resolutions meant so much to party workers and to the people.

After 1947, the focus of the Congress shifted to wielding the reins of power, and over the years, it became disconnected from the people. For many decades, in an environment of Congress domination, the BJP honed its party machinery with a greater focus on engagement with the people. The RSS never took the reins of power, which helped improve the idealism of the individuals who came into the RSS and ensured that the RSS was constantly focused on people and not the spoils of power. The RSS held the same views as Syama Prasad Mookerjee on this issue.

BJP's strategy for the 2019 elections was built on the above philosophy of connecting with the people and consisted of two elements. The first element focused on communicating the welfare programmes of the Modi government to voters in general, and particularly in establishing a connection with 'beneficiaries'. PM Modi was determined to ensure last-mile delivery, and government schemes were tailored to ensure it happened efficiently. This helped bring real positive change to the lives of people and added to BJP's appeal in the eyes of the public.

The second element consisted of gearing up for the largest ever organizational complexity in India's electoral history, as the party had succeeded in getting over 110 million members. This created the challenge of getting a vast machine to work coherently, of overcoming agency problems at multiple levels of the organization. Coordination and coherent work between 110 million members were mammoth tasks.

Election preparation required a robust internal communication system to strengthen the flow of information, plans, instructions and feedback between the top leadership, karyakartas and primary members. The party leadership deliberated on this and came up with the idea of Project Samvad Kendra (Communication Centre). Bhupender Yadav, the co-author, was given charge of the Samvad Kendra project launched by Amit Shah, which facilitated the systematic collection, digitization, verification of personal details of all primary members, and mapping them to polling booths for the two levels of elections, Vidhan Sabha and Lok Sabha. What was novel was the efficient processes that were brought to bear on this. The project began from BJP headquarters in Delhi on 16 July 2018; on 9 August the first Samvad Kendra was set up in Gujarat, and the people present at the National Executive meeting on 8 September 2018 at Ambedkar Bhawan in Delhi were briefed about the project.

Primary members, karyakartas and beneficiaries of government schemes were assembled into a linked database. This data collection exercise was made possible through 193 Samvad Kendras (thirty-two at the state level and 161 at the Lok Sabha level) across the country. At each centre, there was a team which built databases, and originated personalized calls to individuals. In total, there were 15,000 call centre operators making calls.[3]

Apart from phone calls, other channels were also used to reach each beneficiary household. There was one *Pradesh Samvad Kendra* for every state of India, followed by one Lok Sabha *Samvad Kendra* (Lok Sabha Communication Centre) for each pair of Lok Sabha constituencies, and one *Shakti Kendra* (Power Centre) for every five booths. A technology platform called the Contact Centre and Data Management System (CCDMS) was established to host the data and enable the entire process of communication.

This outreach plan did not involve a high-pressure campaign by the BJP. Instead, it softly asked households for feedback on a given scheme. This was effectively a kind of social audit of subsidy programmes, which helped generate feedback about implementation failures. In addition, party workers physically contacted people and encouraged them to give missed calls on dedicated numbers, if they so desired, to reflect their support for PM Modi.

Campaign activities were communicated to persons in the neighbourhood also using these call centres. This mechanism enabled calls to be placed at least once to 220 million recipients of subsidies, 110 million primary members and 20 million party workers. The project started with 0.5 million attempted calls per day and ramped up to a peak of 3.5 million by the end of the campaign. In the 2019 campaign, the Samvad Kendras made 248 million calls, sent 123 million voice messages and 106 million text messages. About 100 million persons were invited to PM Modi's rallies and about 10 million were invited to Shah's rallies.[4]

Parallelly, the senior figures of the party were given well defined management responsibilities. Each party office-bearer had to manage the campaign for thirty to forty Lok Sabha seats. The various sub-organizations such as the Mahila Morcha, Kisan Morcha, SC/ST Morcha, etc. were given specific tasks within the overall campaign. At the booth level, thirty to forty BJP workers were dedicated to each booth.

From 2014 to 2018, the BJP analysed each Lok Sabha seat minutely and worked on the party's expansion, organizational stability and public acceptance. Over these four years, party president Amit Shah visited most districts and held meetings with district in-charges. The two held discussions over areas where the party could be strengthened. There was a special focus on districts where the Congress was losing ground.

To keep the ground-level karyakartas motivated, there was a special effort to connect the workers to the leaders. The top leadership of the party shared meals with the booth workers. PM Modi shared a meal with party workers in 2016 in his constituency of Varanasi. Over 26,000 BJP workers brought their own lunch to the meeting. The Prime Minister also carried his own packed lunch. This helped the ordinary party worker feel kinship with the party leadership, which was different from how the leadership held itself in many other parties. The exercise was also fruitful in micromanagement of ground level mobilization by the top leadership of the party. This was both a formal and informal way of party workers and leaders establishing a line of free exchange of ideas.

Building upon PM Modi's days in Gujarat where he had introduced a consultative process by forming panels with participation from block to the district level, the BJP implemented the same approach at the national level. The party forums were open platforms to put forth ideas and opinions. All big decisions were taken by the BJP Parliamentary Board. During the four years, the government and party worked in close coordination sharing similar objectives. When the government implemented new schemes, the party ensured the message was communicated to the ground level. The party organized programmes around important days identified by the organization to ensure effective messaging about the schemes.

On 14 April 2018, the BJP government embarked upon a massive outreach to cover the backward and weaker sections of society under the key welfare schemes of the BJP government. PM Modi called it the Gram Swaraj Abhiyan (Village Self-Rule Mission). The BJP identified 21,058 villages where scheduled castes and scheduled tribes constituted more than 50 per cent of the population. BJP MPs, including Union ministers, were asked to ensure that everyone in these villages was covered under the schemes aimed at providing LPG connection, vaccination for children, Jan Dhan accounts and power for households. The schemes chosen for special intervention included: *Pradhan Mantri Jan Dhan Yojana* (National Mission for Financial Inclusion), *Pradhan Mantri Jeevan Jyoti Bima Yojana*

(Prime Minister Jeevan Jyoti Insurance Scheme) and *Pradhan Mantri Bima Suraksha Yojana* (Prime Minister's Safety Insurance Scheme).

While MPs spent at least a night each in such villages under the campaign that went on till 5 May, Union ministers spent two nights each in different parts of the country. This campaign helped to increase the BJP's connection with poorer voters of other classes.[56]

As the largest national party, BJP decided not to run things only from Delhi but break down its messages in local languages for wider reach. During the pravas programmes, Shah and other party office bearers interacted with regional media. These interactions helped BJP's messages to percolate beyond Delhi. By June 2018 a detailed plan was in place for Amit Shah's next round of pravas (tours) in various states in view of the upcoming Lok Sabha elections. Lok Sabha teams were constituted in each state to coordinate the visits. Among the issues that Shah took up during the tour were planning of Lok Sabha management, list of beneficiaries, detailed list of membership, status of tasks to be completed at booth level, political and social issues of the state and BJP's presence and relations with the media.

During this phase, the BJP worked in close coordination with the RSS. RSS support on the ground has always been an important aspect of the BJP's electoral success.

The BJP government also implemented plans, programmes and schemes that were part of the party's long-standing developmental and ideological agenda. While the work of governance and party building was underway, the BJP's commitment to building a Ram Mandir remained. There were two opinions on the issue. One which believed that a law be brought in Parliament for the construction of the temple. The BJP government stood by its commitment for a Ram temple in Ayodhya but also maintained that the matter should be adjudicated by the court. A lot of debate and discussion followed and eventually a consensus was reached that the legal option was the best way forward.

Before the 2014 election, in its internal survey, BJP found that digital media had a significant impact in around 160 of the 543 constituencies particularly in states like Gujarat, Haryana, Himachal Pradesh, Karnataka, Andhra Pradesh, Maharashtra, Delhi and Punjab. The BJP then built digital tools like recorded video and audio speeches of top leaders to relay on mobile phones. The party engaged a network of volunteers to aid in the exercise. For the 2014 elections, many volunteers from the diaspora sent text messages, used social media and made calls to ensure voters, particularly in the 'digital seats' turned out to vote for the BJP. In the 2019 Lok Sabha campaign, members from the diaspora also played an active role.

Congress's Campaign against BJP

In the pre-election period, Rahul Gandhi tried to make allegations of corruption against Modi in the purchase of Rafale fighters, but these allegations failed to stick and helped turn the elections into a referendum on Modi's probity.[7] When Rahul Gandhi coined the slogan *Chowkidar chor hai* the BJP responded by using the slogan *Main bhi chowkidar* (I'm also the nation's guard). Short video ads were released, showing people from different walks of life who had turned into chowkidars to do their bit for the country, like Modi. People found an instant connect with the BJP's slogan as it resonated with the public's perception of BJP's clean image and saw it as an attack on PM Modi.

In carrying out numerous rallies, with constant engagement through ground-level karyakartas as well as top leaders, the implicit message was that voting for the BJP would ensure continued progress and development. In the analysis of the loss of 2004, the BJP had realized that while a lot of work was done on the ground, the party had not been successful in communicating it to the people. In 2019, the BJP was determined to not succumb to that problem again. Campaigns and rallies were focused on special demographics such as women, youth and farmers. In 'Pariksha Pe Charcha 2.0' (Discussion on examinations), PM Modi ran a conversation with students, parents and teachers on 29 January 2019 at Talkatora Stadium in New Delhi, for the second time. Arrangements were made across schools in the city to broadcast this session to students of grade 8 and above. This was a pathway to mass mobilization, to get messages into a diverse array of families that could otherwise have been insulated from BJP's messaging. Through this the BJP was able to connect with young voters who were voting for the first time after they turned eighteen.

From 12 February to 2 March 2019, the BJP ran a campaign named *Mera Parivar, Bhajpa Parivar* (My family is the BJP family). The campaign involved the BJP party workers visiting one household at a time, drinking tea, and discussing the achievements of the BJP government. About 50 million party workers were asked to hoist the BJP flag in their homes.

Another event was organized to involve voters and party workers by facilitating *samvad* or dialogue with members, party workers and voters. The nationwide *Kamal Jyoti Sankalp* campaign was launched on 26 February 2019. In this campaign, party cadre reached out to beneficiaries and lit lamps in each beneficiary household. On 28 February 2019, PM Modi addressed millions of party workers and volunteers at the booth level in a nationwide conference. Large meetings known as *Maha-samvad* which were held at 15,000 locations spread over the nation. The PM asked party workers to connect with every voter in their region and make them aware of the government's welfare initiatives. This Maha-samvad was termed the world's biggest video conference. The video conference had a provision for people to send questions directly to PM Modi using the NaMo app.

Continuing with campaigns that spurred community engagement of party workers with voters, the party organized the *Vijay Sankalp Bike Rally* to show the strength of the BJP's ground level karyakartas and to mobilize the youth. On 2 March, a bike rally was organized under this programme at 3,500 locations.

In May 2018, the party again reached out to people. It asked them to express their support through the *Sampark for Samarthan* programme. The day marked four years of the Narendra Modi government in power. The campaign saw about 4,000 BJP functionaries, who included state chief ministers and Union ministers, contact over 1,00,000 people of extraordinary achievement in their fields. Party leaders who met eminent personalities not only asked for their support but also sought their feedback on the performance of the government. The party publicized these meetings through various social media handles, which included bringing the BJP into the mind space of the followers of the eminent people.

The February Attack

The campaign was unfolding when a tragedy struck India. On 14 February, an Indian Army convoy was in transit from Jammu with seventy-eight vehicles carrying 2,547 CRPF security personnel, who belonged to the 76th Battalion. At Lethpora, in Pulwama, a vehicle laden with over eighty kilogrammes of explosives veered into the Jammu–Srinagar highway and rammed a vehicle in the convoy. The terrorist who drove the vehicle was Adil Ahmad Dar and he lived kilometres away from the site. Forty security personnel were killed and many more were injured. Pakistan-based terrorist organization Jaish-e-Mohammed claimed responsibility for the attack.

On 15 February, when the bodies arrived in Delhi, BJP ministers and MPs attended the last rites of the security personnel belonging to their respective constituencies.

The BJP had long criticized Congress for being soft on terrorist attacks and on Pakistan. When the Army base came under attack in Uri in 2016, the Modi government had ordered 'surgical strikes'. The government decided to give Pakistan a strong reply. On 19 February, PM Modi gave National Security Adviser Ajit Doval the green light for decisive action. On 26 February, at 3 a.m., twelve Mirage 2000 aircraft bombed targets inside Pakistan Occupied Kashmir, across the LoC.[8] Before the break of dawn, the operation was complete, and the Indian aircraft were back in Indian territory. The next day, Pakistani planes bombed uninhabited areas of Rajouri and Naushera. Indian planes were scrambled in response, and an Indian pilot, Abhinandan Varthaman, was captured in Pakistan. The mood across the nation was once again sombre. When Pakistan released Abhinandan the very next day, it was seen as a diplomatic win for India.

For long years, the BJP had positioned itself as a nationalist party that was tough on terrorism and tough on Pakistan. BJP's response to the series of events convinced the electorate that the party provided a strong and determined leadership. The global response to the surgical strikes was sympathetic towards India.[9] Reasserting its zero-tolerance policy on terrorism, a few days after the strike, India decided to boycott the South Asian Association for Regional Cooperation (SAARC) meeting that was scheduled to take place in Islamabad.[10]

Party Manifesto

The party decided to make the people a part of the manifesto drafting process. On 3 February, Amit Shah and Rajnath Singh launched a drive to crowdsource suggestions for the BJP's election manifesto, with the tagline 'Bharat ke Mann ki Baat, Modi ke Saath' from a Delhi hotel. As part of the programme, drop boxes were sent across India in 300 raths. Over 7,000 drop boxes were placed across India. The first person to give his suggestion through the drop box was a staff member of the hotel in which the event was held. Suggestions were also collected through the party's website, via email and social media.

Priority areas for suggestions were listed out by Singh and included development and good governance, agriculture, youth, women empowerment, inclusive growth, health and education, economy and trade, infrastructure, among others. Senior ministers were given charge of departments earmarked for suggestions.

The BJP in its manifesto focused on the long standing promises that had been on the party's agenda. The manifesto titled *Sankalp Patra* stressed on national security, border security, terrorism, farmer welfare, the construction of Ram Mandir and abrogation of Article 370 and Article 35A in Jammu and Kashmir. The manifesto said, 'We are committed to annulling Article 35A of the Constitution of India as the provision is discriminatory against non-permanent residents and women of Jammu and Kashmir. We believe that Article 35A is an obstacle in the development of the state.'

On the issue of Ram Mandir, the Sankalp Patra said, 'We will explore all possibilities within the framework of the Constitution and all necessary efforts to facilitate the expeditious construction of the Ram Temple in Ayodhya.'

In addition, the party manifesto also addressed issues that faced the economy and different sectors. For example, in agriculture, the BJP also promised to double farmers' income by 2022. The manifesto said, 'At the very beginning of our current term, prime minister Modi embarked on a mission to double farmers' income. We will make all efforts to achieve this goal by 2022.' It promised, 'Rs 25 lakh crore investment in agri-rural sector. We are committed to making an investment of Rs 25 lakh crore to improve the productivity of the farm sector.'

Further, the manifesto promised economic growth and aspired to build India into a $5 trillion economy. It said, 'Within five years, we have turned India into a bright spot that is not only the fastest growing major economy of the world but also enjoys macroeconomic stability. We have already become the world's sixth largest economy and will soon be among the top five. We aspire to make India the third largest economy of the world by 2030. This implies that we commit to make India a US $5 trillion economy by 2025 and US $10 trillion economy by 2032.'

Head of the party's 20-member manifesto committee Rajnath Singh said the government led by Prime Minister Narendra Modi was fully committed to nationalism and zero tolerance towards terrorism. 'Our "Sankalp Patra" is a vision document that lists the expectations of 130 crore Indians,' Singh said.[11]

A Remarkable Outcome

The BJP entered the 2019 election with a report card of the government's accomplishments over the last five years. The government had worked on introducing major reforms amid sustained opposition attacks and efforts to stall the government's work.

Before the elections came the stage of 'ticket distribution', of choosing the candidates for all the constituencies. The BJP pushed forward on its generational transition, and twenty-two senior party leaders were denied tickets.

The Lok Sabha elections were held between 11 April and 19 May. While there were fifteen parties that made up the NDA, this election was primarily about the popularity of Modi. The top BJP leaders worked on a punishing schedule of campaigning. Modi flew 0.15 million km, and addressed 142 rallies, during the campaign. Shah visited 312 Lok Sabha constituencies, addressed 161 rallies and travelled 0.16 million km.[12]

The BJP's hard work paid off in the 120 seats that the party had never won. The BJP won Congress bastions like Amethi in Uttar Pradesh, Nizamabad in Telangana, Guna in Madhya Pradesh. In Haryana, the party won the Rohtak seat. In West Bengal, the party managed to win eighteen seats against two in 2014. When the votes were counted on 23 May, the BJP gained twenty-one seats compared with the 2014 outcome; it got 303 seats of the 437 it contested.[13]

Table 1: Lok Sabha Elections of 2019[14]

Political Party	LS 2014		LS 2019	
	Vote Share	Seats Won	Vote Share	Seats Won
Bharatiya Janata Party	31.34%	282	37.76%	303
Indian National Congress	19.52%	44	19.7%	52
Bahujan Samaj Party	4.19%	0	3.67%	10

In Indian elections, generally a party is quite competitive at a 30 per cent vote share, and wins clearly at a 40 per cent vote share. Even though the Congress improved its vote share slightly to get to 19.7 per cent, this vote share did not result in a significant number of seats; the Congress only got to fifty-two seats.

The BJP thus became the first non-Congress full majority party to get re-elected with a stronger majority. In the past, only two prime ministers had been re-elected with majorities: Nehru and Indira Gandhi. In those two episodes, the Congress vote share had risen by 2 and 2.9 percentage points; in contrast, Modi's re-election came with a gain of 6.4 percentage points.[15]

In thirteen states and union territories, the BJP's vote share exceeded 50 per cent. That is, in these locations, even if all the opposition parties had stitched up a coalition, they would not have won.

The results showed a concentration in favour of fewer parties. Sixty per cent of the seats in Lok Sabha were won by the National Democratic Alliance consisting of the BJP and its fifteen supporting parties. The remaining 40 per cent were won by twenty-five political parties. The vote share of parties other than the BJP and the

Congress, which had already been on the decline, fell further. From 2004 to 2019, the total vote share garnered by parties other than the Congress and the BJP fell from 51 per cent to 43 per cent. While the Congress did not see dramatic shifts in its vote share, the BJP saw an increase in vote share from 22 per cent in 2004 to 37 per cent in 2019.[16]

In UP, the SP-BSP alliance had succeeded in winning the Gorakhpur and Phulpur by-elections in 2018 fanning opposition hopes of cobbling a joint front to defeat the BJP. However, the caste-based calculations of the BSP and SP in UP failed in the 2019 election; they did worse together as compared with how they fared separately, five years ago.[17][18] Electoral alliances, that depended on transfer of votes by each party's voters to its alliance partners, did not work in expected ways.

The coalitions formed to counter the BJP failed in Bengal for the Communist–Congress alliance, in UP for the Congress–SP alliance, in Karnataka, Bihar, UP and Maharashtra.

The successes the Congress had gained in Rajasthan and Madhya Pradesh were reversed in the Lok Sabha elections. Along with its ally, the Rashtriya Loktantrik Party, the BJP won all twenty-five Lok Sabha seats of Rajasthan. In Madhya Pradesh, the BJP won twenty-eight of the twenty-nine seats.[19] The results of the 2019 Lok Sabha elections proved yet again that Indian voters voted differently in the national and regional elections. In 2004 and 2009, the Congress had also lost state elections but had gone on to hold power at the Centre with the help of its allies. In 2019, despite the Modi wave, in states like Odisha, Andhra Pradesh, Arunachal Pradesh and Sikkim, where assembly elections were held simultaneously, people voted differently at the state and national level.

On the evening of 23 May, Modi addressed the nation from the BJP headquarters in Delhi and asked to be judged for his intentions. The BJP had won based on the trust people had reposed in the party. He said, 'I will not do anything with ill intention or bad desire. I may make mistakes. I will not do anything for myself but I assure you, every moment of my life and every cell in my body will work non-stop to ensure that the country keeps moving forward.'

A new government had to be installed now. Some senior party leaders could not join the new government. Venkaiah Naidu had taken over as India's vice-president in 2017. Sushma Swaraj had not contested elections on the advice of doctors. Arun Jaitley expressed the inability to dedicate himself to ministerial work given his health concerns.

The new Cabinet was sworn in on 30 May and the party stayed with its tradition set during Rajnath Singh's tenure as the BJP president in that young leaders were given key responsibilities. Rajnath Singh took over as defence minister, Amit Shah became the home minister. Nirmala Sitharaman was appointed finance minister. Piyush Goyal, Nitin Gadkari, S. Jaishankar, Dharmendra Pradhan, Smriti Irani, Ravi Shankar Prasad, Dr Harsh Vardhan and Prakash Javadekar also became part of the council of ministers. Among its NDA alliance partners Ram Vilas Paswan from Lok Janshakti Party and Harsimrat Kaur Badal from Shiromani Akali Dal Party were given ministerial berths.

When the elections were over, the samvad kendras were closed systematically over a period of one month. The BJP now began deliberations on the road ahead. During the first term of the Modi government, Amit Shah had taken care of the organization but he had moved to the Union government.

The party now needed a new president. It zeroed in on J.P. Nadda. Nadda was born in Bihar to a family from Himachal Pradesh and educated in Patna University. He went to Himachal Pradesh to pursue his LLB. At Patna University, Nadda was a member of ABVP and had participated in the 1977 students' union election. His association with the ABVP in Himachal Pradesh helped the organization defeat the Students' Federation of India in Himachal Pradesh University for the first time in 1984. He became the president of the students' union. Nadda was the general secretary of the ABVP during 1986-89. He was appointed the president of the Bharatiya

Janata Yuva Morcha in 1991. Two years later, Nadda contested his first election and entered the Himachal Pradesh assembly. He subsequently won the assembly elections in Himachal Pradesh in 1998 and 2007.

J.P. Nadda was appointed the BJP's working president by the party's parliamentary board on 17 June 2019. Amit Shah was requested to continue as the BJP chief till the completion of organizational polls and the membership drive. Nadda was the Union health minister in the first Modi government. Modi had worked closely with Nadda when the former was the party's in-charge for Himachal Pradesh and Nadda a party legislator. Meanwhile, B.L. Santhosh took over as BJP's national general secretary (organization).

With this began a new phase in the life of the party.

Epilogue

The Bharatiya Janata Party has had a unique journey in Indian politics over the last seven decades. The journey started with the coming together of nationalists who began imagining the shape Independent India should take. The India of their imagination was a geographical and cultural entity with a modern outlook rooted in its ethos where each citizen would take pride in the nation's heritage. These nationalists mulled over the shape of politics which would run this modern nation. They drew inspiration from Gandhi's ideals which saw politics only as a means to serve people.

The prominence the Congress gained by participating in the freedom movement ensured for it popular votes as India began organizing national elections. As the party's ideals of nation-building changed, many leaders including Union ministers and party workers began to leave the Congress. Simultaneously, India began to witness the rise of many parties on the national front. Some of these were founded and headed by those who had been Congress members once but had now become disillusioned with the policies the Congress government was implementing. Many other parties also sprung up in the natural course of politics. As years passed, such parties decayed and atrophied because they compromised on their ideologies, allowing corruption, dynasty or individual ambition to assume greater importance than the party organization or its stated objectives.

The Bharatiya Jana Sangh, however, proved to be an aberration. Jana Sangh founder Syama Prasad Mookerjee resigned from the Nehru Cabinet over the Nehru-Liaquat Pact and felt the need to form a political organization based on nationalistic principles. Deen Dayal Upadhyaya later infused in the Jana Sangh ideas of Antyodaya and Integral Humanism which became the party's foundations for governance.

The party was different from other political organizations in some important ways. The most important difference lay in the origins of the party and its links with the RSS. The BJP's journey started with Jana Sangh in 1951 and has been influenced by the morals and ideals of the RSS. The RSS had a long-term cultural agenda, and short-term executive power was not its goal. With a large number of students, farmers, cultural and other organizations affiliated with the RSS, the BJP was not alone in its journey. The association with the RSS has helped the BJP in staying the course. The RSS and BJP do not take decisions on behalf of each other, do not influence each other's financial matters and do not interfere in each other's leadership decisions. The BJP is organizationally linked with the RSS through the post of the organization secretary in the BJP who belongs to the RSS.

While both organizations enjoy independent existence and do not dictate terms to each other, they share a moral bond, engage in ideas exchange and help each other grow. Their ideology is shared among the organizations of the Parivar. Dattopant Thengadi best described the relation when he said, 'We are interrelated, but not interdependent.' The BJP is part of a larger Vichar Parivar and that is why it has remained rooted in its ideology.

The ideological glue ensured that despite merging with the Janata Party in 1977, the Jana Sangh did not disintegrate and merge with the larger whole losing its individual identity. The Jana Sangh emerged from Janata Party as a whole and regrouped itself under a new name and symbol of BJP and lotus respectively. It contested its first general election in 1984 and in the face of a sympathy wave in favour of the Congress following the unfortunate assassination of Indira Gandhi was limited to just two seats. The BJP managed to remain unfazed by the dismissive attitude towards the party and continued to build its organization around its ideological moorings.

In power, the BJP presented a model of politics based on Indian culture and values. In 1999, under Atal Bihari Vajpayee, the BJP formed the first non-Congress coalition government that completed a full term in office. The government and the party organization, however, could not take the message effectively to people and the BJP's opposition parties led by the Congress succeeded in forming a coalition that would keep the BJP out of power for the next ten years.

When Modi assumed charge as the Prime Minister in 2014, he outlined the larger agenda of the government which stated that the approach of all policies would be pro-poor. The BJP's organization worked to ensure the implementation of Deen Dayal Upadhyaya's vision of Antyodaya. As two BJP Prime Ministers, Atal Bihari Vajpayee and Narendra Modi realised these ideals in governance by thinking of the last-person in the sociological and economic order and giving the country value-based politics.

Unleashing the full potential of Digital India, the BJP government introduced key reforms that had been long-pending in the country. Pradhan Mantri Ujjwala Yojana, Jan Dhan accounts, Pradhan Mantri Awas Yojana, Goods and Services Tax, Swachh Bharat Mission and electricity for all were among the pioneering schemes of the government that people benefited from. Benefits of government schemes started reaching the intended beneficiaries without delay and without the involvement of middlemen.

The successful implementation of these policies and programmes backed by a robust communication strategy and ground-level mobilization saw the BJP return to power in 2019 with an even bigger mandate of 303 Lok Sabha seats. In its second term, the BJP government, apart from implementing schemes centred on the poor, also fulfilled many political promises such as the abrogation of Article 370 in Jammu and Kashmir, construction of Ram Temple and outlawing of Triple Talaq.

While BJP's journey has been marked by the active participation of a large number of sister organizations, other parties in India operate mainly as single organizations. The inner party democracy in the BJP has become stronger because unlike other Indian political parties, the BJP is not a family-driven enterprise. To maintain inner party democracy and to not fall victim to dynastic politics the way many other parties have, the BJP follows a set of rules. The party holds elections every three years to choose its office-bearers, including the party president. The party has a core committee, whose membership rotates, and decision-making in the party is based on consensus reached within the core committee. Members of the committee collect feedback from the ground level and make the process inclusive and thorough. It has set a rule of 'one family, one person' when it comes to holding positions in the government or party.

The BJP's journey has seen generational change every fifteen years. New party presidents have brought in new teams with a focus on giving key responsibilities to younger people. The party also made a rule to let only those below seventy-five years of age participate in elections, leaving the elderly to act as a guiding force. The party uses the experience of the elderly leaders as guides (margdarshak) for key policy issues. The party works at all levels to strengthen the organization. It has integrated programmes to induct new members who are then trained in party activities and work culture, and are given a detailed understanding of the party's ethos.

Part of BJP's success both at the level of the government and at the level of the party has been the ease with which it has included technology in its working model. Through digital mediums like NaMo App and outreach programmes like Mann Ki Baat, the party has been able to build a direct connect with its members, voters and supporters. There is a technological thrust at all levels and this has minimized the chances of errors, made operations smooth, increased reach and heightened efficiency.

More recently, particularly since 2014, the party and the government work in tandem. The organizational machinery of the BJP ensures that all messages and projects of the government are communicated to the people. The government focused on better governance and set up technology-based direct benefit transfers to poor people to uplift their standard of living through their bank accounts for toilets, houses, cooking gas, for farmers, for pensioners and for students. Direct benefit transfers reduced pilferage and money reached people straight from the government. The party then connected directly with the beneficiaries. Communication with the people was made possible by mobilization of the party's machinery at all levels: from the party's MPs and national office-bearers to the booth-level party workers. This has made the party a formidable force with a rising vote share among new voters. The BJP's vote share rose from 31 per cent in 2014 to 37.4 per cent in 2019. The BJP, which had long been seen as a party of urban India, saw its vote share in rural constituencies rise by a sharp 7.3 percentage points. The difference between BJP's vote share in urban and rural constituencies fell from 8.9 percentage points in 2014 to merely 3.5 percentage points in 2019.[1]

As India enters the 75th year of its Independence, the BJP is at the centre-stage of national politics. It is expanding numerically and geographically. The BJP has become the world's largest political party. The party has its governments in north, south, east and west of India. While the party has long been accused of intellectual phobia, the BJP is no longer the party that stood isolated in Indian politics. Going forward, the combination of the BJP's dedicated and disciplined cadre, its non-dynastic leadership, its inner party democracy, its relentless activities, training and induction of new members every three years gives it an advantage over other political parties in India.

Notes

Chapter 1: The Jana Sangh

1   M.K. Gandhi, 'His Last Will and Testament', *My Non-Violence* (1960).

2   Maulana Abdul Kalam Azad, in his biography *India Wins Freedom*, delves into the events leading to the Partition of India. He felt that Jawaharlal Nehru ought to share some responsibility for the partition for two reasons. First, in spite of a pre-poll assurance, Nehru refused to include both Chaudhari Khaliquzzaman and Nawab Ismail Khan, members of the Muslim League, in the Uttar Pradesh Cabinet after the first elections held in 1937. Second, Nehru's statement at the Bombay press conference held on 10 July 1946, where he declared that Congress would enter the Constituent Assembly unfettered by the Cabinet Mission Plan or any other agreement, enraged Mohammad Ali Jinnah. In retaliation, the Muslim League Council passed a resolution rejecting the Cabinet Mission Plan, as well as resorted to direct action for the achievement of Pakistan. See A.K. Azad., *India Wins Freedom: The Complete Version* (Orient BlackSwan, 1997), pp. 230–231

3   Around June 1947, Gandhi wrote in a letter, 'Probably no one is more distressed than I am over the impending division of India. But I have no desire to launch a struggle against what promises to be an accomplished fact.' See, M. Gandhi, *The Collected Works of Mahatma Gandhi Vol. 95 (30 April 1947–July 6, 1947)* (Publications Division, Ministry of Information and Broadcasting, Government of India, 1983), p. 194

4   For a discussion on the various factions existing within the Congress before Independence, see A.J. Dastur, 'Twenty-five Years of Indian Socialism', *India Quarterly,* 16(2) (1960), pp. 105–119

5   Sutapa Lahiry, 'Jana Sangh and Bharatiya Janata Party: A Comparative Assessment of Their Philosophy and Strategy and Their Proximity with the Other Members of the Sangh Parivar' *The Indian Journal of Political Science* 66, no. 4 (2005), pp. 831–50.

6   Vijayadashami is celebrated as a day that marks the victory of Ram over Ravana and so is seen as the triumph of good over evil. To this day, the RSS sarsanghchalak delivers an annual address every Vijayadashami.

7   Walter Anderson and Shridhar Damle in, 'Formation and Development of the Rashtriya Swayamsevak Sangh'. *The Brotherhood in Saffron: The Rashtriya Swayamsevak Sangh and Hindu Revivalism,* (Penguin Random House India Private Limited, 2019), pp. 30–31

8   Arun Anand, *The Saffron Surge Untold Story of RSS Leadership* (Prabhat Prakashan, 2019), Chapter 2, p. 67

9   In the 1930s, Hedgewar sent students to universities outside Maharashtra to recruit them in the RSS. Around this time, Golwalkar was recruited while working as lecturer at the Banaras Hindu University. See Walter Andersen, 'The Rashtriya Swayamsevak Sangh: I: Early Concerns', *Economic and Political Weekly,* 7(11) (1972), p. 594

10 Ranga Hari, *The Incomparable Guru Golwalkar* (Prabhat Prakashan, 2018), p. 82

11 Ibid, p. 128

12 Walter Andersen, 'The Rashtriya Swayamsevak Sangh: III: Participation in Politics', *Economic and Political Weekly,* 7(13), (1972), p. 675

13 Statement of M.S. Golwalkar, sarsanghchalak of the RSS, dated 1 February 1948, issued to the press before his arrest. See M.S. Golwalkar, *Justice on Trial: Historic Document of Guruji-Govt. Correspondence,* Appendix III (1968). Available at: http://www.hvk.org/specialarticles/justice/justice.html (accessed on 7 April 2020)

14 Supra note 12, p. 674

15 Supra note 12, p. 675

16 Ibid, p. 677

17 Ibid, pp. 675–676

18 *Organiser.* About Us, The *Organiser*

19 Supra note 12

20 Supra note 13, Appendix IX

21 Christophe Jaffrelot, *Hindu Nationalism: A Reader* (Princeton University Press, 2009), p. 175

22 Udayan Bandyopadhyay, 'The essence of Hindu Rashtravad a Study of the Ideas of the Concept Builders 1920 to 1970', Department of Political Science, University of Calcutta (2017), pp. 161–162

23 Supra note 4

24 S.C. Das, *Bharat Kesri Dr Syama Prasad Mookerjee with Modern Implication* (Abhinav Publications, 2000), p. 77, footnote 28

25 M. Gandhi, *The Collected Works of Mahatma Gandhi Vol. 79* (Jul 16, 1940 - Dec 27, 1940) (Publications Division, Ministry of Information and Broadcasting, Government of India, 1983), p. 285. Available at https://www.gandhiashramsevagram.org/gandhi-literature/mahatma-gandhicollected-works-volume-79.pdf

26 Supra note 12, pp. 679–680

27 Supra note 12, p. 680

28 Prafulla Ketkar, 'Correcting Historical Wrongs', the *Organiser* (2019). Available at: https://www.*Organiser*.org/Encyc/2019/12/16/Correcting-Historical-Wrongs.html (accessed on 20 March 2020)

29 'The Kashmir Issue', in Eminent Parliamentarians Monograph Series: Dr Syama Prasad Mookerjee (Lok Sabha Secretariat, 1990), pp. 109–123. Available at: https://eparlib.nic.in/bitstream/123456789/58670/1/Eminent_Parliamentarians_Series_Syama_Prasad_Mookerjee.pdf (accessed on 26 July 2020).

30 Supra note 12, p. 680

31 B.D. Graham, 'Syama Prasad Mookerjee and the Communalist Alternative' in *Soundings in Modern South Asian History*, edited by D.A. Low (University of California Press, 1968), pp. 346–52

32 Supra note 12, p. 680

33 Supra note 4, pp. 105–119

34 K.N. Kumar, *Political Parties in India (The Ideology and Organization)* (Mittal Publications, 1990), pp. 20–24

35 Walter Andersen, 'The Rashtriya Swayamsevak Sangh: III: Participation in Politics', *Economic and Political Weekly*, 7(13), (1972), pp. 679–680

36 The RSS claimed to be above partisan attachment. Moreover, neither Hedgewar nor Golwalkar wanted the RSS to be too closely associated with a group that would have placed them in direct opposition to the Congress.

See Walter Andersen, 'The Rashtriya Swayamsevak Sangh: II: Who Represents The Hindus?', *Economic and Political Weekly*, 7(12) (1972), p. 635. Also, see supra note 12, pp. 677–678.

37   Koushiki Dasgupta, *Electoral Politics and Hindu Nationalism in India: The Bharatiya Jana Sangh, 1951–1971* (Routledge, 2019), p. 66

38   In an article in the *Organiser*, dated 25 June 1956, Golwalkar reported his discussions with Mookerjee just before the formation of the Jana Sangh. Golwalkar insisted, 'RSS could not be drawn into politics, that it could not play second fiddle to any political or other party, nor could it be a handmaiden to a political party.' In response, Mookerjee insisted that the Jana Sangh could not be subservient to any other organization. Both agreed with each other. See Walter Andersen, 'The Rashtriya Swayamsevak Sangh: IV: Jan Sangh and Other Organisations', *Economic and Political Weekly*, 7(14) (1972), pp. 724–725.

39   Christophe Jaffrelot, *The Hindu Nationalist Movement and Indian Politics: 1925 to the 1990s: Strategies of Identity-Building, Implantation and Mobilization* (with special reference to Central India) (C. Hurst & Co. Publishers, 1996), p. 117

40   Walter Andersen, 'The Rashtriya Swayamsevak Sangh: IV: Jan Sangh and Other Organisations', *Economic and Political Weekly* (1972), p. 725

41   Ibid, p. 725

42   K. Pillai, 'Jan Sangh—A Rightist Opposition to the Congress Party', *The Indian Journal of Political Science*, 27(2) (1966), p. 69

43   Ibid

44   'Why Jansangh?', *Kamal Sandesh,* 5 June 2017. Available at: http://www.kamalsandesh.org/why-jansangh/ (accessed on 29 March 2020)

45   *Party Documents 1951–1972: Principles and Policies, Manifestos and Constitution*, Volume 1, (Bharatiya Jana Sangh, 1973), p. 48

46   Ibid, pp. 47–48

47   Ibid, p. 53

48   Ibid, p. 56

49   Art. 44, Constitution of India, 1950.

50   Mridula Mukherjee, 'Small Men, Narrow Minds, Petty Principles: Nehru in 1951 on Communalism', *National Herald*, 27 May 2019. Available at: https://www.nationalheraldindia.com/jawaharlal-nehru/remembering-jawaharlal-nehru-thecommunal-mind-is-a-small-mind (accessed on 20 February 2020)

51   Supra note 39, p. 70

52   Ibid

53   'Performance of Political Parties' in Statistical Report On General Elections, 1951 To The First Lok Sabha Volume I, Election Commission of India, New Delhi. Available at: https://eci.gov.in/statistical-report/statistical-reports/.

54   Authors' calculations based on various statistical reports, Election Commission of India

55   Bharatiya Jana Sangh 1952–1980, Party Document, History of Bharatiya Jana Sangh, Volume 6, p. 122

56   Supra note 39, p. 70

57   Eminent Parliamentarians Monograph Series: Dr Syama Prasad Mookerjee (Lok Sabha Secretariat, 1990). Available at: https://eparlib. nic.in/bitstream/123456789/58670/1/Eminent_Parliamentarians_Series_ Syam a_Prasad_Mookerjee.pdf

58   At the Kanpur Session in December 1956, where Deen Dayal Upadhyaya was appointed the general secretary of Jan Sangh, Mookerjee remarked, 'If I could get two or three more Deen Dayals, I will change the entire political map of India.' See Deendayal Research Institute, Manthan Volume 20 (1999), p. 89

59   Preeti Trivedi, Architect of a Philosophy: Deendayal Upadhyaya (Bhartiya Sahitya Sangrah, 2017), pp. 63–64

60   For more details on demands of the Praja Parishad Movement, see 'Integrate Kashmir Movement' in Party Documents 1951–1972: Resolutions on Internal Affairs, Volume 4 (Bharatiya Jana Sangh, 1973), pp. 26–29

61   Party Documents 1951–1972: Resolutions on Internal Affairs, Volume 4 (Bharatiya Jana Sangh, 1973), p. 19

62   Party Documents 1951–1972: Resolutions on Internal Affairs, Volume 4 (Bharatiya Jana Sangh, 1973), pp. 20–21

63   Arun Anand, 'Praja Parishad Party—the Forgotten Name Behind the Removal of Article 370 in J&K', ThePrint, 14 November 2020. Available at: https://theprint.in/india/praja-parishad-party-theforgotten-name-behind-the-removal-of-article-370-in-jk/543732/

64   Devesh Khadelwa, Pledge for Integrated India (1st edition, Prabhat Prakashan, 2016), p. 180

65   The Inner Line permit is an official travel document issued by the Government of India, granting Indian citizens the permission to enter Kashmir.

66 Dr Syama Prasad Mookerjee, One Country One Constitution (Research
    Foundation, 2019), p. 24. Available at: https://www.spmrf.org/wp-
    content/uploads/2019/10/Booklet-on-A370_SPMRF_ENG.pdf

67 Details of by-elections from 1952–1995. Available at: https://eci.gov.in/
    files/file/2511-details-of-bye-elections-from-1952-to-1995/

68 K.R. Malkani, 'Dr. Syama Prasad Mookerji & The Unholy Trinity', Political
    Mysteries (Prabhat Prakashan, 2016), p. 55

69 Tathagata Roy, Syama Prasad Mookerjee, Life and Times (Penguin
    Random House, 2018) p. 384.

70 Padmini Harish Chander, Dr Syama Prasad Mookerjee: A Contemporary
    Study (Noida News, 2000), p. 206

71 Ibid, p. 127

72 Ibid

Chapter 2: The Jana Sangh after Mookerjee

1   Padmini Harish Chander, Dr Syama Prasad Mookerjee: A Contemporary
    Study (Noida News, 2000), p. 127

2   'Poll-O-Meter: 1st visually-challenged MP', Deccan Herald, 11 May 2019.
    Available at: https://www.deccanherald.com/lok-sabha-election-2019/
    poll-o-meter-1st-visually-challengedmp-733284.html

3   K. Raman Pillai, 'Jan Sangh—A Rightist Opposition to the Congress
    Party', The Indian Journal of Political Science Vol. 27, No. 2 (1966), p. 70

4   Mahesh Chandra Sharma, Deendayal Upaddhayay: Kartavya Avam
    Vichar (2015 edition; Prabhat Prakashan, 2018), p. 114

5   Craig Baxter, The Jana Sangh: A Biography of an Indian Political Party
    (University of Pennsylvania Press, 1969), pp. 153–154

6   Dr Suchitra Kulkarni, RSS–BJP Symbiosis on the Cusp of Culture and
    Politics (1st edition, Prabhat Prakashan, 2020), p. 97

7   Supra note 5, p. 141

8   K. Raman Pillai, 'Jan Sangh—A Rightist Opposition to the Congress
    Party', The Indian Journal of Political Science Vol. 27, No. 2 (1966), p. 71

9   Supra note 5, p. 141

10 Supra note 5, p. 146

11 Ramachandra Gowda, 'Jagannath Rao Joshi, an inspiring memory:
    An ideal swayamsevak, great orator, mass leader', Organiser, 2010.
    Available at: https://www.Organiser.org/archives/dynamic/modulesd5f7.
    html?name=Content&pa=showpa ge&pid=355&page=12

12 Praveen Davar, 'The liberation of Goa', *The Hindu*, 31 December 2017. Available at: https://www.thehindu.com/opinion/op-ed/the-liberation-of-goa/article22339624.ece

13 Ashok K. Singh, 'Nehru's First Cabinet: An Ideal That Failed', *livehistoryindia.com*, 5 May 2021. Available at: https://www.livehistoryindia.com/story/mmi-cover-story/nehrus-first-cabinet/

14 Supra note 5, p. 128

15 H.S. Fartyal, *Role of the Opposition in the Indian Parliament* (Chaitanya Publishing House, 1971), p. 41

16 Supra note 5, p. 130

17 Ibid, p. 131

18 Ibid

19 Eminent Parliamentarians Monograph Series: Dr Syama Prasad Mookerjee (Lok Sabha Secretariat, 1990), p. 8. Available at: https://eparlib.nic.in/bitstream/123456789/58670/1/Eminent_Parliamentarians_Series_Syama_ Prasad_Mookerjee.pdf

20 Balraj Madhok, *Dr. Syama Prasad Mookerjee: A Biography* (Deepak Prakashan, 1954), pp. 48, 51, 100

21 Verinder Grover, *Political System in India* (Deep & Deep Publications, 1989), p. 221

22 Craig Baxter, *The Jana Sangh: A Biography of an Indian Political Party* (University of Pennsylvania Press, 1969), p. 153

23 Supra note 5, p. 162

24 'Performance of Political Parties' in *Statistical Report on General Elections, 1957 to the Second Lok Sabha Volume I*, Election Commission of India, New Delhi. Available at: https://eci.gov.in/statistical-report/statistical-reports/.

25 Supra note 5, p. 163

26 V.R. Raghavan, *Conflicts in Jammu and Kashmir: Impact on Polity, Society and Economy* (film edition, VIJ Books (India) Ltd, 2012), p. 192, footnote 15

27 Supra note 5, p. 179

28 *Organiser*, XI:8 (4 November 1957) and XI:9 (11 November 1957)

29 Craig Baxter, *The Jana Sangh: A Biography of an Indian Political Party* (University of Pennsylvania Press, 1969) p. 179

30 Supra note 5, p. 179

31 V. Krishna Ananth, *India Since Independence: Making Sense of Indian Politics* (First edition, Pearson Education, 2010), p. xiii

32   'Performance of Political Parties' in *Statistical Report on General Elections, 1962 to the Third Lok Sabha Volume I*, Election Commission of India, New Delhi. Available at: https://eci.gov.in/statistical-report/statistical-reports/.

33   Walter Andersen and Shridhar Damle, *The RSS: A View to the Inside* (Penguin Viking, 2018), p. 145

34   B.N. Jog, *Pt. Deendayal Upadhyay Ideology & Preception - Part - 6: Politics for Nation's Sake* (Suruchi Prakashan, 2014), pp. 46–49

35   Ibid, 'Defence Preparedness', pp. 48–49

36   V.N. Khanna, *Foreign Policy of India* (7th Edition; Vikas Publishing House, 2018), p. 125

37   *Organiser*, Volume 44 (Bharat Prakashan, 1992), p. 152

38   Walter Andersen and Shridhar Damle, *The RSS: A View to the Inside* (Penguin Viking, 2018), p. 146

39   Walter Anderson and Shridhar Damle, *The Brotherhood in Saffron: The Rashtriya Swayamsevak Sangh and Hindu Revivalism* (Penguin Random House India Private Limited, 2019), p. 167

40   Craig Baxter, *The Jana Sangh: A Biography of an Indian Political Party* (University of Pennsylvania Press, 1969), p. 248

41   Manjari Katju, *Vishva Hindu Parishad and Indian Politics* (Orient Blackswan Private Limited - New Delhi, 2nd edition, 2010), p. 15

42   'Save-the-cow' mob in Delhi rampage', *Sydney Morning Herald*, 8 November 1966. Available at: https://www.newspapers.com/clip/48432319/save-the-cow-mob-in-delhi-rampage/

43   Manjari Katju, *Vishva Hindu Parishad and Indian* Politics (Orient Blackswan Private Limited - New Delhi, 2nd edition, 2010), pp. 15–40

44   'Save-the-cow' mob in Delhi rampage', *The Sydney Morning Herald*, 8 November 1966. Available at: https://www.newspapers.com/clip/48432319/save-the-cow-mob-in-delhi-rampage/

45   Koushiki Dasgupta, *Electoral Politics and Hindu Nationalism in India: The Bharatiya Jana Sangh, 1951–1971* (Routledge, 2020), pp. 125–126

46   Ramashray Roy, 'Congress Defeat in Farrukhabad: A Failure of Party Organisation', *EPW*, Vol. 17, Issue No. 22 (29 May 1965). Available at: https://www.epw.in/system/files/pdf/1965_17/22/congress_defeat_in_farrukhabada_failure_of_party_organisation.pdf

47   *Bharatiya Jana Sangh (1952–1980) Vol: 6: History of Jana Sangh* (Bharatiya Janata Party, 2005), p. 275

48   Craig Baxter, *The Jana Sangh: A Biography of an Indian Political Party* (University of Pennsylvania Press, 1969), pp. 267, 268

49 'Performance of Political Parties' in *Statistical Report on General Elections, 1967 to the Fourth Lok Sabha Volume I*, Election Commission of India, New Delhi. Available at: https://eci.gov.in/statistical-report/statistical-reports/.

50 *Bharatiya Jana Sangh* (1952–1980) Vol: 6: *History of Jana Sangh (Bharatiya Janata Party, 2005)*, p. 286

51 *Statistical Report on General Elections, 1967 to the Legislative Assembly of Rajasthan,* Election Commission of India, New Delhi. Available at: https://eci.gov.in/statistical-report/statistical-reports/.

52 'Performance of Political Parties' in *Statistical Report on General Elections, 1967 to the Fourth Lok Sabha Volume I*, Election Commission of India, New Delhi. Available at: https://eci.gov.in/statistical-report/statistical-reports/.

53 Supra note 50, p. 287

54 Mridula Sinha and Vijayaraje Scindia, *Royal to Public Life* (First edition, Prabhat Prakashan, 2016), p. 165

55 Walter Anderson and Shridhar Damle, *The Brotherhood in Saffron: The Rashtriya Swayamsevak Sangh and Hindu Revivalism* (Penguin Random House India Private Limited, 2019), p. 169

56 Craig Baxter, *The Jana Sangh: A Biography of an Indian Political Party* (University of Pennsylvania Press, 1969), p. 271

57 A. A. Parvathy, *Hindutva: Ideology and Politics* (Deep & Deep Publications, 2004), p. 150

58 Party Documents 1951–1972: Resolutions on Internal Affairs, Volume 4 (Bharatiya Jana Sangh, 1973), p. 194

59 Gopal Prasad Singh, *Power and Politics: Congress Rule in Bihar, 1973–85* (Academic Excellence, 2005), p. 33

60 Sunita Aron. 'A Tale of Coalitions.' In *Ballots and Breakups: The Games Politicians Play* (Bloomsbury India, 2019), p. 75

61 Eminent Parliamentarians Monograph Series: Dr Syama Prasad Mookerjee, (Lok Sabha Secretariat, 1990). Available at: https://eparlib. nic.in/bitstream/123456789/58670/1/Eminent_Parliamentarians_Series_ Syama_Prasad_Mookerjee.pdf

62 Thomas Blom Hansen, *The Saffron Wave: Democracy and Hindu Nationalism in Modern India*, (Princeton University Press, 1999), p. 129

63 'JanSangh President'. Deendayalupadhyay.org

64 Deendayal Upadhyay, *Political Diary* (Suruchi Prakashan, 2014), pp. 9–13

65 Ibid, p. 10

66   Deendayal Upadhyay, 'Lecture II' in Integral Humanism (23 April 1965). Available at: http://www.chitrakoot.org/download/IntegralHumanism. pdf (accessed on 7 April 2020)

67   Deendayal Upadhyaya, 'Lecture IV' in Integral Humanism (25 April 1965). Available at: http://www.chitrakoot.org/download/IntegralHumanism. pdf (accessed on 7 April 2020)

68   Ullekh N.P., *The Untold Vajpayee: Politician and Paradox* (Penguin Random House India, 2016), p. 62

69   Preeti Trivedi, *Architect of A Philosophy* (Bhartiya Sahitya Sangrah, 2017), p. 82, footnote 79

70   Shiv Lal, *Indian Elections Since Independence*, Volume 2 (Election Archives, 1972), p. 21

71   *Bharatiya Jana Sangh (1952–1980) Vol. 6: History of Jana Sangh* (Bharatiya Janata Party, 2005), pp. 307–308

72   Various statistical reports on Legislative Assembly Elections, Election Commission of India, New Delhi. Available at: https://eci.gov.in/ statistical-report/statistical-reports/.

73   Ullekh N.P., *The Untold Vajpayee: Politician and Paradox* (Penguin Random House India, 2016), p. 51

74   Ibid

75   Ibid

76   Erik S. Herron, Robert Pekkanen and Matthew Soberg Shugart, *The Oxford Handbook of Electoral Systems* (Oxford University Press, 2018), p. 708

77   Sujit Choudhry, Madhav Khosla and Pratap Bhanu Mehta, *The Oxford Handbook of the Indian Constitution* (1st edition, OUP Oxford, 2016), p. 417

78   Ajay Singh, 'Atal Bihari Vajpayee's Most Profound Creative Disruptions in Indian Politics: A camaraderie that built a legacy', *Firstpost*, 21 August 2018. Available at: https://www.Firstpost.com/politics/atal-bihari-vajpayees-most-profound-creative-disruptions-in-indian-politics-a-camaraderie-that-built-a-legacy-5010681.html

79   'Performance of Political Parties' in *Statistical Report on General Elections, 1971 to the Fifth Lok Sabha Volume I*, Election Commission of India, New Delhi. Available at: https://eci.gov.in/statistical-report/statistical-reports/.

80   Christophe Jaffrelot, *The Hindu Nationalist Movement and Indian Politics: 1925 to the 1990s* (Penguin Books, 1999), p. 236

81   Madhu Dandavate, *Jayaprakash Narayan: Struggle with Values: A Centenary Tribute* (Allied Publishers Pvt. Ltd., 2002), p. 44

82 Upendra Mishra, *Caste and Politics in India: A Study of Political Turmoil in Bihar, 1967–1977* (Uppal Publishing House, 1986), p. 335

83 Lalan Tiwari, *Democracy and Dissent (A Case Study of the Bihar Movement, 1974–75)* (Mittal Publications, 1987), pp. 33–34

84 Coomi Kapoor, *The Emergency: A Personal History* (Penguin Books Limited, 2016), p. 190

85 D.R. Mankekar and Kamla Mankekar, *Decline and Fall of Indira Gandhi* (Vision Books, 1977), p. 15

86 Shaan Kashyap, 'Here is what Balasaheb Deoras wrote to Indira Gandhi during Emergency', *Organiser*, June 26, 2018. https://www.*Organiser*.org/Encyc/2018/6/26/-Shri-Balasaheb-Deoras-wrote-to-Smt-Indira-Gandhi-.html

87 L.K. Advani, *A Prisoner's Scrap-Book* (Prabhat Prakashan, 2016), pp. 255–256

88 'Performance of Political Parties' in *Statistical Report on General Elections, 1977 to the Sixth Lok Sabha Volume I*, Election Commission of India, New Delhi. Available at: https://eci.gov.in/statistical-report/statistical-reports/.

89 'Performance of Political Parties' in *Statistical Report on General Elections, 1977 to the Sixth Lok Sabha Volume I*, Election Commission of India, New Delhi. Available at: https://eci.gov.in/statistical-report/statistical-reports/.

90 *Bharatiya Jana Sangh (1952–1980) Vol. 6: History of Jana Sangh* (Bharatiya Janata Party, 2005), p. 196

91 S.H. Patil, *The Constitution, Government and Politics in India* (Vikas Publishing House, 2016), p. 141

92 *Bharatiya Jana Sangh (1952–1980) Vol. 6: History of Jana Sangh* (Bharatiya Janata Party, 2005), pp. 451–452

Chapter 3: A Party Is Born

1 G.G. Mirchandani, *320 Million Judges: Analysis of 1977 Lok Sabha and State Elections in India* (New Delhi: Abhinav Publications, 2003). pp. 176–191

2 Janak Raj Jai, *Presidents of India 1950–2003* (Regency Publications, 2003), p. 141

3 'Constitutional Government and Democracy in India', in *Union Executive: Prime Minister*. ed. Abhay Prasad Singh and Krishna Murari (Pearson India Education Services Pvt Ltd, 2019), p. 190

4 Shanti Bhushan, 'The Prime Minister and his Senior Colleagues Wait for Each Other's Death with Bated Breath' in *Courting Destiny: A Memoir* (Penguin India, 2008), pp. 190–191

5 G.G. Mirchandani, *320 Million Judges: Analysis of 1977 Lok Sabha and State Elections in India* (Abhinav Publications, New Delhi, 2003), p. 243

6 Shanti Bhushan, 'The Prime Minister and his Senior Colleagues Wait for Each Other's Death with Bated Breath' in *Courting Destiny: A Memoir* (Penguin India, 2008), p. 190

7 Mohammad Yunus, *Persons, Passions & Politics* (Vikas Publishing House, 1980), p. 317

8 Harsh Singh Lohit, *Chronology & Milestones in the Life of Charan Singh 23 December 1902 – 29 May 1987* (Chaudhary Charan Singh Archive, Harsh Singh Lohit, 2018), p. 12

9 Rajmata Vijayaraje Scindia and Mridula Sinha, *Royal to Public Life* (Prabhat Prakashan, 2016), p. 247

10 Ajaz Ashraf, 'Lesson from 1979 Janata Party Fiasco: Coalitions are Sunk by National Parties not Regional Ones', *Scroll*, 12 February 2019. Available at: https://Scroll.in/article/912542/modi-may-mock-opposition-alliances-but-janata-party-fiasco-in-1979-underlines-a-different-reality (accessed on 6 October 2020)

11 A.G. Noorani, 'The Crisis of India's Party System', *Asian Affairs: An American Review*, 7:4 (1980), p. 243

12 Mahendra Prasad Singh, *Split in a Predominant Party: The Indian National Congress in 1969* (New Delhi: Abhinav Publications, 1981), pp. 8–9

13 A.G. Noorani, 'Appointing a PM', *The Frontline*, 3 July 2009. Available at: https://frontline.thehindu.com/books/article30187407.ece (accessed on 5 October 2020).

14 Madhu Dandavate, '1977: Victory of Democracy', in *Dialogue with Life*, (Allied Publishers (P) Ltd., New Delhi, 2005), p. 92

15 A.G. Noorani, 'Appointing a PM', *Frontline*, 3 July 2009. Available at: https://frontline.thehindu.com/books/article30187407.ece (accessed on 5 October 2020)

16 Ananth V. Krishna, *India Since Independence: Making Sense of Indian Politics* (Pearson Education, 2010), p. 231

17 Ibid, pp. 232–233

18 Shanti Bhushan, 'The Prime Minister and his Senior Colleagues Wait for Each Other's Death with Bated Breath' in *Courting Destiny: A Memoir* (Penguin India, 2008), p. 194

19 'Forty Years Ago, August 21, 1979: Charan Govt Resigns', *Indian Express*, 21 August 2019. Available at: https://indianexpress.com/article/opinion/

editorials/forty-years-ago-august-21-1979-charan-govt-resigns-5921778/ (accessed on 5 October 2020).

20 S. Venkata Narayan and Prabhu Chawla, 'I wish Harijans had become Brahmins: Jagjivan Ram', *India Today*, September 15, 1979. Available at: https://www.indiatoday.in/magazine/interview/story/19790915-i-wish-harijans-had-become-brahmins-jagjivan-ram-822581-2014-02-21

21 'Performance of Political Parties' in *Statistical Report on General Elections, 1980 to the Seventh Lok Sabha Volume I*, Election Commission of India, New Delhi. Available at: https://eci.gov.in/statistical-report/statistical-reports/.

22 M.R. Masani, 'India's Second Revolution', *Asian Affairs: An American Review* (1977), p. 19. DOI: 10.1080/00927678.1977.10554000

23 Peu Ghosh, *Indian Government and Politics* (PHI Learning, 2017), p. 325

24 'Performance of Political Parties' in *Statistical Report on General Elections, 1980 to the Seventh Lok Sabha Volume I*, Election Commission of India, New Delhi. Available at: https://eci.gov.in/statistical-report/statistical-reports/.

25 Jyotirindra Das Gupta. 'The Janata Phase: Reorganization and Redirection in Indian Politics.' *Asian Survey* 19, no. 4 (1979), pp. 390–403 (accessed 23 June 2021). DOI:10.2307/2643859.

26 Vijay Kumar Malhotra and J.C. Jaitli, *Evolution of BJP, Party Documents Vol. 10* (Bharatiya Janata Party, 2006), p. 1

27 Ibid, p. 242

28 Ibid

29 Avijit Ghosh, 'How Ayodhya Changed India's Politics', *Times of India*, 10 November 2019. Available at: https://timesofindia.indiatimes.com/india/how-the-opening-of-a-lock-became-the-key-to-the-rise-of-indias-right/articleshow/71987040.cms?intenttarget=no

30 Imtiaz Ahmad, 'India's Secular Journey', *Sociological Bulletin* (2017), Vol 66, Issue 3, pp. 257–270. DOI:10.1177/0038022917726933

31 V. Krishna Ananth, *India Since Independence: Making Sense of Indian Politics* (Pearson Education, 2010), p. 189

32 Shiv Lal, *The Election Archives*, Issues 41–52 (1980), p. 115

33 A.G. Noorani, *The RSS and the BJP: A Division of Labour* (LeftWord Books, 2000), p. 34

34 *Bharatiya Jana Sangh (1952–1980) Vol: 6: History of Jana Sangh* (Bharatiya Janata Party, 2005), p. 500

35 Ibid, p. 499

36 V. Krishna Ananth, *India Since Independence: Making Sense of Indian Politics* (Pearson Education, 2010), p. 239

37 *Statistical Report on General Elections, 1977 to the Legislative Assembly of Madhya Pradesh*, Election Commission of India, New Delhi. Available at: https://eci.gov.in/statistical-report/statistical-reports/.

38 Vijay Kumar Malhotra and J.C. Jaitli, *Evolution of BJP, Party Documents, Vol. 10* (Bharatiya Janata Party, 2006), p. 1

39 *Indian Herald*, 26 June 1975, p. 1

40 Vijay Kumar Malhotra and J.C. Jaitli, *Evolution Of BJP, Party Documents, Vol. 10* (Bharatiya Janata Party, 2006), p. 3

41 Pratap Chandra Swain, *Bharatiya Janata Party: Profile and Performance* (APH Publishing Corporation, 2001), p. 90

42 The phrase *sarva dharma sama bhava* translates to 'equal treatment by the state towards all religions' and also conveys a pluralistic approach towards religion.

43 Supra note 41

44 Chagla, a respected liberal lawyer and jurist, was chief justice of the Bombay High Court from 1947 to 1958 and a judge of the International Court of Justice at The Hague from 1957 to 1960. Chagla was minister of education (1963–66), leader of the Indian delegation to the United Nations Security Council during debates on the disputed region of Kashmir (1964–65), and minister for external affairs (1966–67). While serving under Prime Minister Indira Gandhi in 1966–67, Chagla became highly critical of her increasingly authoritarian government. Available at: https://www.britannica.com/biography/M-C-Chagla

45 'The Challenge of 1981', *Times of India*, 18 January 1981.

46 Vijay Kumar Malhotra and J.C. Jaitli, *Evolution of BJP, Party Documents, Vol. 10* (Bharatiya Janata Party, 2006), p. 3

47 Mahatma Gandhi authored *Hind Swaraj*, a small book of 30,000 words in Gujarati in the year 1909, which was later translated to English. The three central themes in the book were colonial imperialism, industrial capitalism, and rationalist materialism. The book mainly describes Gandhi's philosophy of life which focuses on the concepts of self-rule and political and economic freedom. Among other things, Gandhi shares his philosophy on a range of topics including, Indian civilization, Satyagraha, Swadeshi etc. Available at: https://www.mkgandhi.org/articles/hind%20swaraj.htm

48 Vijay Kumar Malhotra and J.C. Jaitli, *Evolution of BJP, Party Documents, Vol. 10* (Bharatiya Janata Party, 2006), p. 20

49 Ibid, p. 135

50 Statistical Reports, Election Commission of India. Available at: https://eci. gov.in/statistical-report/statistical-reports/#collapse

51 Ajit Roy, 'Clear Polarisation', *Economic and Political Weekly*, Vol. No.17, No. 22 (1982), p. 886. Available at: http://www.jstor.org/stable/4370952

52 Jayanta Kumar Ray, *Aspects of India's International relations 1700 to 2000: South Asia and the World* (New Delhi: Pearson, 2007), p. 484

53 Gordon Kerr, 'The Making of a Nation, Indira Gandhi's Return to Power', in *A Short History of India: From the Earliest Civilisations* and Myriad Kingdoms, *to Today's Economic Powerhouse* (Pocket Essentials, 2017), pp. 171–172

54 Sumit Ganguly, 'The Crisis of Indian Secularism', *Journal of Democracy 14,* No. 4 (2003), p. 16

55 Zoya Hasan, *Congress After Indira: Policy, Power, Political Change (1984 -2009)* (Oxford University Press, 2014), p. 11

56 Bharatiya Jana Sangh, National Executive in New Delhi on 14 November 1984.

57 'The Making of a Nation, Indira Gandhi's Return to Power', in *A Short History of India: From the Earliest Civilisations to Today's Economic Powerhouse*, ed. Gordon Kerr (Pocket Essentials, 2017), p. 172

58 F. Tomasson Jannuzi, *India in Transition: Issues of Political Economy in a Plural Society* (Routledge, 2018), p. 29

59 'Watch: Had late former PM Rajiv Gandhi 'justified' the 1984 anti-Sikh riots?', *India Today,* 20 November 2015. Available at: https://www. indiatoday.in/fyi/story/watch-had-late-pm-rajiv-gandhi-justified-the-1984-anti-sikh-riots-273632-2015-11-20

60 'Performance of Political Parties' in *Statistical Report on General Elections, 1984 to the Eighth Lok Sabha Volume I,* Election Commission of India, New Delhi. Available at: https://eci.gov.in/statistical-report/statistical-reports/.

61 Pratap Chandra Swain, *Bharatiya Janata Party: Profile and Performance* (APH Publishing Corporation, 2001), p. 198

62 'Performance of Political Parties' in *Statistical Report on General Elections, 1984 to the Eighth Lok Sabha Volume I,* Election Commission of India, New Delhi. Available at: https://eci.gov.in/statistical-report/statistical-reports/.

63 Vijay Kumar Malhotra and J.C. Jaitli, *Evolution of BJP, Party Documents, Vol. 10* (Bharatiya Janata Party, 2006), p. 17

64 Vijay Kumar Malhotra and J.C. Jaitli, *Evolution of BJP, Party Documents, Vol. 10* (Bharatiya Janata Party, 2006), pp. 17–18

65 Shiv Lal, *Election Activity in India 1993, Volume 2* (Election Archives, 1996), p. 117

66 Vijay Kumar Malhotra and J.C. Jaitli, *Evolution of BJP, Party Documents, Vol. 10* (Bharatiya Janata Party, 2006), p. 19

67 Pratap Chandra Swain, *Bharatiya Janata Party: Profile and Performance* (APH Publishing Corporation, 2001), p. 90

68 Zoya Hassan, *Congress After Indira: Policy, Power, Political Change (1984 -2009)* (Oxford University Press, 2014), p. 15

69 Ibid , p. 2

70 Ibid p. 16

71 For detailed facts of the case, see 'Report of the Joint Committee to Inquire into the Bofors Contract' (Lok Sabha Secretariat, 1988) pp. 4–23. Available at: http://loksabhaph.nic.in/writereaddata/InvestigativeJPC/Bofors.pdf (accessed on 7 October 2020)

72 Ibid. pp. 189–192

73 The AIDMK is a regional party operating in the southern Indian state of Tamil Nadu. The Rajya Sabha is the Upper House of the Parliament of India.

74 T.N. Ninan, 'Bofors inquiry: Joint Parliamentary Committee report reveals more than it conceals', *India Today*, 15 May 1988. Available at: https://www.indiatoday.in/magazine/special-report/story/19880515-bofors-inquiry-joint-parliamentary-committee-report-reveals-more-than-it-conceals-797272-1988-05-15 (accessed on 7 October 2020)

75 Prabhu Chawla, 'HDW submarine deal assumes centre stage again. An exclusive inside story', *India Today*, 15 March 1990. Available at: https://www.indiatoday.in/magazine/special-report/story/19900315-hdw-submarine-deal-assumes-centre-stage-again.-an-exclusive-inside-story-812418-1990-03-15 (accessed on 7 October 2020)

76 V.P. Singh, 'Walk the Talk with V.P. Singh', *NDTV*, July 2005, (Shekhar Gupta, Interviewer). Retrieved from: https://www.NDTV.com/video/shows/walk-the-talk/walk-the-talk-with-vp-singh-aired-july-2005-303898 (accessed on 17 April 2020)

Chapter 4: Decade of Growth (1986–1996)

1 Zoya Hasan, 'Minority Identity, Muslim Women Bill Campaign and the Political Process', *Economic and Political Weekly* (7 January 1989), Vol. 24, No. 1, pp. 44–50

2   Zoya Hasan, Congress After Indira: Policy, Power, Political Change
    (1984–2009) (Oxford University Press, 2014), p. 17
3   Zoya Hasan, *Congress After Indira: Policy, Power, Political Change
    (1984–2009)* (Oxford University Press, 2014), p. 17
4   See Supreme Court of India, *Mohd. Ahmed Khan vs Shah Bano Begum.*
    AIR 1985 SC 945.
5   These included Maulana Abul Lais, Emir of the Jamaat-e-Islami-Hind;
    Maulana Asad Madani, president of Jamiat-ul-Ulema-e-Hind; Maulana
    Abul Hasan Ali Hasani Nadwi, president of All India Muslim Personal
    Law Board; Maulana Obaidullah Khan Azmi, founder of All-India
    Muslim Personal Law Conference; Maulana Ziaur Rahman Ansari, Union
    Minister of State for Environment; Najma Heptullah, deputy chairperson
    of Rajya Sabha, Begum Abida Ahmed, prominent leader of Congress Syed
    Shahabuddin, Janata Party Lok Sabha member, Dr. Sharifunnisa Ansari,
    head of the department of Persian Studies, Osmania University, Ibrahim
    Sulaiman Sait, president of Indian Union Muslim League (IUML), and
    Gulam Muhammad Banatwala, general secretary of IUML.
6   Fasihur Rahman, 'Mired in Controversy', *Pioneer,* 24 July 2019.
    Available at: https://www.dailypioneer.com/2019/columnists/mired-in-
    controversy.html (accessed on 17 April 2020)
7   Shekhar Gupta, Inderjit Badhwar and Farzand Ahmed Gupta, 'Shah
    Bano Judgement Renders Muslims a Troubled Community, Torn by
    an Internal Rift', *India Today,* 31 January 1986. Available at: https://
    www.indiatoday.in/magazine/cover-story/story/19860131-shah-bano-
    judgement-renders-muslims-a-troubled-community-torn-by-an-
    internal-rift-800516-1986-01-31 (accessed on 17 April 2020)
8   Bipan Chandra, Aditya Mukherjee and Mridula Mukherjee, *India Since
    Independence* (Penguin Books, 2008), p. 362
9   SC verdict; Full text of Ayodhya verdict, The Hindu, 9 November 2019,
    Available   at: https://www.thehindu.com/news/resources/full-text-of-
    ayodhya-verdict/article29929786.ece
10 Charles B. Strozier et al., *The Fundamentalist Mindset: Psychological
    Perspectives on Religion, Violence, and History* (United Kingdom: Oxford
    University Press USA, 2010), p. 209
11 S.P. Udayakumar, 'Historicizing Myth and Mythologizing History: The
    'Ram Temple' Drama', *Social Scientist,* (August 1997), Vol No. 25 7/8,
    p. 14
12 'Role of Arun Nehru, Rajiv in Opening Masjid Ignored', *The Hindu,* 25
    November 2009. Available at: https://www.thehindu.com/news/national/

Role-of-Arun-Nehru-Rajiv-in-opening-masjid-ignored/article16894059. ece (accessed on 17 April 2020)

13 SC verdict; Full text of Ayodhya verdict, The Hindu, 9 November 2019, Available at: https://www.thehindu.com/news/resources/full-text-of-ayodhya-verdict/article29929786.ece

14 Vinay Sitapati, *Jugalbandi: The BJP Before Modi* (Penguin Random House, 2020), p. 138

15 BJP National Executive Meeting, Resolutions 9 -11, 1989 (Palampur), pp. 14–17

16 Ibid, pp. 306–307

17 *BJP Political Resolutions*, (Bharatiya Janata Party 2004), p. 306

18 Zoya Hasan, *Congress After Indira: Policy, Power, Political Change (1984 -2009)* (Oxford University Press, 2014), p. 19

19 V.P. Singh, 'Walk the Talk with V.P. Singh Singh', *NDTV*, July 2005 (Shekhar Gupta, Interviewer). Retrieved from: https://www.*NDTV*. com/video/shows/walk-the-talk/walk-the-talk-with-vp-singh-aired-july-2005-303898 (accessed on 17 April 2020)

20 Prabhu Chawla, 'HDW Submarine Deal Assumes Centre Stage Again. An Exclusive Inside Story', *India Today,* 15 March 1990. Available at: https://www.indiatoday.in/magazine/special-report/story/19900315-hdw-submarine-deal-assumes-centre-stage-again.-an-exclusive-inside-story-812418-1990-03-15 (accessed on 7 October 2020).

21 Fickett, L.P., 'The Rise and Fall of the Janata Dal', *Asian Survey* (1993), 33 (12), p. 1151

22 Ibid p. 1152

23 U.N. Gupta, *Indian Parliamentary Democracy* (Atlantic Publishers & Dist., 2003), p. 124

24 Ibid p. 11

25 'Performance of Political Parties' in *Statistical Report' on General Elections, 1989 to the Ninth Lok Sabha Volume I,* Election Commission of India, New Delhi. Available at: https://eci.gov.in/statistical-report/statistical-reports/.

26 For a detailed discussion on the formation of the National Front government in 1989, see, U.N. Gupta, *Indian Parliamentary Democracy* (Atlantic Publishers & Dist., 2003), p. 14–17

27 Rajiv Gandhi, 'Breaking Up My Country', *Outlook,* 8 June 2006. Available at: https://www.*Outlook*india.com/website/story/breaking-up-my-country/231503

28 Nilanjan Mukopadhyay, *The RSS: Icons of The Indian Right* (Tranquebar, 2019), pp. 284–285

29 Vijat Chauthaiwale, 'Deoras: The Man Behind BJP's Rise', *Deccan Chronicle*, 9 June 2016. Available at: https://www.deccanchronicle.com/opinion/op-ed/090616/deoras-the-man-behind-bjp-s-rise.html

30 VHP was set up in 1964 by M.S. Golwalkar and S.S. Apte. During the setting up of VHP, the RSS adopted a slogan: *Na Hindu patito bhavet* (no Hindu shall remain untouchable).

31 'Pseudo-Secularism has Weakened unity: Advani', *The Hindu*, 25 December 1990.

32 Andy Marino, *Narendra Modi: A Political Biography* (HarperCollins, 2014), pp. 75–76

33 'Ayodhya Yatra not against Muslims: Advani', *Hindustan Times*, 24 January 2009. Available at: https://www.hindustantimes.com/india/ayodhya-yatra-not-against-muslims-advani/story-mkAV9ocqVwkMuMT5wfBGFO.html (accessed on 19 April 2020)

34 Zoya Hasan, 'Gender, Religion and Democratic Politics in India.' *Third World Quarterly 31*, no. 6 (2010), pp. 939–54. Available at: http://www.jstor.org/stable/27896590.

35 Advani's *rath yatra* in 1990 received overwhelming press coverage. As time passed, newspapers, like *Amar Ujala*, increased the number of pages devoted to covering the yatra. Since 13 October 1990, *Indian Express* regularly carried the rath yatra on its front page. Many journalists opined that the response to the yatra was dream-like, unimaginable, matchless and would give a strong base to the party. A *Times of India* report, dated 16 October 1990, described the rath yatra as religious bhakti and not communal shakti. Rajdeep Sardesai describes his experience covering the rath yatra, 'As a young reporter tracking L.K. Advani on his journey to stardom, I was struck with the finesse with which the BJP handled the travelling media. Every little detail of the yatra was meticulously planned and the journalists were provided the kind of professional support which would have done a corporate communication office proud.'

36 Rajdeep Sardesai, 'Consumed by the Media', *Deccan Herald*, 3 September 2009. Available at: https://www.deccanherald.com/content/23244/consumed-media.html (accessed on 19 April 2020)

37 Barbara Crossette, 'India's Cabinet Falls as Premier Loses Confidence Vote, by 142–346, and Quits', *New York Times*, 8 November 1990. Available at: https://www.nytimes.com/1990/11/08/world/india-s-cabinet-falls-as-premier-loses-confidence-vote-by-142-346-and-quits.html

38 'Performance of Political Parties' in *Statistical Report on General Elections, 1991 to the Tenth Lok Sabha Volume I*, Election Commission of India,

New Delhi. Available at: https://eci.gov.in/statistical-report/statistical-reports/.

39 See Table 2 (Lok Sabha Elections of 1991), Chapter 4, p. 66

40 Karsevak is derived from the Sanskrit words *kar* (hand) and *sevak* (servant). A karsevak is someone who offers services for free to a religious cause.

41 Shashi Shekhar, 'We Fall, Get Up and March Forward', *Livemint,* 12 December 2016. Available at: https://www.Livemint.com/Opinion/v3i0ojYgZQhHh1DLlhb0yO/We-fall-get-up-and-march-forward.html

42 Aviral Virk, 'Ayodhya Part 6: The Making of "Mulla Mulayam"', *Quint,* 11 November 2017. Available at: https://www.thequint.com/videos/short-doqs/ayodhya-deqoded-part-6-the-making-of-mullah-mulayam

43 'Decision to Order Firing in Ayodhya Painful: Mulayam Singh Yadav', *Times of India*, 28 August 2016. Available at:https://timesofindia.indiatimes.com/city/lucknow/Decision-to-order-firing-in-Ayodhya-painful-Mulayam-Singh-Yadav/articleshow/53892287.cms

44 Shriram Janmabhumi Mukti Andolan 1. Available at: https://web.archive.org/web/20150321180231/http://vhp.org/shriram-janmabhumi-mukti-andolan/mov1-shriram-janmabhumi-mukti-andolan

45 *Statistical Report on General Elections, 1991 to the Legislative Assembly of Uttar Pradesh*, Election Commission of India, New Delhi. Available at: https://eci.gov.in/statistical-report/statistical-reports/.

46 'All 32 Acquitted in Babri Demolition Case due to "lack of proof"; Defence Claims Singhal, Advani Tried to Save Structure', *Firstpost,* 30 September 2020. Available at: https://www.Firstpost.com/india/babri-masjid-verdict-all-32-accused-including-advani-joshi-acquitted-cbi-court-observes-incident-not-pre-planned-8865681.html

47 Rajnath Singh's speech in Lok Sabha, Available at https://www.youtube.com/watch?v=GZ-HIIqNofk

48 Arun Jaitley's speech in Rajya Sabha, Available at https://www.youtube.com/watch?v=Zpt-DWciNwU

49 Zoya Hasan, *Congress After Indira: Policy, Power, Political Change (1984–2009)* (Oxford University Press, 2014), p. 33

50 Harivansh and Ravi Dutt Bajpai, *Chandra Shekhar—The Last Icon of Ideological Politics* (Rupa Publications India, 2019), p. 216

51 'How the Chandra Sekhar Govt in 1990 Came on the Cusp of Solving the Ayodhya Dispute', *Week,* 9 November 2019. Available at: https://www.

theweek.in/news/india/2019/11/09/how-the-chandra-sekhar-govt-1990-came-on-the-cusp-resolving-ayodhya-dispute.html

52 L.K. Advani 'The 1980s: the BJP's Phoenix-Like Rise', in *My Country My Life* (Rupa Publications, 2008), p. 320

53 Vinay Sitapati, *Half Lion: How PV Narasimha Rao Transformed India* (Penguin Books India, 2016), pp. 85–86

54 Supreme Court of India. P.V. Narasimha Rao Vs. State (Cbi/Spe), AIR 1998 SC 229

55 'Chapter 11: The Balance of Payments Crisis of 1991' in RBI History Volume 4 (1981–1997). Available at: https://www.rbi.org.in/scripts/RHvol-4.aspx

56 Vinay Sitapati, *Half Lion: How PV Narasimha Rao Transformed India* (Penguin Books India, 2016), p. 106

57 Montek S. Ahluwalia, 'The 1991 Reforms: How Home-grown Were They?', *Economics and Political Weekly*, Vol. 51, Issue No. 29 (2016)

58 36 percent of the Indian population was below the poverty line in 1991. By 2011, this share was down to about twenty-one percent; RBI Publications. Available at: https://www.rbi.org.in/scripts/PublicationsView.aspx?id=16603

59 L.K. Advani 'The Entry and Exit of Two Prime Ministers in Two Years', in *My Country My Life* (Rupa Publications, 2008), p. 468

60 Andy Marino, 'The Yatra to Power', in Narendra Modi: A Political Biography (HarperCollins, 2014), pp. 77–78

61 *Statistical Report on General Elections, 1995 to the Legislative Assembly of Maharashtra*, Election Commission of India, New Delhi. Available at: https://eci.gov.in/statistical-report/statistical-reports/.

62 *Statistical Report on General Elections, 1995 to the Legislative Assembly of Bihar*, Election Commission of India, New Delhi. Available at: https://eci.gov.in/statistical-report/statistical-reports/.

63 *Statistical Report on General Elections, 1995 to the Legislative Assembly of Gujarat*, Election Commission of India, New Delhi. Available at: https://eci.gov.in/statistical-report/statistical-reports/.

64 *Statistical Report on General Elections, 1990 to the Legislative Assembly of Gujarat, Election Commission of India*, New Delhi. Available at: https://eci.gov.in/statistical-report/statistical-reports/.

65 *Statistical Report on General Elections, 1995 to the Legislative Assembly of Gujarat*, Election Commission of India, New Delhi. Available at: https://eci.gov.in/statistical-report/statistical-reports/.

66 Andy Marino, *Narendra Modi: A Political Biography* (HarperCollins, 2014), pp. 86–87

67 Andy Marino, *Narendra Modi: A Political Biography* (HarperCollins, 2014), pp. 89

68 Peu Ghosh, *Indian Government and Politics* (PHI Learning, 2017), p. 38

69 Sunil K. Choudhary, *The Changing Face of Parties and Party Systems: A Study of Israel and India* (Singapore: Palgrave Macmillan, 2017), pp. 158–59

70 L.K. Advani 'The Entry and Exit of Two Prime Ministers in Two Years', in *My Country My Life* (Rupa Publications, 2008), pp. 472–473

71 Party Document, Election Manifesto 1991, Page 341

72 N.K. Singh, 'Advani Gambles on Rath Yatra as Party Tries to Repair Hawala Damage in Run-Up to Elections', *India Today*, 31 March 1996.

73 Dev Goswami, 'When Atal Bihari Vajpayee Showed the World How to Resign in Style', *India Today*, 17 August 2018. Available at: https://www.indiatoday.in/india/story/atal-bihari-vajpayee-parliament-trust-vote-1996-speech-resign-1316838-2018-08-17

74 'Performance of Political Parties' in *Statistical Report on General Elections, 1996 to the Eleventh Lok Sabha Volume I*, Election Commission of India, New Delhi. Available at: https://eci.gov.in/statistical-report/statistical-reports/.

Chapter 5: BJP in Government (1995–2004)

1 The thirteen parties were Janata Dal, Samajwadi Party, DMK, Telugu Desam Party, CPI, CPI(M), Ahom Gana Parishad, All India Indira Congress (Tiwari), Tamil Maanila Congress, Forward Bloc, Socialist Party, National Conference and Maharashtrawadi Gomantak Party

2 Sumit Mitra, 'Sitaram Kesri Pulls Down UF Govt, Deve Gowda Goes Down Fighting', *India Today*, 30 April 1997. Available at: https://www.indiatoday.in/magazine/coverstory/story/19970430-sitaram-kesri-pulls-down-uf-govt-deve-gowda-goes-down-fighting831321-1997-04-30 (accessed on 22 April 2020).

3 I.K. Gujral, *Matters of Discretion: An Autobiography* (Hay House India, 2011), p. 386

4 'Keeping Politics on Top', *Economic and Political Weekly*, Issue No. 15, Vol. 32, 12 April 1997. Available at: https://www.epw.in/journal/1997/15/uncategorised/keeping-politics-top.html?0=ip_login_no_cache%3D02bd73bd0d882de96eebb226e2159a89

5   Zafar Agha, 'Hung assembly verdict in UP sends major parties into tailspin', *India Today*, 31 October 1996. Available at: https://www. indiatoday.in/magazine/nation/story/19961031- hung-assembly-verdict-in-up-sends-major-parties-into-tailspin-834040-1996-10-31

6   Venkitesh Ramakrishnan Praveen Swami, 'A Crisis Defused', *Frontline*, 1 November 1997. Available at: https://frontline.thehindu.com/other/article30160288.ece

7   Harinder Baweja and Farzand Ahmed, 'K.R. Narayanan Returns Cabinet Resolution Seeking Imposition of President's Rule in Bihar', *India Today*, 5 October 1998. Available at: https://www.indiatoday.in/magazine/cover-story/story/19981005-k.r.-narayanan-returnscabinet-resolution-seeking-imposition-of-presidents-rule-in-bihar-827153-1998-10-05

8   'Cabinet Reverses Decision on President's Rule in UP', *Rediff*, 23 October 1997. Available at: https://m.*Rediff*.com/news/oct/22up.htm

9   *Statistical Report on General Elections, 1996 to the Legislative Assembly of Uttar Pradesh*, Election Commission of India, *New Delhi*. Available at: https://eci.gov.in/statistical-report/statistical-reports/.

10 R. Keerthana, 'Rajiv's death – a revisit.' *The Hindu*, 21 March 2014

11 Prabhu Chawla, 'Rajiv Gandhi Killing: Jain Commission Report Indicts DMK for Colluding with LTTE', *India Today*, 17 November 1997. Available at: https://www.indiatoday.in/magazine/cover-story/story/19971117-rajiv-gandhi-killing-jaincommission-report-indicts-dmk-for-colluding-with-ltte-832134-1997-11-17

12 S. Gupta, 'His decency set him apart—why we can't forget I.K. Gujral, India's Truly Accidental PM', *ThePrint*, 4 December 2019. Available at: https://theprint.in/opinion/the-factivist/hisdecency-set-him-apart-why-we-cant-forget-ik-gujral-indias-truly-accidental-pm/329803/ (accessed on 22 April 2020).

13 I.K. Gujral, *Matters of Discretion: An Autobiography* (Hay House India, 2011), p. 464

14 'Delhi High Court Quashes Hawala Charges Against Advani, Shukla', *Rediff*. Available at: https://m.*Rediff*.com/news/apr/08hawala.htm

15 'Delhi High Court Quashes Hawala Charges Against Advani, Shukla', *Rediff*.

16 *The Yatra's Raison D'Etre* in 'Shri L K Advani – Chairman BJP Parliamentary Party'. Available at: https://www.bjpchandigarh.org/shri-lk-advani/

17 Vijay Kumar Malhotra and J.C. Jaitli, *Evolution of BJP, Party Documents, Vol. 10* (Bharatiya Janata Party, 2006), pp. 40–41

18   Vijay Kumar Malhotra and J.C. Jaitli, *Evolution of BJP, Party Documents, Vol. 10* (Bharatiya Janata Party, 2006), p. 40. Available at: http://library. bjp.org/jspui/bitstream/123456789/275/2/Evolution%20of%20BJP%20 -%20Full.pdf

19   Author's calculations based on *Statistical Report on General Elections - 1996 & 1998* https://eci.gov.in/statistical-report/statistical-reports/.

20   'Performance of Political Parties' in *Statistical Report on General Elections, 1998 To The Twelfth Lok Sabha Volume I*, Election Commission of India, New Delhi. Available at: https://eci.gov.in/statistical-report/statistical-reports/.

21   Archis Mohan, 'George Fernandes: The Trade Unionist They Thought would be the PM', *Business Standard*, 29 January 2019.

22   Nistula Hebbar, 'George Fernandes: The Giant-Killer Who Straddled Multiple Identities', *The Hindu*, 29 January 2019. Available at: https://www. thehindu.com/news/national/george-fernandes-obituary-1930-2019/ article26120571.ece

23   Bidyut Chakrabarty, *Forging Power: Coalition Politics in India* (New Delhi: Oxford University Press, 2006), p. 196

24   Atal Bihari Vajpayee's Lok Sabha speech. Available at: http://164.100.47.194/ Loksabha/Debates/Result12.aspx?dbsl=248

25   Press Information Bureau Archives. Available at: http://pibarchive.nic.in/ archive/releases98/lyr98/l0598/PIBR110598.html

26   Summary of Annual Report of the RBI, 1998–99. Available at: https:// www.rbi.org.in/scripts/AnnualReportPublications.aspx?Id=20

27   Pami Dua and Arunima Sinha, 'East Asian Crisis and Currency Pressure: The Case of India', Centre for Development Economics Department of Economics, Delhi School of Economics (2007), Working Paper No. 158, p. 28, table 3. Available at: http://www.cdedse.org/pdf/ work158.pdf

28   Ibid p. 26, figure 7

29   Desh Gupta, 'Has India Escaped the Asian Economic Contagion?', *South Asia: Journal of South Asian Studies* (2000), 23:s1, 179–192. DOI: 10.1080/00856400008723407, p. 186, table 2. Available at: https://www. tandfonline.com/doi/pdf/10.1080/00856400008723407\

30   Supra note 27, p. 30 table 6

31   Charan D. Wadhva, 'Costs of Economic Sanctions: Aftermath of Pokhran II', *Economic and Political Weekly* (1998), Vol. 33, No. 26, pp. 1604–1607. Available at: https://www.jstor.org/stable/4406922?seq=1#metadata_ info_tab_contents

32 U.S. President Bill Clinton in Germany discussing the International Crime Control Strategy on 12 May 1998. Available at: https://clintonwhitehouse3.archives.gov/WH/New/html/19980512-6632.html

33 Summary of Annual Report of RBI, 1998–99. Available at: https://www.rbi.org.in/scripts/AnnualReportPublications.aspx?Id=20

34 These bonds were floated on 5 August 1998 with a tenure of five years.

35 Shefali Rekhi, 'Vajpayee Government Woos NRIs with Resurgent India Bonds, Makes Impressive Gains', *India Today*, 24 June 1998. Available at: https://www.indiatoday.in/magazine/economy/story/19980831-vajpayee-government-woosnris-with-resurgent-india-bonds-makes-impressive-gains-826991-1998-06-24

36 Prabhakar Sinha, 'All's Well with RIB Redemptions: SBI', *Times of India*, 13 September 2003. Available at: 24 https://timesofindia.indiatimes.com/business/india-business/Alls-well-with-RIB-redemptionsSBI/articleshow/179528.cms

37 'Moody Blues', *The Economist*, 9 July 9 1998, Asia section. Available at: https://www.economist.com/asia/1998/07/09/moody-blues

38 Amberish K. Diwanji, 'If Govt is Going to Amend its Budget, Then Where Is Its Sanctity?', *Rediff On The Net*, 12 June 1998, Budget '98 section. Available at: https://www.*Rediff*.com/budget/1998/jun/12bud4.htm

39 Rajesh Ramachandran 'Import levy will Hurt Foreign Investment, Joint Ventures', *Rediff On The Net*, 8 June 1998, Budget '98 section. Available at: https://www.Rediff.com/budget/1998/jun/08budget.htm

40 'Special Import Duty Slashed, Urea Price Hike Withdrawn', *Rediff On The Net*, 12 June 1998, Budget '98 section. Available at: https://www.*Rediff*.com/budget/1998/jun/12bud3.htm

41 Jonathan Karp, 'India Rolls Back Tariffs, Price Increases; Reversal Casts Doubt on BJP's Resolve', *WSJ*, 15 June 1998. Available at: https://www.wsj.com/articles/SB89785433616229500

42 Party Documents 1951–1972: Resolution on Economic Affairs, Volume 2 (Bharatiya Jana Sangh, 1972), p. 119

43 Party Documents 1951–1972: Resolution on Economic Affairs, Volume 2 (Bharatiya Jana Sangh, 1972), p. 174. Delhi, August 30, 1969, C.W.C, Resolution No. 69.15

44 Party Documents 1951–1972: Resolution on Economic Affairs, Volume 2 (Bharatiya Jana Sangh, 1972), pp. 15–16

45 Foreign Exchange Management Act, 1999 (FEMA). Available at: http://www.helplinelaw.com/business-law/FEMA/foreign-exchange-management-act-1999- fema.html

46 'When NDA's First PM Atal Bihari Vajpayee Lost No-Confidence Motion by 1 vote', *Hindustan Times*, 20 July 2018. Available at: https://www.hindustantimes.com/india-news/when-nda-s-first-pm-atal-bihari-vajpayee-lost-no-confidence-motion-by-1-vote/story-wIzcIvDLfNv7kbuNFmoHxI.html

47 Pranab Mukherjee, *The Coalition Years 1996–2012* (Rupa Publications India, 2017)

48 Meera Mohanty, 'Giridhar Gamang, who Voted Against Vajpayee Govt in 1999, says Pranab's Book Exonerated Him', *The Economic Times*, 16 April 2019. Available at: https://economictimes.indiatimes.com/news/politics-and-nation/giridhar-gamang-who-votedagainst-vajpayee-govt-in-1999-says-pranabs-book-exonerated-him/articleshow/68912475 (accessed on 22 April 2020)

49 PTI, 'Not me, Saifuddin Soz Responsible for Vajpayee Govt's Fall: Giridhar Gamang', *Economic Times*, 30 May 2015. Available at: https://economictimes.indiatimes.com/news/politics-andnation/not-me-saifuddin-soz-responsible-for-vajpayee-govts-fall-giridhargamang/articleshow/47482694

50 Line of Control is a de facto military control line on the border of India and Pakistan.

51 'Performance of Political Parties' in *Statistical Report on General Elections, 1999 to the Thirteenth Lok Sabha Volume I*, Election Commission of India, New Delhi. Available at: https://eci.gov.in/statistical-report/statistical-reports/.

52 M.P. Singh and Rekha Saxena, *India at the Polls: Parliamentary Elections in the Federal Phase* (New Delhi: Orient Longman Pvt. Ltd., 2003), pp. 198–99

53 L. K. Advani's 'Presidential Address to the BJP National Executive Meeting', New Delhi, Office Secretary, BJP, April 11, 2000, p. 253. Available at: http://library.bjp.org/jspui/handle/123456789/247

54 Saba Naqvi Bhaumik, 'Once Counsellor to the Cadres, New BJP President Kushabhau Thakre to be a Subservient Crutch for the Government', *India Today*, 27 April 1998. Available at: https://www.indiatoday.in/magazine/nation/story/19980427-once-counsellor-to-the-cadres-new-bjp-president-kushabhau-thakre-to-be-a-subservient-crutch-for-the-government-826250-1998-04-27

55 The South East Asian economic crisis refers to the 1997 financial contagion that began in Thailand and then spread to its neighbouring countries.

A series of currency devaluations in the region started with Thailand's decision to float its currency and remove its currency peg to the U.S. dollar.

56 Union Budget Speech 1999–2000. Available at: https://www.indiabudget.gov.in/budget_archive/ub1999-2000/bs/bs26.htm

57 David Szakonyi and Johannes Urpelainen, 'India's power sector reforms: Who reaped the benefits?', *Ideas for India*, 2 May 2014. Available at: https://www.ideasforindia.in/topics/governance/indias-power-sector-reforms-who-reaped-thebenefits.html (accessed on 2 July 2020).

58 'Resolution of the National Executive Meeting at Nagpur, 27–28 August 2000', in *Economic Resolutions Party Documents Volume 6* (Bharatiya Janata Party, 2005), pp. 86–87. Available at: http://library.bjp.org/jspui/bitstream/123456789/265/1/BJPEconomics%20Resolutions.pdf

59 'Resolution of the National Executive Meeting at Bangalore, 2–3 January 1999', in *Economic Resolutions Party Documents Volume 6* (Bharatiya Janata Party, 2005), pp. 90–91

60 'Resolution of the National Executive Meeting at Bangalore, 28–30 August 1982', in *Economic Resolutions Party Documents Volume 6* (Bharatiya Janata Party, 2005), pp. 281, 312, 341,342

61 Oliver Heath, 'Anatomy of BJP's Rise to Power: Social, Regional and Political Expansion', *Economic and Political Weekly* 34, no. 34/35 (1999), pp. 2511–517, (accessed 11 August 2021. http://www.jstor.org/stable/4408347.

62 'PM Modi turns 68; From Humble Upbringing to Leading a Country of Over 130 Crore Population; Here's All you Need to Know About the Charismatic Leader', *India TV*, 17 September 2018. Available at: https://www.indiatvnews.com/news/india-pm-modi-turns-68-from-humbleupbringing-to-leading-a-country-of-over-130-crore-population-here-s-all-you-need-to-knowabout-the-charismatic-leader-463562

63 'Vajpayee Felt Gujarat Riots Was A 'Mistake' *Deccan Herald*, 4 July 2015. Available at: https://www.deccanherald.com/national/vajpayee-felt-gujarat-riots-was-a-mistake468519.html

64 'BJP Lost in 2004 Due to Modi, Gujarat Riots: Nitish', *Rediff*.com, 25 June 2012. Available at: https://www.Rediff.com/news/slide-show/slide-show-1-bjp-lost-in2004-due-to-modi-gujarat-riots-nitish/20120620.htm

65 Atul Kohli, 'India Defies the Odds: Enduring Another Election', *Journal of Democracy* (1998), Vol. 9, No. 3. DOI: 10.1353/jod.1998.0047

66 E. Sridharan, 'Coalition Politics, Seminar', No. 437, January 1996, pp. 54–55

67   Bharatiya Janata Party 1980–2005, Presidential Speeches Part II, Party
     Document - Volume 3, p. 371
68   Shri Atal Bihari Vajpayee, Bharatiya Janata Party (2004), p. 371. Available
     at: http://lib.bjplibrary.org/jspui/handle/123456789/250
69   Julia Brummer, 'India's Negotiating Position at WTO' (paper presented
     at Dialogue on Globalization, Briefing Papers FES Geneva, November
     2005).
70   Statement by Murasoli Maran, minister of commerce and industry at the
     fourth Ministerial Conference in Doha from 9–13 November 2001.
71   'WTO: Swadeshi Team to Camp at Cancun', Rediff, 11 August 2003.
     Available at: https://www.Rediff.com/money/2003/aug/11wto.htm.
72   'Development Must be Centre Stage at Cancun', Inaugural address by Arun
     Jaitley, minister of commerce and industry at the National Symposium
     on 'Trade and Globalisation: Agenda towards Cancun 2003', New Delhi,
     18–19 August 2003.
73   Ranjit Devraj, 'WTO-CANCUN: India Takes Lead in Opposing Farm
     Subsidies', IPS News, 10 September 2003. Available at: http://www.
     ipsnews.net/2003/09/wto-cancun-india-takeslead-in-opposing-farm-
     subsidies/
74   Ibid

Chapter 6: The Loss of 2004

1   Bharatiya Janata Party 1980–2005, Presidential Speeches Part II, Party
     Document - Volume 3, p. 357
2   'I am about mission, not ambition: Modi', Hindustan Times, 12 December
     2002. Available at: https://www.hindustantimes.com/india/i-am-about-
     mission-not-ambition-modi/story-20w77ry9ogsOWODngscerM.
     html
3   V. Venkatesan, 'A Pracharak as Chief Minister', Frontline, 13 October
     2001.
4   Andy Marino, Narendra Modi: A Political Biography (New Delhi:
     HarperCollins Publishers India, 2014), p. 94
5   'Gujarat riot death toll revealed', BBC News, 11 May 2005
6   Manas Dasgupta, '140 killed as Gujarat bandh turns violent', The Hindu, 1
     March 2002.
7   Resolution on Godhra and its aftermath passed at the national executive
     meeting held in Goa between 12 and 14 April 2002 (BJP Political

Resolutions, Party Document Volume 5), p. 32. Available at: http://library.
bjp.org/jspui/handle/123456789/264

8   *Statistical Report On General Elections, 2002 To The Legislative Assembly of
     Gujarat*, Election Commission of India, New Delhi. Available at: https://eci.
     gov.in/statistical-report/statistical-reports/.

9   *Statistical Report On General Elections, 1998 To The Legislative Assembly
     of Gujarat*, Election Commission of India, New Delhi. Available at: https://
     eci.gov.in/statistical-report/statistical-reports/.

10   Reserve Bank of India, Recent Economic Developments, 23 December 2004,
     Available   at: https://www.rbi.org.in/Scripts/PublicationReportDetails.
     aspx?ID=402

11   *Statistical Report on General Elections, 2003 to the Legislative Assembly of
     Madhya Pradesh*, Election Commission of India, New Delhi. Available at:
     https://eci.gov.in/statistical-report/statistical-reports/.

12   महेश पांडे, 'मध्य प्रदेश में भाजपा को भारी बहुमत', *BBC Hindi,* 4 December
     2003.   Available   at: https://www.bbc.com/hindi/regionalnews/
     story/2003/12/031204_elect_madhypradesh

13   *Statistical Report on General Elections, 2003 to the Legislative Assembly of
     Madhya Pradesh*, Election Commission of India, New Delhi. Available at:
     https://eci.gov.in/statistical-report/statistical-reports/.

14   *Statistical Report on General Elections, 2003 to the Legislative Assembly
     of Chhattisgarh*, Election Commission of India, New Delhi. Available at:
     https://eci.gov.in/statistical-report/statistical-reports/.

15   *Statistical Report on General Elections, 2003 to the Legislative Assembly
     of Rajasthan*, Election Commission of India, New Delhi. Available at:
     https://eci.gov.in/statistical-report/statistical-reports/.

16   Various statistical reports on General Elections, 2003 to the Legislative
     Assembly of Chhattisgarh, Madhya Pradesh and Rajasthan. Available at:
     https://eci.gov.in/statistical-report/statistical-reports/.

17   BS Political Bureau, 'BJP won semi-final on tribal power', *Rediff,* 10 December
     2003. Available at: 'https://www.*Rediff*.com/election/2003/dec/10bjp.htm

18   BJP 1980–2005: Presidential Speeches Part II, Party Document - Volume
     3, p. 330

19   Ajit Kumar Jha, 'NDA rides on Vajpayee's popularity, appears set to sweep
     elections 2004: *India Today* poll', *India Today,* 9 February 2004. Available
     at: https://www.indiatoday.in/magazine/india/mood-of-the-nation/
     story/20040209-vajpayee-bjp-set-for-landslide-win-in-forthcoming-
     2004-elections-790960-1999-11-30

20 Rajat Arora, 'NaMos Net worth', *Financial Express,* 16 March 2014. Available at: https://www.financialexpress.com/archive/namos-net-worth/1233661/

21 'The feel good factory', *Frontline,* 6 February 2015. Available at: https://frontline.thehindu.com/economy/the-feel-good-factory/article6805284.ece

22 Priya Sahgal and Ajit Kumar Jha, 'Atal Bihari Vajpayee favourite with young Indian voters: Survey', *India Today,* 3 May 2004. Available at: https://www.indiatoday.in/magazine/cover-story/story/20040503-atal-bihari-vajpayee-favorite-among-young-indian-voters-790201-1999-11-30

23 Rajeev Deshpande and Lakshmi Iyer, 'Elections 2004: BJP rides on India Shining plank, Cong counters feel-good line', *India Today,* 22 March 2004. Available at: https://www.indiatoday.in/magazine/cover-story/story/20040322-game-plan-of-congress-bjp-in-electio ns-2004-790276-2004-03-22'

24 Bhuvan Bagga, 'What makes NDA's "India Shining" campaign the "worst" poll strategy in Indian history', *India Today,* 14 May 2013. Available at: https://www.indiatoday.in/india/story/nda-india-shining-worst-poll-strategy-162922-2013-05-14

25 Vikas Pandey, 'India's colourful election slogans', *BBC,* 22 April 2014. Available at: https://www.bbc.com/news/world-asia-india-27018561

26 Rajeev Deshpande and Lakshmi Iyer, 'Elections 2004: BJP rides on India Shining plank, Cong counters feel-good line', *India Today,* 22 March 2004. Available at: https://www.indiatoday.in/magazine/cover-story/story/20040322-game-plan-of-congress-bjp-in-electio ns-2004-790276-2004-03-22

27 Pradeep Kaushal, 'L.K. Advani: Organiser to primary member', *The Indian Express,* 11 June 2013. Available at: http://archive.indianexpress.com/news/l-k-advani-organiser-to-primary-member/1127507/4

28 'Advani's Bharat Uday Yatra generates political heat', *Outlook India,* 9 March 2004. Available at: https://www.outlookindia.com/newswire/story/advanis-bharat-uday-yatra-generates-political-heat/206493

29 'Votes Polled by Parties In States/UTs' in *Statistical Report on General Elections, 2004 to the 14th Lok Sabha Volume I,* Election Commission of India, New Delhi. Available at: https://eci.gov.in/statistical-report/statistical-reports/.

30 'Performance of Political Parties' in *Statistical Report on General Elections, 2004 To The 14th Lok Sabha Volume I,* Election Commission of India,

New Delhi. Available at: https://eci.gov.in/statistical-report/statistical-reports/.

31 'Votes Polled by Parties in States/UTs' in *Statistical Report on General Elections, 2004 to the 14th Lok Sabha Volume I*, Election Commission of India, New Delhi. Available at: https://eci.gov.in/statistical-report/statistical-reports/.

32 L.K. Advani, *My Country My Life* (Rupa 2008), p. 772

Chapter 7: Building the Party (2004–2008)

1 Minhaz Merchant, 'Congress: Why 2004 was a false dawn', *The Economic Times*, 9 November 2013. Available at https://economictimes.indiatimes.com/blogs/headon/congress-why-2004- was-a-false-dawn/

2 Dhananjay Mahapatra, 'Phone-tapping case: Amar Singh withdraws allegations against Congress', *Times of India*, 9 February 2011. Available at: https://timesofindia.indiatimes.com/india/phone-tapping-case-amar-singh-withdraws-allegations-against-congress/articleshow/7459923.cms

3 'The pragmatic comrade is dead', *The Economic Times*, 2 August 2008. Available at: https://economictimes.indiatimes.com/news/politics-and-nation/the-pragmatic-comrade-isdead/articleshow/3317263.cms?from=mdr

4 L.K. Advani, *My Country My Life* (New Delhi: Rupa and Co, 2008), pp. 779–781

5 Radhika Ramaseshan, 'Advani salutes "secular" Jinnah', *Telegraph Online*, 4 June 2005. Available at: https://www.telegraphindia.com/india/advani-salutes-secular-jinnah/cid/873488

6 Sundeep Dougal, 'Cracks in the Parivar', *Outlook*, 7 June 2005. Available at: https://www.Outlookindia.com/website/story/cracks-in-the-parivar/227597

7 Ibid

8 'Vajpayee supports Advani on Jinnah', *Outlook*, 7 June 2005. Available at: https://www.Outlookindia.com/newswire/story/vajpayee-supports-advani-on-jinnah/302871

9 Priya Sahgal, 'LK Advani's tryst with Mohammad Ali Jinnah robs BJP of its ideology', *India Today*, 20 June 2005. Available at: https://www.indiatoday.in/magazine/coverstory/story/19700101-lk-advani-tryst-with-mohammad-ali-jinnah-robs-bjp-of-its-ideology-787453- 2005-06-20

10 'LK Advani quits as BJP president', *Business Standard*, 6 February 2013. Available at: https://www.business-standard.com/article/economy-policy/lk-advani-quits-as-bjp-president105060801087_1.html

11 L.K. Advani, *My Country, My Life* (New Delhi: Rupa and Co, 2008), pp. 812, 813, 814

12 The BJP Statement', *Outlook*, 10 June 2005. Available at: https://www.Outlookindia.com/website/story/the-bjp-statement/227609

13 'Uma Bharti walks out of meet after spat with Advani', *Rediff*, 10 November 2004 . Available at: https://www.Rediff.com/news/2004/nov/10bjp.htm

14 Devesh Kumar, 'Fair deal: BJP announces 33% reservation for women', *Economic Times*, 23 September 2007. Available at: https://economictimes.indiatimes.com/dateline-india/fair-dealbjp-announces-33-reservation-for-women/articleshow/2394041.cms?from=mdr

15 BJP Political Resolution, 17 September 2005. Available at: https://www.bjp.org/en/articledetail/148781/Political-Resolution

16 Ibid

17 Priya Sahgal, Malini Bhupta and Aditi Pai, 'Sneak peek of the shooting of the charismatic BJP leader Pramod Mahajan', *India Today*, 8 May 2006. See also, 'Mahajan's death prompts BJP to cancel yatras', Outlook India, May 4, 2006.

18 'NDA leaders meet Kalam, say Parliament adjourned to save Sonia', *Outlook*, 22 March 2006. Available at: https://www.*Outlook*india.com/newswire/amp/nda-leaders-meet-kalam-sayparliament-adjourned-to-save-sonia/372110 (accessed on 24 December 2020).

19 'Performance of Political Parties' in *Statistical Report To General Election, 2004 to the Legislative Assembly of Karnataka* (Election Commission of India, 2004), pp. 11–12. Available at: https://eci.gov.in/files/file/3782-karnataka-2004/ (accessed on 9 November 2020)

20 On forming a coalition government with the Congress, Deve Gowda said, 'We joined hands to keep the communal forces in check.' See Stephen David, 'Congress-JD(S) coalition government in Karnataka fights over cabinet berths', *India Today*, 14 June 2004. Available at: https://www.indiatoday.in/magazine/states/story/20040614-congress-jds-coalition-governmentin-karnataka-fights-over-cabinet-berths-789807-2004-06-14 (accessed on 9 November 2020)

21 The decision to withdraw support came after a change of guard within the JD(S), with Deve Gowda appointing his son, H.D.Kumaraswamy, as the state president. In protest, Deve Gowda resigned as JD(S) national

president. See Stephen David, 'H.D. Kumaraswamy becomes Karnataka CM, may face problems from coalition partner BJP', *India Today*, 13 February 2006. See also, Stephen David, 'Kumaraswamy breaks Karnataka's first coalition govt, BJP looks to debut in south India', *India Today*, 30 January 2006.

22   'Performance of Political Parties' in *Statistical Report To General Election, 2008 to the Legislative Assembly of Karnataka* (Election Commission of India, 2008), pp. 11–12. Available at: https://eci.gov.in/files/file/3783-karnataka-2008/ (accessed on 9 November 2020)

23   'Performance of Political Parties' in *Statistical Report to General Election, 2005 to the Legislative Assembly of Jharkhand* (Election Commission of India, 2005), pp. 8–10. Available at: https://eci.gov.in/files/file/3785-jharkhand-2005/ (accessed on 9 November 2020)

24   Amberish K. Diwanji, 'How NDA pulled off Operation Decoy', *Rediff*, 7 March 2005. Available at: https://www.*Rediff*.com/election/2005/mar/03decoy.htm (accessed on 9 November 2020).

25   Ibid

26   *Statistical Report on General Elections, 2005 (February) to the Legislative Assembly of Bihar,* Election Commission of India, New Delhi. Available at: https://eci.gov.in/statistical-report/statistical-reports/.

27   *Statistical Report on General Elections, 2005 (October) to the Legislative Assembly of Bihar*, Election Commission of India, New Delhi. Available at: https://eci.gov.in/statistical-report/statistical-reports/.

28   Milan Vaishnav and Saksham Khosla, 'Battle for Bihar', *Carnegie Endowment for International Peace,* 30 September 2015. Available at: https://carnegieendowment.org/2015/09/30/battle-forbihar/iid1 (accessed on 09/11/2020).

29   *Statistical Report on General Elections, 2005 to the Legislative Assembly of Bihar*, Election Commission of India, New Delhi. Available at: https://eci.gov.in/statistical-report/statistical-reports/.

30   Mathaai Mathiyazhagan, 'Recent State Assembly Elections in India: How Big a Setback for the Congress?' ISAS Brief No. 6 Institute of South Asian Studies (8 March 2007). Available at: https://www.files.ethz.ch/isn/29439/6.pdf (accessed on 09/11/2020).

31   '"Maut ke saudagar" may have hurt Congress', *The Times of India,* 24 December 2007. Available at:https://timesofindia.indiatimes.com/india/maut-ke-saudagar-may-have-hurt-congress/articleshow/2646136.cms

32 Christophe Jaffrelot, 'Gujarat: The Meaning of Modi's Victory', *Economic and Political Weekly*, vol. 43, no. 15, 2008, pp. 12–17. Available at: http://www.jstor.org/stable/40277329

33 *Statistical Report on General Elections, 2007 to the Legislative Assembly of Gujarat*, Election Commission of India, New Delhi. Available at: https://eci.gov.in/statistical-report/statistical-reports/.

34 National Executive Political Resolution, 29 January 2008

35 'BJP plans to woo Muslims', *Outlook India*, 1 April 2008. Available at: https://www.*Outlook*india.com/newswire/story/bjp-plans-to-woo-muslims/558752

36 *Social, Economic and Educational Status of the Muslim Community of India*, Prime Minister's High Level Committee Cabinet Secretariat Government of India (November 2006), pp. 25, 187, 241.

37 BJP Resolution, National Executive at Bengaluru on 13 September 2008. Available at: https://www.bjp.org/en/resolutionarticledetail/1413/Bengaluru-Karnataka-

38 Ibid

39 'UPA Govt Wins Trust Vote', *India Today*, 22 July 2008. Available at: https://www.indiatoday.in/latest-headlines/story/upa-govt-wins-trust-vote-27529-2008-07-22

40 'SP–Cong deal on Nuke deal in Mulayam's interest: Mayawati', *Hindustan Times*, 4 July 2008. Available at: https://www.hindustantimes.com/lucknow/sp-cong-deal-on-nuke-deal-in-mulayams-interest-maya/story-I1Kkaw26bMYDiPMbNTAc3O.html (accessed on 9 November 2020).

41 'Congress misused CBI to save Mulayam Singh: BJP', *Hindustan Times*, 10 February 2009. Available at: https://www.hindustantimes.com/india/congress-misused-cbi-to-save-mulayamsingh-bjp/story-QdqhndqyDd4GCpoqPKARdL.html (accessed on 9 November 2020).

42 'UPA trying to put me behind bars: Mulayam', *Indian Express*, 27 February 2009. Available at: https://indianexpress.com/article/india/india-others/upa-trying-to-put-me-behind-bars-mulayam/ (accessed on 9 November 2020).

43 'I supported UPA in crisis, but it has put CBI after me: Mulayam', *Firstpost*, 19 March 2013. Available at: https://www.Firstpost.com/politics/i-supported-upa-in-crisis-but-it-has-put-cbi-afterme-mulayam-679015.html

44 'Revisiting the night of Mumbai terror attack: When 10 Pak terrorists attacked India's financial capital', *Economic Times*, 26 November 2019. Available at: https://economictimes.indiatimes.com/news/

defence/revisiting-the-night-of-mumbai-terror-attack-when-10-pak-terrorists-attacked-indias-financial-capital/articleshow/72235424.cms?from=mdr

45 Aman Sharma, 'Government had intelligence inputs on 26/11 Mumbai attacks, says former NSA M.K. Narayanan', *Economic Times*, 21 January 2014. Available at: https://economictimes.indiatimes.com/news/politics-and-nation/government-had-intelligenceinputs-on-26/11-mumbai-attacks-says-former-nsa-mk-narayanan/articleshow/29127352.cms

46 The Central Vigilance Commission (CVC) is a statutory body that deals with corruption in the government. It monitors vigilance activity under the Central Government and advises Central Government organizations on various matters.

47 The Comptroller and Auditor General of India (CAG) conducts internal as well as external audits of the expenses of the national and state governments.

48 Ajoy Ashirwad Mahaprashasta, 'Mega Scam', *Frontline*, 10 September 2010. Available at: https://frontline.thehindu.com/the-nation/article30181732.ece

49 Ravi Shankar and Mihir Srivastava, 'Payoffs & bribes cast a shadow on CWG', *India Today*, 16 August 2010. Available at: https://www.indiatoday.in/magazine/sport/story/20100816-payoffsbribes-cast-a-shadow-on-cwg-743744-2010-08-07

50 'Performance Audit Report on the Issue of Licences and Allocation of 2G Spectrum', Comptroller and Auditor General of India, 16 November 2010. Available at:https://www.thehindu.com/news/Performance-Audit-Report-on-the-Issue-of-Licences-andAllocation-of-2G-Spectrum-CAG-Report/article15689218.ece

51 Pragya Srivastava, 'The great 2G scam: What it was, and what changed after that', *Financial Express*, 19 March 2018. Available at: https://www.financialexpress.com/industry/thegreat-2g-scam-what-it-was-and-what-changed-after-that/984319/

52 Nagendar Sharma, 'CAG scan of the 2G spectrum scam', *Hindustan Times*, 18 November 2010. Available at: https://www.hindustantimes.com/india/cag-scan-of-the-2g-spectrumscam/story-a245gc1ahDfoQjrAHyFlLO.html

53 Subhajti Sengupta and Suhas Munshi, '2G Scam Explained', *News18*, https://www.News18.com/news/immersive/2g-scam-explained.html

54 'CBI to file 80,000-page charge sheet against Raja, others on April 2', *The Hindu*, 30 March 2011. Available at: https://www.thehindu.com/news/national/CBI-to-file-80000-page-chargesheet-against-Raja-others-on-April-2/article14966499.ece

55 'Performance Audit of Allocation of Coal Blocks and Augmentation of Coal Production', Comptroller and Auditor General of India, 17 August 2012. Available at: https://www.sourcewatch.org/images/4/40/Draft_CAG_report_Pt_1.pdf

56 'What is coal scam?', *Indian Express*, 22 May 2017. Available at: https://indianexpress.com/article/what-is/manmohan-singh-cbi-coalgate-coal-block-allocationcag-report-what-is-coal-scam-4668265/

57 Deeptiman Tiwary, 'Coal blocks allocation cases explained: The allegations, investigation, and what next', *Indian Express*, 19 October 2020. Available at: 41 https://indianexpress.com/article/explained/explained-recalling-the-coal-blocks-allocation-casesallegations-investigation-and-what-now-6723961/

58 Alok Ray, 'Core issues in the coal scam', *Hindu BusinessLine*, 27 August 2012. Available at:https://www.thehindubusinessline.com/opinion/core-issues-in-the-coalscam/article22994776.ece

59 'Performance Audit of Allocation of Coal Blocks and Augmentation of Coal Production', Comptroller and Auditor General of India, 17 August 2012, p. 21.

60 Deepalakshmi K., 'Adarsh scam: The story of a posh high-rise with not-so-posh occupants', *The Hindu*, 29 April 2016. Available at: https://www.thehindu.com/news/national/adarsh-scambackgrounder/article14264528.ece

61 Rahi Gaikwad, 'Adarsh, a classic case of fence eating crop: CAG', *The Hindu*, 25 December 2011. Available at: https://www.thehindu.com/news/national/adarsh-a-classic-case-of-fenceeating-crop-cag/article2745204.ece

62 Ibid

63 'What is the Adarsh scam?', *Indian Express*, 22 December 2017. Available at: https://indianexpress.com/article/what-is/what-is-the-adarsh-scam-4994206/

64 'Adarsh housing society case: A timeline of events', *Livemint*, 22 December 2017. Available at:https://www.*Livemint*.com/Politics/BJwWQeCPJxSUlXBTqS15LJ/Adarsh-housing-societycase-A-timeline-of-events.html

65 BJP Political Resolution, 6 February 2009. Available at: https://www.
    bjp.org/en/articledetail/132011/Political-Resolution-passed-at-the-BJP-
    NationalCouncil-Meeting-in-Nagpur-Maharashtra-

Chapter 8: The Road to Resurgence (2009–2014)

1   Shekhar Iyer, 'LK Advani is BJP's man for PM post', *Hindustan Times*, 11
    December 2007. Available at:https://www.hindustantimes.com/india/lk-
    advani-is-bjp-s-man-for-pm-post/story-ADT4qJZ49CABoxRljKSmGI.
    html
2   Agriculture Resolution passed at the BJP National Council meeting
    in Nagpur on 6 February 2009. Available at: https://www.bjp.org/en/
    articledetail/132015/Agriculture-Resolution-passed-at-the-BJP-National-
    Council-Meeting-in-Nagpur-Maharashtra-
3   Priya Sahgal, 'The hits and misses', *India Today Bureau*, 17 May 2009.
    Available   at: https://www.indiatoday.in/magazine/election-news/
    story/20090525-the-hits-and-misses-739767- 2009-05-17
4   Performance of National Parties, *Statistical Report on General Elections,
    2009 to the 15th Lok Sabha Volume I*, Election Commission of India, New
    Delhi. Available at: https://eci.gov.in/statistical-report/statistical-reports/
5   'Performance of Political Parties' in *Statistical Report on General Elections,
    2009 To The 15th Lok Sabha Volume I*, Election Commission of India,
    New Delhi. Available at: https://eci.gov.in/statistical-report/statistical-
    reports/
6   'At his hour of ignominy, BJP stands by Advani', *Rediff*, 16 May
    2009. Available at: http://election.Rediff.com/report/2009/may/16/
    loksabhapoll-bjp-concedes-defeat-virtually.htm   (accessed   on   20
    November 2020).
7   'Advani not keen to be leader of opposition: Rajnath Singh', *Rediff*,
    May, 2009. Available at: http://election.Rediff.com/report/2009/may/16/
    loksabhapoll-advani-doesnt-want-to-be-leader-ofopposition.htm
    (accessed on 20 November 2020)
8   Onkar Singh, 'Advani agrees to become Opposition Leader', *Rediff*, 18
    May 2009. Available at: http://election.Rediff.com/report/2009/may/18/
    loksabhapoll-advani-remains-oppositionleader.htm   (accessed   on   20
    November 2020)
9   BJP Political resolution moved at National Executive in New Delhi, 20
    June 2009. Available at: https://www.bjp.org/en/articledetail/132010/

Political-Resolution-passed-at-the-BJP-NationalExecutive-Meeting-in-Parliament-Annexe-New-Delhi-

10 Purnima Joshi, 'NDA fractured after defeat', *India Today*, 18 May 2009. Available at: https://www.indiatoday.in/elections-north/delhi/story/nda-fractured-after-defeat-47891-2009-05- 18 (accessed on 20 November 2020).

11 'Swipe at Advani, RSS slams Net campaign', *Indian Express*, 26 May 2009. Available at: http://archive.indianexpress.com/news/swipe-at-advani-rss-slams-net-campaign/465997/ (accessed on 20 November 2020)

12 Shivaji Sarkar, 'The party that expands nationally has better chance to rule', *Organiser*, 31 May 2009. Available at: https://www.Organiser.org/archives/dynamic/modules5992.html?name=Content&pa=showpage&pid=293&page=9 (accessed on 20 November 2020).

13 Rajendra Prabhu, 'In the sunrise of bipolar politics, BJP has the best chance to be the alternative', *Organiser*, 31 May 2009. Available at: https://www.Organiser.org/archives/dynamic/modules80ec.html?name=Content&pa=showpage& pid=293&page=7 (accessed on 20 November 2020).

14 Gautam Sen, 'The challenge before BJP', *Organiser*, 31 May 2009. Available at: https://www.Organiser.org/archives/dynamic/modules2221.html?name=Content&pa=showpage& pid=293&page=10 (accessed on 20 November 2020).

15 Bharatiya Janata Party Political Resolution passed at the BJP National Executive Meeting at New Delhi on 20 June 2009. Available at: https://www.bjp.org/en/articledetail/132010/PoliticalResolution-passed-at-the-BJP-National-Executive-Meeting-in-Parliament-Annexe-New-Delhi- (accessed on 20 November 2020)

16 Election Commission of India, Available at: https://eci.gov.in/files/file/3724-maharashtra-2009/

17 Election Commission of India, Available at: https://eci.gov.in/files/file/3826-haryana-2009/

18 See Article 19, Constitution and Rules, Bharatiya Janata Party 2012

19 At least twenty members of electoral colleges of not less than five states, where elections to the National Council have been concluded, must make the nomination with the consent of the candidate. See, ibid

20 See Article 21, Constitution and Rules, Bharatiya Janata Party 2012

21 *Statistical Report on General Election, 2010 to the Legislative Assembly Bihar*, Election Commission of India.

22 Ibid

23 'BJP National Executive Meeting in Guwahati BJP to focus on fighting corruption 2G scam, CWG scam, Adarsh Scam and Sonia's Bofors connection', *Organiser*, 23 January 2011. Available at: https://www.Organiser.org/archives/dynamic/modulesbf35. html?name=Content&pa=showpage&pid=381&page=2

24 'North-East India Sampark Cell of BJP launched Make sure foreigners are not enumerated in census- LK Advani', *Organiser*, 5 September 2010. Available at: https://www.Organiser.org/archives/dynamic/modulesf60b. html?name=Content&pa=showpage&pid=360&page=39

25 Anirban Ganguly and Shiwanand Dwivedi, *Amit Shah and the March of BJP* (Bloomsbury India, 2019), pp. 53–54

26 'SIT gives clean chit to Modi, 57 others', *Livemint*, 10 April 2012. Available at: https://www.*Livemint*.com/Politics/hJNWc0iH34a25I9E6Tpr1K/SIT-gives-clean-chit-to-Modi-57- others.html

27 'Amit Shah gets CBI clean chit in Ishrat Jahan encounter case', *The Times of India*, 8 May 2014. Available at: https://m.economictimes.com/news/politics-and-nation/amit-shah-gets-cbi-cleanchit-in-ishrat-jahan-encounter-case/articleshow/34804000.cms

28 'Bill Summary: The Lokpal & Lokayuktas Bill 2011 (as passed by Lok Sabha)', *PRS Legislative Research*. Available at: https://prsindia.org/files/bills_acts/bills_parliament/Lokpal_&_Lokayukta_Bill_Summary.pdf

29 'Hunger strike over Lokpal Bill as thousands protest corruption', *Reuters*, 5 April 2011, Available at: https://in.reuters.com/article/idINIndia-56135720110405

30 'Ramdev reaches Delhi, UPA to placate him', *New Indian Express*, 1 June 2011, Available at: https://www.newindianexpress.com/nation/2011/jun/01/ramdev-reaches-delhi-upa-to-placatehim-258597.html

31 'Midnight police swoop on Baba Ramdev ends protest', *Times of India*, 5 June 2011, Available at: https://timesofindia.indiatimes.com/india/Midnight-police-swoop-on-Baba-Ramdevends-protest/articleshow/8730121.cms

32 'Ramdev arrested: Opposition slams police crackdown on Ramdev, BJP targets PM, Sonia', *The Economic Times*, 5 June 2011. Available at: https://economictimes.indiatimes.com/news/politics-and-nation/ramdev-arrested-opposition-slams-police-crackdown-on-ramdev-bjp-targets-pm-sonia/articleshow/8736375.cms?from=mdr

33 Pradeep K. Chibber and Rahul Verma, *Ideology & Identity: The Changing Party Systems of India* (Oxford University Press, 2018), pp. 42, 201–205

34 'Delhi gang rape: Violence erupts at India Gate, protesters clash
    with police', *The Times of India,* 23 December 2012, Available at:
    https://timesofindia.indiatimes.com/city/delhi/Delhi-gangrape-
    Violence-erupts-at-India-Gate-protesters-clash-with-police/
    articleshow/17731094.cms

35 Abhinav Bhatt, 'Advani, Sushma Swaraj bat for Nitin Gadkari as
    allegations mount', *NDTV,* 24 October 2012. Available at: https://www.
    NDTV.com/india-news/lk-advani-sushma-swaraj-batfor-nitin-gadkari-
    as-allegations-mount-502677

36 Gautam Chintamani, *Rajneeti: A Biography of Rajnath Singh* (Penguin
    Random House, 2019), p. 184–186

37 'Advani will be next PM, says Modi', *The Indian Express,* 18 January 2009.
    Available at: http://archive.indianexpress.com/news/advani-will-be-next-
    pm-says-modi/412013/

38 'Rahul Gandhi trashes ordinance, shames government', *The Times of
    India*, 28 December 2013, Available at: https://timesofindia.indiatimes.
    com/india/Rahul-Gandhi-trashes-ordinanceshames-government/
    articleshow/23180950.cms

39 Shri Narendra Modi lays foundation stone of the world's tallest statue
    'Statue of Unity'. *YouTube*, 31 October 2013.

40 Various statistical reports on general elections, 2013 to the Legislative
    Assembly of Delhi, Election Commission of India, New Delhi.

41 'With eye on polls, Vasundhara Raje starts 58-Day yatra today', *NDTV*,
    4 August 2018. Available at: https://www.NDTV.com/india-news/
    with-eye-on-polls-vasundhara-raje-to-begin-58-day-yatra-from-
    tomorrow-1894943

42 *Statistical Report on General Elections, 2013 to the Legislative Assembly of
    Rajasthan*, Election Commission of India, New Delhi.

43 Ashok K. Mishra, 'Serial blasts in Patna kill 6 ahead of maiden
    Narendra Modi rally', *Economic Times*, 28 October 2013. Available
    at: https://economictimes.indiatimes.com/news/politics-and-nation/
    serial-blasts-in-patna-kill-6-ahead-of-maiden-narendra-modi-rally/
    articleshow/24785834.cms?from=mdr

44 Uday Mahurkar, 'Modi's 3D campaign was a first in Indian electoral
    history', *India Today*, 30 November 1999. Available at: https://
    www.indiatoday.in/magazine/nation/story/20121217-gujarat-
    elections-narendra-modi-3d-campaign-first-in-indian-electoral-
    history-761012-1999-11-30

45 Maulik Pathak, 'Modi's innovative campaign rakes up controversy', *Livemint*, 20 November 2012. Available at: https://www.Livemint.com/ Politics/9pCe3fdwkJ6Dm63kPDDeHN/Modis-3D-meeting-may-have-cost-just-14-crore.html

46 '10-ft tall Narendra Modi to cast 3D magic in Shimla, Delhi on Monday', *India Today*, 7 April 2014. Available at: https://www.indiatoday.in/ elections/highlights/story/narendra-modi-to-cast-3d-magic-in-shimla-delhi-on-monday-187972-2014-04-07

47 Jayanth Jacob, 'BJP way ahead of competition on social media in 2014, says Stanford Univ study', *Hindustan Times*, 17 May 2017. Available at: https://www.hindustantimes.com/india-news/bjp-way-ahead-of-competition-on-social-media-in-2014-says-stanford-university-study/ story-6Uq81HOwstzCwgCmiSyMWI.html

48 Various statistical reports, Election Commission of India

49 'Furore in A'bad co-op bank over deposits in MMCB', *The Times of India*, 23 September 2001. Available at: https://timesofindia.indiatimes.com/ city/ahmedabad/Furore-in-Abad-co-op-bank-over-deposits-in-MMCB/ articleshow/567368177.cms

50 Anirban Ganguly and Shiwanand Dwivedi, *Amit Shah and the March of BJP* (Bloomsbury, 2019), pp. 191–196

51 'Performance of National Parties', *General Elections, 2014 to the 16th Lok Sabha Volume I*, Election Commission of India, New Delhi. Available at: https://eci.gov.in/statistical-report/statistical-reports/

52 Author's calculations based on data from statistical reports, Election Commission of India. Available at: https://eci.gov.in/statistical-report/ statistical-reports/

53 'Performance of National Parties', *General Elections, 2014 to the 16th Lok Sabha Volume I*, Election Commission of India, New Delhi. Available at: https://eci.gov.in/statistical-report/statistical-reports/

54 'Largest Mass Outreach Campaign in Electoral History of a Democracy', Narendramodi.in, 29 April 2014. Available at:https://www.narendramodi. in/largest-mass-outreach-campaign-in-electoral-history-of-a-democracy-3136

Chapter 9: Working in Unison: Party and Government (2014)

1 'Narendra Modi bows as he enters Parliament for first time', *The Economic Times*, 20 May 2014. Available at: https://economictimes.indiatimes.com/

news/politics-and-nation/narendra-modi-bows-as-heenters-parliament-for-first-time/articleshow/35387870.cms?from=mdr

2   BJP Political Resolution passed in BJP National Council Meeting at Jawaharlal Nehru Stadium, New Delhi on 9 August 2014. Available at: https://www.bjp.org/en/articledetail/101169/Political-Resolution-passed-in-BJP-National-Council-Meeting-at-Jawaharlal-Nehru-Stadium-New-Delhi

3   Piyush Srivastava, 'BJP wipes out UP with 71 seats', *India Today*, 17 May 2014. Available at: https://www.indiatoday.in/elections/story/bjp-wipesout-up-with-71-seats-193280-2014-05-17

4   Kumar Uttam, 'Amit Shah named BJP's new president', *Hindustan Times*, 10 July 2014. Available at: https://www.hindustantimes.com/india/amit-shah-named-bjp-s-new-president/storyY3f67WIcJqQyTwlfMciThL.html (accessed on 14 February 2021).

5   'Performance of National Parties', General Elections, 2014 to the 16th Lok Sabha Volume I, Election Commission of India, New Delhi. Available at: https://eci.gov.in/statistical-report/statistical-reports/

6   Authors' calculations based on various statistical reports (Election Commission of India, New Delhi) https://eci.gov.in/statistical-report/statistical-reports/.

7   Political resolution passed in BJP National Council Meeting at Jawaharlal Nehru Stadium, New Delhi on 9 August 2014. Available at:https://www.bjp.org/en/articledetail/101169/Political-Resolution-passed-in-BJP-National-Council-Meeting-at-Jawaharlal-Nehru-Stadium-New-Delhi

8   Bhalchandra Krishna Kelkar, *Pandit Deen Dayal Upadhyaya: Vichar Darshan Volume 3* (New Delhi: Aschi Prakashan), p. 80

9   BJP National Council meeting held on 9 August 2014. Available at: https://vimeo.com/125258831

10 'Financial Inclusion in India – An Assessment 1', *RBI Docs*. Available at: https://rbidocs.rbi.org.in/rdocs/Speeches/PDFs/MFI101213FS.pdf

11 Financial Inclusion Annual Report. Available at: https://financialservices.gov.in/sites/default/files/Financial%20Inclusion_annual%20report_material31.3.2019_0.pdf

12 Alistair Scrutton, 'As India booms, social welfare struggles to catch up', *Reuters, 20* April 2010. Available at: https://www.reuters.com/article/us-india-welfare-idUSTRE63I70620100419

13 Devanik Saha, '3 years of Swachh Bharat: 2.5 lakh villages declared open defecation free, but 1.5 lakh claims not verified', *Hindustan Times*, 2 October 2017. Available at: https://www.hindustantimes.com/india-news/3-years-

of-swachh-bharat-2-5-lakh-villages-declared-open-defecation-free-but-
1-5-lakh-claims-not-verified/story-brpTIcdIoZ9YhpkgXGfg4I.html

14 UN Deputy Secretary Eliasson emphasized the need to talk about open
defecation and toilets in public in 2013 saying that we needed to break
this taboo and break away from the shame that accompanied it. Laura
Paddison, 'We need to talk about open defecation', *Guardian*, 10 September
2013. Available at: https://www.theguardian.com/globaldevelopment-
professionals-network/2013/sep/10/open-defecation-sanitation-un

15 *Ek Bharat Shreshtha Bharat: Sabka Sath Sabka Vikas, Election Manifesto
2014*, Bharatiya Janata Party, p. 26. Available at: http://library.bjp.org/
jspui/bitstream/123456789/252/1/bjp_lection_manifesto_english_
2014.pdf

16 Amrita Chowdhury, 'Design thinking can help Swachh Bharat', *Livemint*,
3 October 2016. Available at: https://www.livemint.com/Politics/
IQ0CW3VEpLwcz1YKsc8RVM/Designthinking-can-help-Swachh-
Bharat.html

17 'Swachh Bharat: Picking up a clean habit', *Economic Times*, 30 March
2017. Available at: https://economictimes.indiatimes.com/blogs/et-
commentary/swachh-bharat-picking-up-aclean-habit/

18 Krishnanand Tripathi, 'Swachh Bharat Mission: Modi government has
spent this much to build over 9 crore toilets', *Financial Express*, 7 February
2019. Available at: https://www.financialexpress.com/india-news/swachh-
bharat-mission-modi-government-hasspent-this-much-to-build-over-9-
crore-toilets/1480286/

19 'Clarification on estimates of Toilet Costs under Swachh Bharat Mission',
Ministry of Drinking Water & Sanitation, April 27, 2018. Available at:
https://pib.gov.in/PressReleaseIframePage.aspx?PRID=1530548

20 'Resolution of the National Executive Meeting at Vijayawada, 2–4 January,
1987', in *Economic Resolutions Party Documents Volume 6* (Bharatiya
Janata Party, 2005), pp. 122, 251, 259, 197.

21 'Jan Dhan Scheme completes six years, benefits 40.35 crore people', *Times
of India*, 28 August 2020. Available at: https://timesofindia.indiatimes.
com/business/indiabusiness/jan-dhan-scheme-completes-six-years-
benefits-40-35-crorepeople/articleshow/77798377.cms (accessed on 14
February 2021).

22 BJP Political Resolution passed in BJP National Council Meeting at
Jawaharlal Nehru Stadium, New Delhi on 9 August 2014. Available at:
https://www.bjp.org/en/articledetail/101169/Political-Resolution-passed-

in-BJP-National-Council-Meeting-at-Jawaharlal-Nehru-Stadium-New-Delhi

23 BJP Political Resolution passed in BJP National Council Meeting at Jawaharlal Nehru Stadium, New Delhi on 9 August 2014. Available at: https://www.bjp.org/en/articledetail/101169/Political-Resolution-passed-in-BJP-National-Council-Meeting-at-Jawaharlal-Nehru-Stadium-New-Delhi

24 'PM Narendra Modi launches BJP's membership drive', *narendramodi.in*, 1 November 2014.

25 Anirban Ganguly and Shiwanand Dwivedi, *Amit Shah and The March of BJP* (Bloomsbury India, 2019), p. 120

26 'Modi launches BJP membership drive, seeks representation for all', *India Today*, 1 November 2014. Available at: https://www.indiatoday.in/india/story/pm-narendra-modi-launch-bjpmembership-drive-delhi-amit-shah-225469-2014-11-01

27 'BJP membership drive blasts off, 60 lakh join party', *India Today*, 8 November 2014. Available at: 53 https://www.indiatoday.in/india/story/bjp-membership-drive-blasts-off-60-lakh-join-party-226297-2014-11-08

28 Speech by Shri Amit Shah addressing Sadasyata Abhiyan on 22 November 2014. Available at: https://www.bjp.org/en/speechdetail/239604/Speech-Shri-Amit-Shah-addressing-SadasyataAbhiyan

29 Parvez Sultan, 'Delhi BJP to create 19 departments, 10 cells for smooth functioning', *Hindustan Times,* 10 July 2017.

30 Anirban Ganguly and Shiwanand Dwivedi, *Amit Shah and the March of BJP* (Bloomsbury Publishing, 2019), p. 162

31 'BJP to include 'Namami Gange' & 'Beti Bachao, Beti Padhao' as mass contact theme', *The Daily Pioneer*, 14 May 2015. Available at: https://www.dailypioneer.com/2015/state-editions/bjpto-include-namami-gange-and-beti-bachao-beti-padhao-as-mass-contact-theme.html

32 Gyan Varma, 'Amit Shah unveils new BJP team; Varun Gandhi dropped', *Livemint,* 16 August 2014. Available at: https://www.livemint.com/Politics/NBQzUBallWRT1xcvlI5ocL/Amit-Shahannounces-new-team-before-assembly-polls.html (accessed on 14 February 2021).

33 Venkat Ananth, 'The anatomy of an alliance: The BJP-Shiv Sena story', *Livemint*, 22 September 2014. Available at: https://www.livemint.com/Politics/VbrxNc2FSZuGroknO7I97M/The-anatomy-of-analliance-The-BJPShiv-Sena-story.html (accessed on 14 February 2021).

34 Kavitha Iyer, 'Why Gopinath Munde's death spells gloom for BJP in Maharashtra', *Firstpost*, 5 June 2014.

35 Pallavi, 'This is how BJP leader Gopinath Munde died: Do not go by EVM hacking drama', *India Today,* 22 January 2019. Available at: https://www.indiatoday.in/india/story/bjp-leader-gopinathmunde-car-crash-1436506-2019-01-22 (accessed on 14 February 2021).

36 'Bal Thackeray passes away; funeral on Sunday', *The Hindu*, 17 November 2012. Available at: https://www.thehindu.com/news/national/other-states/bal-thackeray-passes-away- 54 funeral-on-sunday/article4105003.ece (accessed on 14 February 2021)

37 Election Commission of India, General Elections 2014 (16th Lok Sabha): State Wise Seat Won & Valid Votes Polled by Political Parties, pp. 8–9

38 'Maharashtra assembly polls 2014: Shiv Sena-BJP alliance headed for rocky waters amid trust deficit', *The Economic Times*, 24 September 2014. Available at: https://economictimes.indiatimes.com/news/politics-and-nation/maharashtra-assembly-polls2014-shiv-sena-bjp-alliance-headed-for-rocky-waters-amid-trustdeficit/articleshow/43355975.cms?from=mdr (accessed on 14 February 2021)

39 'Ready to be chief minister: Uddhav', *Mumbai Mirror*, 14 September 2014. Available at: https://mumbaimirror.indiatimes.com/mumbai/other/ready-to-be-chief-ministeruddhav/articleshow/42400667.cms

40 Sanjay Jog, 'BJP, Shiv Sena break alliance of 25 years', *Business Standard*, 26 September 2014. Available at: https://www.business-standard.com/article/politics/bjp-shiv-sena-alliance-endsafter-seat-sharing-talks-fail-114092501055_1.html (accessed on 14 February 2021).

41 'Maharashtra assembly polls 2014: NCP ends alliance with Congress', *The Economic Times*, 25 September 2014. Available at: https://economictimes.indiatimes.com/news/politicsand-nation/maharashtra-assembly-polls-2014-ncp-ends-alliance-withcongress/articleshow/43448370.cms?utm_source=contentofinterest&utm_medium=text&utm_ca mpaign=cppst (accessed on 14 February 2021).

42 'Small in size but big in impact: These parties play crucial role in democracy', *Indian Express,* 28 September 2019. Available at: https://indianexpress.com/elections/small-in-sizebut-big-in-impact-these-parties-play-crucial-role-in-democracy-6035338/ (accessed on 14 February 2021).

43 Maharashtra 2014 assembly election results, *Election Commission of India*.

44 Election Commission of India, General Elections 2014 (16th Lok Sabha): State Wise Seat Won & Valid Votes Polled by Political Parties, 2014), p. 4

45 'Kuldeep Bishnoi-led Haryana Janhit Congress snaps ties with BJP', *Indian Express,* 28 August 2014. Available at: https://indianexpress.com/article/india/politics/kuldeepbishnoi-led-haryana-janhit-congress-snaps-ties-with-bjp/ (accessed on 15 February 2021).

46 India TV News Desk (Nov. 2014). Give me 'full majority', I'll give you 'full development', says Narendra Modi at Chaibasa, Jharkhand. India TV. Available at: https://www.indiatvnews.com/politics/national/narendra-modi-live-jharkhand-assembly-elections-2014-chaibasa--22863.html https://www.indiatvnews.com/politics/national/narendra-modi-live-jharkhand-assembly-elections-2014-chaibasa--22863.html (accessed on 15 February 2021).

47 'BJP-AJSU alliance gets clear majority, to form government in Jharkhand', *The Economic Times,* 23 December 2014.

48 *Statistical Report on General Elections, 2014 to the Legislative Assembly of Jammu & Kashmir,* Election Commission of India, New Delhi.

49 Jharkhand assembly 2014 election result, *Election Commission of India*

50 'Modi, Amit Shah redefining BJP's language of business', *India Today,* 22 October 2014

51 'Make BJP world's largest party, says Amit Shah to party men', *The Economic Times,* 3 January 2015

52 Political resolution passed in BJP National Executive Meeting at Bengaluru on 4 April 2015. Available at: https://www.bjp.org/en/pressreleasesdetail/295602/Political-resolution-passed-in-BJP-National-Executive-Meeting-at-Bengaluru-Karnataka-

53 Political resolution passed in BJP National Executive Meeting at Bengaluru on 4 April 2015. Available at: https://www.bjp.org/en/pressreleasesdetail/295602/Political-resolution-passed-in-BJP-National-Executive-Meeting-at-Bengaluru-Karnataka-

54 Pragya Kaushika, 'Knocking on voters' doors: Amit Shah leaving nothing to chance in Gujarat campaign', *ThePrint,* 5 November 2017.

55 'Page Pramukhs: Amit Shah's Silent Army to Reach The Last Voter in Gujarat', *News18,* 12 November 2017. Available at: https://www.news18.com/news/politics/page-pramukhs-amitshahs-silent-army-to-reach-every-last-voter-in-gujarat-1574109.html

Chapter 10: Expansion and Outreach (2015)

1   Political resolution passed in the BJP National Executive meeting at Bengaluru on 4 April 2015. Available at: https://www.bjp.org/en/

pressreleasesdetail/295602/Political-resolution-passed-in-BJP-National-Executive-Meetingat-Bengaluru-Karnataka-

2 'Performance of Political Parties' *Statistical Report on General Election, 2013, to the Legislative Assembly of Government of NCT of Delhi*, Election Commission of India.

3 Ibid

4 'Delhi election results: 5 reasons why AAP winning Delhi is historic', *India Today*, 10 February 2015 Available at: https://www.indiatoday.in/assembly-elections-2015/delhi/story/delhi-electionsarvind-kejriwal-5-reasons-aap-winning-delhi-historic-239592-2015-02-10

5 Aadil Ikram Zaki Iqbal, 'Delhi Assembly Elections 2015: Top 5 things BJP, AAP and Congress are promising Delhi voters', *India.com*, 6 February 2015. Available at: https://www.india.com/viral/delhi-assembly-elections-2015-top-5-things-bjp-aap-and-congressare-promising-delhi-voters-271803/ (accessed on 15 February 2020).

6 Gargi Parsai, 'Kiran Bedi is BJP's CM candidate', *The Hindu*, 19 January 2015. Available at: https://www.thehindu.com/elections/assembly2014/former-ips-officer-kiran-bedi-is-chiefministerial-candidate-says-bjp-chief-amit-shah/article6802588.ece (accessed on 15 February 2020).

7 'Performance of Political Parties' *Statistical Report on General Election, 2015, to the Legislative Assembly of Government of NCT of Delhi*, Election Commission of India

8 The vote share of Congress fell from 24.67 per cent to 9.70 per cent between 2013 and 2015. See, Election Commission of India (2015). Performance of Political Parties in *Statistical Report on General Election, 2015, to the Legislative Assembly of Government of NCT of Delhi*, Election Commission of India; Election Commission of India (2013). Performance of Political Parties in *Statistical Report on General Election, 2013, to the Legislative Assembly of Government of NCT of Delhi*, Election Commission of India.

9 'Kiran Bedi loses in BJP bastion of Krishna Nagar, apologizes', *Livemint*, 10 February 2015

10 *Statistical Report on General Elections, 2015 to the Legislative Assembly of Delhi*, Election Commission of India, New Delhi. Available at: https://eci.gov.in/statistical-report/statistical-reports/

11 Sandipan Sharma, 'Achche din no more: BJP will lose aam aadmi with Land Acquisition Bill', *Firstpost*, 25 February 2015. Available at: https://www.Firstpost.com/politics/achche-din-no-more-bjpwill-lose-aam-aadmi-with-land-acquisition-bill-2120917.html (accessed on 15 February 2020).

12   Swapan Dasgupta, Javed M. Ansari and Farzand Ahmed, 'Laloo Prasad Yadav mocks democracy by anointing wife Rabri Devi as successor', *India Today,* 4 August 1997, Available at: https://www.indiatoday.in/magazine/cover-story/story/19970804-laloo-prasad-yadav-mocksdemocracy-by-anointing-wife-rabri-devi-as-successor-831820-1997-08-04

13   M. Rajshekhar, 'Bihar is struggling to improve the lives of the poor even after 27 years of backward caste rule', *Scroll.in,* 14 June 2017. Available at: https://Scroll.in/article/839031/bihar-is-struggling-to-improve-the-lives-of-the-poor-even-after-27-years-of-backward-caste-rule (accessed on 15 February 2020).

14   'Elections 2014: Nitish Kumar was left with no option, says Ram Vilas Paswan', *Economic Times,* 17 May 2014. Available at: https://economictimes.indiatimes.com/news/politics-and-nation/elections-2014-nitish-kumar-wasleft-with-no-option-says-ram-vilaspaswan/articleshow/35270825.cms?utm_source=contentofinterest&utm_medium=text&utm_ca mpaign=cppst (accessed on 15 February 2020).

15   'बिहार बीजेपी: प्यादों पर पैनी नजर', *Aaj Tak,* 18 September 2015. Available at: https://www.aajtak.in/india-today-hindi/special-report/story/bihar-election-2015-bjp-is-focus-on-every-trick-through-its-micromanagement-313167-2015-09-18

16   Pragya Kaushika, 'Knocking on voters' doors: Amit Shah leaving nothing to chance in Gujarat campaign', *ThePrint,* 5 November 2017

17   'Nitish, Lalu clinch deal: JD(U), RJD join hands for Bihar polls, seat sharing talks 8n cards', *Firstpost,* 8 June 2015. Available at: https://www.Firstpost.com/politics/nitish-lalu-clinchdeal-jdu-rjd-join-hands-for-bihar-polls-seat-sharing-talks-on-cards-2283878.html (accessed on 15 February 2020).

18   Rahul Shrivastava and Sidharth Pandey, 'Bihar Deal: BJP Wins Over Jitan Ram Manjhi, Now Paswan Upset, Say Sources', *NDTV,* 14 September 2015. Available at: https://www.NDTV.com/bihar/dealdone-bjp-jitan-ram-manjhi-agree-on-seat-sharing-for-bihar-1217297 (accessed on 15 February 2020)

19   Madan Kumar, 'PM Modi addressed 31 rallies in Bihar, nearly twice of Sonia-Rahul duo's 16 ', *The Times of India,* 4 November 2015.

20   *Statistical Report on General Elections, 2015 to the Legislative Assembly of Bihar,* Election Commission of India, New Delhi. Available at: https://eci.gov.in/statistical-report/statistical-reports/.

21   Performance of Political Parties, in *Statistical Report on General Election, 2015, to the Legislative Assembly of Government of Bihar*. Election Commission of India (2015)

22   'Modi shutting the Planning Commission: All you need to know about the central body', *Firstpost*, 19 August 2014. Available at: https://www. Firstpost.com/business/corporatebusiness/modi-shutting-the-planning-commission-all-you-need-to-know-about-the-centralbody-1984401.html

23   Speech of Gujarat chief minister, Narendra Modi at the fifty-seven meeting of the National Development Council on 27 December 2012, published by the Planning Commission, Government of India, New Delhi.

24   Press note on Global Multidimensional Poverty Index and India, *NITI Aayog*, 7 September 2020. Available at: https://pib.gov.in/PressReleasePage. aspx?PRID=1651981#:~:text=According%20to%20Glo bal%20MPI%20 2020,(2015%2F16)%20data.&text=As%20the%20Nodal%20agency%20 for,Index%20Coordination%20Committee%20(MPICC) https://ophi. org.uk/multidimensional-poverty-index/

25   Shreya Nandi and Utpal Bhaskar, 'Centre claims to have saved over ₹51,000 crore through DBT in F19', *Livemint*, 11 June 2019.

26   The Mistry reports refers to the High-level Committee on 'Making Mumbai an International Financial Centre' headed by Percy Mistry.
       See also, The Rajan report refers to 'A Hundred Small Steps Report of the Committee on Financial Sector Reforms', Government of India, Planning Commission, New Delhi (SAGE Publications India Pvt Ltd, 2009).

27   Ila Patnaik, 'Maintaining macroeconomic stability', *Getting India Back on Track: An Action Agenda for Reform*, ed. Bibek Debroy, Ashley J. Tellis and Reece Trevor (Random House India, 2014), p. 38

28   'Agreement on Monetary Policy Framework Between the Government of India and the Reserve Bank of India', 20 February 2015. Available at: https://www.finmin.nic.in/sites/default/files/MPFAgreement28022015.pdf

29   'Bihar, where Amit Shah's one-size-fits all strategy failed', *The Hindustan Times*, 8 November 2015. Available at: https://www.hindustantimes.com/ analysis/bihar-poll-results-why-the-verdictcan-make-or-break-amit-shah/story-Qa3FCzbn0p0jRM6NtaglVP.html

30   'Vision & Mission' Available at: https://rmponweb.org/vision-and-mission/

31   Maha Prashikshan Abhiyan, amitshah.co.in.

32   'BJP to launch leadership training campaign for party members', *The Economic Times*, 12 June 2015. Available at: https://economictimes.

indiatimes.com/news/politics-and-nation/bjp-to-launch-leadership-training-campaign-for-party-members/articleshow/47645763.cms

33 Yojna Gusai, 'Maha Prashikshan Abhiyan: BJP to hold oratory classes for its leaders', *Deccan Chronicle,* 27 November 2016. Available at: https://www.deccanchronicle.com/nation/currentaffairs/271116/maha-prashikshan-abhiyan-bjp-to-hold-oratory-classes-for-its-leaders.html

34 BJP to Launch Leadership Training Campaign for Party Members', *NDTV,* 12 June 2015. Available at: https://www.NDTV.com/india-news/bjp-to-launch-leadership-training-campaign-forparty-members-771124

35 'PM urges well-off to give up LPG subsidy', *Hindu BusinessLine,* 3 January 2018. Available at: https://www.thehindubusinessline.com/news/pm-urges-welloff-to-give-up-lpgsubsidy/article7065578.ece

36 Ibid

37 Ibid

38 'Give-it-Up: Over 1 crore LPG users gave up their subsidies', *Economic Times,* 21 April 2016. Available at: https://economictimes.indiatimes.com/industry/energy/oil-gas/give-itup-over-1-crore-lpg-users-gave-up-their-subsidies/articleshow/51929960.cms?from=mdr

39 'Give-it-Up: Over 1 crore LPG users gave up their subsidies', *Economic Times,* 21 April 2016. Available at: https://economictimes.indiatimes.com/industry/energy/oil-gas/give-it-up-over1-crore-lpg-users-gave-up-their-subsidies/articleshow/51929960.cms?from=mdr

40 'BJP to hold 'Jan Kalyan Parv' from 26 May on completion of one year of Narendra Modi government', *The Economic Times,* 14 May 2015.

41 'BJP to celebrate JP birth anniversary as "Save Democracy Day"', *Business Standard,* 7 October 2015. Available at: https://www.business-standard.com/article/pti-stories/bjpto-celebrate-jp-birth-anniversary-as-save-democracy-day-115100701280_1.html (accessed on 15 February 2021).

42 'The 140th birth anniversary of Sardar Vallabhbhai Patel is being celebrated across the country, with PM Modi flagging off the "Run for Unity" at Rajpath', *Times of India,* 31 October 2015. Available at: https://timesofindia.indiatimes.com/The-140th-birth-anniversary-of-Sardar-Vallabhbhai-Patel-is-being-celebrated-across-the-country-with-PM-Modi-flagging-off-the-Run-For-Unity-at-Rajpath-/articleshow/49604638.cms

43 'PM Narendra Modi to flag off "Run for Unity" tomorrow on Sardar Patel's birth anniversary', *Economic Times,* 30 October 2015. Available at: https://economictimes.indiatimes.com/news/politics-and-nation/pm-

narendra-modi-to-flag-off-run-for-unity-tomorrow-on-sardar-patels-birth-anniversary/articleshow/49600557.cms?from=mdr

Chapter 11: Winning the States (2016–2018)

1   Election Commission of India, Available at: file:///C:/Users/Administrator/Downloads/State%20wise%20seat%20won%20and%20valid%20v otes%20polled%20by%20political%20party.pdf

2   Samudra Gupta Kashyap, 'Tarun Gogoi's ex-confidante Himanta Biswa Sarma joins BJP in style' *Indian Express*, 29 August 2015. Available at: https://indianexpress.com/article/india/indiaothers/tarun-gogois-ex-confidante-himanta-biswa-sarma-joins-bjp-in-style/ (accessed on 17 February 2021).

3   'BJP departs from practice, names Sarbananda Sonowal as Assam CM candidate', *Economic Times*, 28 January 2016. Available at: https://economictimes.indiatimes.com/news/politics-and-nation/bjp-departs-from-practicenames-sarbananda-sonowal-as-assam-cmcandidate/articleshow/50761663.cms?utm_source=contentofinterest&utm_medium=text&utm_c 61 ampaign=cppst (accessed on 16 February 2021)

4   'BJP Alliance to Get Majority in Assam, Says ABP-Nielsen Survey', *Quint*, 30 March 2016. Available at: https://www.thequint.com/news/politics/bjp-alliance-to-get-majority-in-assam-says-abp-nielsen-survey (accessed on 17 February 2021)

5   'Congress and BJP neck and neck in Assam, opinion poll projects', *Times of India*, 1 April 2016. Available at: https://timesofindia.indiatimes.com/elections-2016/assam-elections-2016/Congress-BJP-neck-and-neck-in-Assam-opinion-poll-projects/articleshow/51651280.cms (accessed on 17 February 2021)

6   'Performance of Political Parties', *Statistical Report on General Election, 2016, to the Legislative Assembly of Government of Assam*, Election Commission of India, 2016

7   'India's BJP wins landmark Assam victory', *BBC*, 19 May 2016, Available at: https://www.bbc.com/news/world-asia-india-36319405

8   *Statistical Report on General Elections, 2016 to the Legislative Assembly of Assam*, Election Commission of India, New Delhi. Available at: https://eci.gov.in/statistical-report/statistical-reports/

9   'Performance of Political Parties', *Statistical Report on General Election, 2016, to the Legislative Assembly of Government of West Bengal*, Election Commission of India, 2016

10 'Performance of Political Parties', *Statistical Report on General Election, 2016, to the Legislative Assembly of Government of Kerala*, Election Commission of India, 2016

11 'Performance of Political Parties', *Statistical Report on General Election, 2014, to the Legislative Assembly of Government of Arunachal Pradesh*, Election Commission of India, 2014, p. 8.

12 Utpal Parashar, 'BJP takes another Northeast state as Arunachal CM Khandu joins BJP with 33 MLAs', *Hindustan Times*, 1 January 2017. Available at: https://www.hindustantimes.com/india-news/bjp-takes-another-northeastern-state-as-arunachal-s-khandu-joins-with-33-mlas/story-USOUNxK9dc2e6yRDxeZXOL.html (accessed on 11 August 2021).

13 Makarand Paranjape, 'Award wapsi: What really happened is still a mystery!', *DNA*, 11 August 2018. Available at: https://www.dnaindia.com/analysis/column-award-wapsi-what-reallyhappened-is-still-a-mystery-2648215

14 The Sahitya Akademi is an autonomous organization under the Central government of India. Its mandate is to work towards the development of Indian letters, set high literary standards, foster and co-ordinate literary activities in all the Indian languages

15 'JNU row: BJP's Jan Swabhiman Abhiyan begins today', *Deccan Chronicle*, 18 February 2016

16 'Amit Shah blasts Rahul Gandhi, Owaisi in his speech at BJP's National Executive meeting - Top 10 quotes', *Zee News*, 20 March 2016. Available at: https://zeenews.india.com/news/india/amit-shah-blasts-rahul-gandhi-owaisi-in-his-speech-atbjps-national-executive-meeting-top-10-quotes_1867690.html (accessed on 16 February 2021)

17 Political Resolution passed in BJP National Executive Meeting at NDMC Convention Centre, New Delhi on 20 March 2016. Available at: https://www.bjp.org/en/pressreleasesdetail/296444/Political-Resolution-passed-in-BJP-NationalExecutive-Meeting-at-NDMC-Convention-Centre-New-Delhi

18 Lt. Gen Satish Dua (Retired), *India's Bravehearts: Untold Stories from the Indian Army*, (Juggernaut Books, 2020), p. 4

19 Narendra Modi speech at Kozhikode on 24 September 2016. Availabe at: 62 https://www.youtube.com/watch?v=8u1ATUAmrl8

20 '3 yrs of surgical strikes: When Army sent a strong message, avenged Uri terror attack', *India Today*, 29 September 2019. Available at: https://www.indiatoday.in/india/story/3-yrs-of-surgical-strikes-when-army-sent-a-strong-message-avenged-uri-terror-attack-1604414-2019-09-29

21   Jitesh Jha, 'PM Modi launched Gram Uday Se Bharat Uday Abhiyan
     on Dr. Ambedkar's birth anniversary', *Jagran Josh*, 14 April 2016.
     Available   at: https://www.jagranjosh.com/currentaffairs/pm-modi-
     launched-gram-uday-se-bharat-uday-abhiyan-on-dr-ambedkars-
     birthanniversary-1460624619-1 (accessed on 15 February 2021).

22   Kumar Shakti Shekhar, 'Demonetisation days: All you need to know',
     India Today, 25 November 2016.

23   Ila Patnaik, 'Show me the money', *Indian Express*, 11 November 2016.
     Available at: https://indianexpress.com/article/opinion/columns/ban-on-
     rs-500-rs-1000-notes-pm-modiblack-money-cashless-economy-4368777

24   Friedrich Schneider, Andreas Buehn and Claudio E. Montenegro,
     'Shadow Economies All over the World: New Estimates for 162 Countries
     from 1999 to 2007', Policy Research Working Paper 5356, The World
     Bank Development Research Group, Poverty and Inequality Team,
     & Europe and Central Asia Region Human Development Economics
     Unit, July 2010. Available at: http://documents1.worldbank.org/curated/
     en/311991468037132740/pdf/WPS5356.pdf

25   Arun Kumar, 'Estimation of the Size of the Black Economy in India, 1996–
     2012', *Economic and Political Weekly*, Vol. 51, Issue No. 48, (2016). Available
     at: https://www.epw.in/system/files/pdf/2016_51/48/Estimation_of_the_
     Size_of_the_Black_Econ omy_in_India%2C_1996- 2012_0.pdf?0=ip_
     login_no_cache%3D3e3ced44a50d4ff417c445e75fa7954d

26   'Full text: PM Modi's 2016 demonetisation speech that shocked India',
     Business Standard, 8 November 2017. Available at: https://www.
     business-standard.com/article/economypolicy/full-text-pm-modi-
     s-2016-demonetisation-speech-that-shocked-india117110800188_1.
     html

27   'Government study pegs face value of fake currencies at Rs 400 crore',
     Economic Times, 2 August 2016. Available at: https://economictimes.
     indiatimes.com/news/economy/finance/government-study-pegs-
     facevalue-of-fake-currencies-at-rs-400-crore/articleshow/53504738.
     cms?from=mdr#:~:text=Sign%20in-,Government%20study%20p egs%20
     face%20value%20of%20fake%20currencies%20at%20Rs,Finance%20
     Arjun%20Ra m%20Meghwal%20said.

28   Areendam Chanda and C. Justin Cook, 'Who Gained from India's
     Demonetization? Insights from Satellites and Surveys', Departmental
     Working Papers 2019-06, Department of Economics, Louisiana State
     University (2019).

29 'यूपी: 17000 किलोमीटर चलकर थमीं BJP की परिवर्तन यात्राएं', *ABP Live*, 25 December 2016. Available at: https://www.abplive.com/news/states/uttar-pradesh-bjp-parivartan-yatra-ends-in-lu cknow-524728

30 'Performance of Political Parties', *Statistical Report on General Election, 2017, to the Legislative Assembly of Government of Uttar Pradesh*, Election Commission of India, 2017

31 *Statistical Report on General Elections, 2017 to the Legislative Assembly of Uttar Pradesh* Election Commission of India, New Delhi. Available at: https://eci.gov.in/statistical-report/statistical-reports/

32 Gurpreet Singh Nibber, 'Punjab election 2017: BJP fails to stay afloat', *Hindustan Times*, 12 March 2017. Available at: https://www. hindustantimes.com/assembly-elections/punjab-election-2017-bjp-fails-to-stay-afloat/story-OFrEFdP4hnJblj3QtJUAdI.html (accessed on 16 February 2021).

33 'Performance of Political Parties', *Statistical Report on General Election, 2017, to the Legislative Assembly of Government of Uttarakhand*, Election Commission of India, 2017

34 Kavita Upadhyay, 'Trivendra Singh Rawat takes oath as Uttarakhand Chief Minister, *The Hindu*, 18 March 2017. Available at: https://www. thehindu.com/elections/uttarakhand-2017/trivendra-rawat-takes-oath-as-uttarakhand-chief-minister/article17526906.ece (accessed on 11 August 2021)

35 Performance of Political Parties,: *Statistical Report on General Election, 2017, to the Legislative Assembly of Government of Goa*, Election Commission of India, 2017

36 Debashish Panigrahi and Nida Khan, 'Assembly elections 2017: Congress, BJP in tug of war to form government in Goa', *Hindustan Times*, 11 March 2017. Available at: https://www.hindustantimes.com/assembly-elections/assembly-elections-2017-cong-comes-first-in-goa-but-bjp-hopes-to-form-govt/story-KNIUfptVEpSXcHPWsZXcLP.html (accessed on 16/02/2021).

37 Sangeeta Barooah Pisharoty, 'BJP Crafts North East Democratic Alliance to Make the Region "Congress Mukt"', *Wire*, 25 May 2016. Available at: https://thewire.in/politics/bjp-crafts-north-east-democratic-alliance-to-make-the-region-congress-mukt (accessed on 16/02/2021).

38 Various statistical reports on the Legislative Assembly of Manipur, Election Commission of India, New Delhi. Available at: https://eci.gov.in/statistical-report/statistical-reports/

39 Amarnath Tewary, 'Live updates: BJP backs Nitish, Tejashwi says RJD will stake Claim', *The Hindu,* 26 July 2017. Available at: https://www.thehindu.com/news/national/nitish-kumar-resigns-as-bihar-cm/article19364717.ece (accessed on 16 February 2021).

40 'After resignation, Modi-Nitish's Twitter bonhomie: PM approves, Bihar CM thanks', *India Today,* 26 July 2017. Available at: https://www.indiatoday.in/india/story/narendra-modi-lauds-nitish-kumar-fighting-corruption-after-resignation-1026465-2017-07-26 (accessed on 16 February 2021)

41 *Statistical Report on General Elections, 2012 to the Legislative Assembly of Gujarat,* Election Commission of India, New Delhi. Available at: https://eci.gov.in/statistical-report/statistical-reports/

42 'Rahul Gandhi's temple run: Did the Congress really gain?', *The Indian Express,* 19 December 2017. Available at: https://indianexpress.com/elections/gujarat-assembly-elections-2017/rahul-gandhis-temple-run-congress-won-in-9-seats-4989335/

43 'BJP kickstarts Gujarat election campaign with Gaurav Yatra', *Livemint,* 1 October 2017. Available at: https://www.livemint.com/Home-Page/AZnvfDBBpgrt8j5LLQguQJ/BJP-kickstarts-Gujarat-election-campaign-with-Gaurav-Yatra.html

44 *Statistical Report on General Elections, 2017 to the Legislative Assembly of Himachal Pradesh,* Election Commission of India, New Delhi. Available at: https://eci.gov.in/statistical-report/statistical-reports/

45 *Statistical Report on General Elections, 2017 to the Legislative Assembly of Gujarat,* Election Commission of India, New Delhi. Available at: https://eci.gov.in/statistical-report/statistical-reports/vae

46 *Statistical Report on General Elections, 2017 to the Legislative Assembly of Gujarat,* Election Commission of India, New Delhi). Available at: https://eci.gov.in/statistical-report/statistical-reports/

47 'BJP plans aggressive expansion with offices in all 630 districts', *Livemint,* 19 May 2015. Available at: https://www.*Livemint*.com/Politics/FLRo8F50KmdqL1CWIKEfPM/BJP-plans-aggressive-expansion-with-offices-in-all-630-distr.html

48 'PM Modi, Amit Shah lay foundation stone for new BJP headquarters in New Delhi', *Indian Express,* 18 August 2016. Available at: https://indianexpress.com/article/india/india-news-india/pm-modi-amit-shah-lay-foundation-stone-for-new-bjp-headquarters-in-new-delhi-2982541/

49 *Kamal Sandesh,* Vol. 12, No. 12, 16–30 June 2017.

50   'The general on the warpath', *New Indian Express*, 16 July 2017.

51   Anirban Ganguly and Shiwanand Dwivedi, *Amit Shah and the March of BJP*, Bloomsbury Publishing, 2019, p. 90

52   Prerna Katiyar, 'Amit Shah's game of political chess reaches its endgame', *Economic Times,* 6 August 2017.

53   'Amit Shah taking battle to rivals' bastions during 95-day tour', *The Economic Times,* 15 May 2017. Available at:https://economictimes. indiatimes.com/news/politics-and-nation/amit-shah-taking-battle-to-rivals-bastions-during-95-day-tour/articleshow/58675176.cms

54   'Lokniti-CSDS-ABP News Mood of the Nation Survey', 25 January 2018. Available at: http://www.lokniti.org/media/upload_files/Lokniti-CSDS-ABP-News-Mood-oftheNationSurvey2018-A-Report.pdf

55   *Ek Bharat Shreshtha Bharat: Sabka Sath Sabka Vikas, Election Manifesto 2014,* Bharatiya Janata Party, p. 15. Available at: http://library.bjp.org/jspui/bitstream/123456789/252/1/bjp_lection_manifesto_english_2014. p. 26 df

56   Utpal Bhaskar, 'PM highlights Ujjwala success; reaches out to women, poor, Muslims', *Livemint,* 28 May 2018. Available at:https://www.livemint.com/Politics/OVJ1CPuxjSCNtdggALEm6N/PM-Modi-says-10-crore-LPG-connections-given-in-4-years-again.html

57   'Meet Sunil Deodhar, the man who changed the BJP's fate in Tripura', *Business Standard,* 16 February 2018. 'Accessed on 25 August 2021'. Available at:https://www.business-standard.com/article/politics/meet-sunil-deodhar-the-man-who-changed-the-bjp-s-fate-in-tripura-118021600281_1.html

58   *Statistical Report on General Elections, 2018 to the Legislative Assembly of Tripura* Election Commission of India, New Delhi. Available at: https://eci.gov.in/statistical-report/statistical-reports/

59   'Performance of Political Parties', *Statistical Report on General Election, 2018, to the Legislative Assembly of Government of Tripura,* Election Commission of India, 2018

60   'Performance of National Parties', *Election Commission of India, General Elections, 2014 (16th LOK SABHA)* Election Commission of India, New Delhi. Available at: shttps://eci.gov.in/statistical-report/statistical-reports/

61   Various statistical reports on the Legislative Assembly of Madhya Pradesh and Rajasthan, Election Commission of India, New Delhi.

62   Author's calculations based on statistical reports, Election Commission of India. Available at: https://eci.gov.in/statistical-report/statistical-reports/

Chapter 12: The Campaign for Lok Sabha 2019

1   Jimmy Jacob, '"Don't Worry About Who Will Be PM": Mamata Banerjee at Opposition Rally - 10 Facts', *NDTV*, 19 January 2019. Available at: https://www.ndtv.com/india-news/trinamool-chief-mamata-banerjee-to-hold-mega-rally-of-opposition-parties-today-10-points-1979933

2   'लोकसभा संचालन समिति के पदाधिकारियों द्वारा किये जाने वाले करणीय बिंदु' (Internal party document)

3   'World's Largest Targeted Outreach Initiative: Samvad Kendra' (Internal party document)

4   Ibid.

5   Anirban Ganguly and Shiwanand Dwivedi, *Amit Shah and the March of BJP* (Bloomsbury India, 2019), p. 90

6   Prerna Katiyar, 'Amit Shah's game of political chess reaches its endgame', *The Economic Times*, 6 August 2017. Available at: https://economictimes.indiatimes.com/news/politics-and-nation/amit-shahs-game-of-political-chess-reaches-its-endgame/articleshow/59933126.cms?from=mdr

7   Chayan Kund and Khushdeep Sehgal, 'फैक्ट चेक: राहुल गांधी ने 5 महीने में 4 बार बदली राफेल विमान की कीमत', *Aaj Tak*, 25 September 2018. Available at: https://aajtak.intoday.in/story/fact-file-rafale-deal-controversy-rahul-gandhi-change-price-modi-government-1-1022253.html

8   LoC stands for Line of Control.

9   C. Uday Bhaskar, 'Muted global response on strikes hints Delhi did its homework well', *BloombergQuint*, 30 September 2016. Available at: https://www.thequint.com/news/india/muted-global-response-on-strikes-hints-delhi-did-its-homework-well-uri-terror-attack-surgical-strikes-raheel-sharif

10   Elizabeth Roche, 'Pakistan postpones Saarc Summit after India-led boycott over Uri', *Livemint*, 1 October 2016. Available at: https://www.Livemint.com/Politics/waHWF3HUajmf66JdNwnCqJ/Pakistan-cancels-Saarc-Summit-after-Indialed-boycott-over-U.html

11   'BJP manifesto 2019: Rajnath Singh says 'Sankalp Patra' is a vision document, lists expectations of 130 crore Indians', *Financial Express*, 8 April 2019. Available at: https://www.financialexpress.com/elections/bjp-manifesto-2019-rajnath-singh-says-sankalp-patra-is-a-vision-document-lists-expectations-of-130-crore-indians/1541528/

12   'Amit Shah says Modi's election campaign involved 1.5-lakh km of air travel, 142 rallies', *Business Today*, 17 May 2019. Available at: https://

www.businesstoday.in/latest/economy-politics/story/amit-shah-says-modi-election-campaign-involved-15-lakh-km-of-air-travel-142-rallies-195795-2019-05-17

13   Author's calculations based on data from statistical reports, Election Commission of India. Available at: https://eci.gov.in/statistical-report/statistical-reports/

14   *Performance of National Parties, General Elections, 2019 (17th LOK SABHA)*, Election Commission of India, New Delhi. Available at: https://eci.gov.in/statistical-report/statistical-reports/

15   Author's calculations based on data from statistical reports, Election Commission of India. Available at: https://eci.gov.in/statistical-report/statistical-reports/

16   Author's calculations based on data from statistical reports, Election Commission of India. Available at: https://eci.gov.in/statistical-report/statistical-reports/

17   Gilles Verniers, 'Verdict 2019 in charts and maps: Two-thirds of MPs who re-ran won, half the new MPs are first-timers', *Scroll.in,* 31 May 2019. https://Scroll.in/article/925139/verdict-2019-in-charts-and-maps-two-thirds-of-mps-who-reran-won-half-the-new-mps-are-first-timers

18   Narendra Modi speech, 23 May 2019.

19   'Votes Polled By Parties In States/UTs', *Statistical Report on General Elections, 2019 to the 17th Lok Sabha Volume I,* Election Commission of India, New Delhi. Available at: https://eci.gov.in/statistical-report/statistical-reports/.

Epilogue

1   Sanjay Kumar and Pranav Gupta, 'Where did the BJP get its votes from in 2019?', *Livemint,* 3 June, 2019. Available at: https://www.livemint.com/politics/news/where-did-the-bjp-get-its-votes-from-in-2019-1559547933995.html

Index

Gamang, Giridhar, 91
Gandhi, Indira, 25
    assassination, 46–51
    declared internal emergency, 31
Gandhi, Mahatma
    assassination of, 5
    Independence movement by, 2
    returned to India from South
        Africa, 1–2
    Swaraj, 2
Gandhinagar National Executive, 45
Gandhi, Rahul, 152, 155, 207, 212,
    237
Gandhi, Rajiv
    assassination, 70
    Congress Party under, 51–53
    as prime minister in late 1984,
        47–48
    in Shah Bano Case, 55–56
Gandhi, Sanjay, 32
Gandhi, Sonia, 115,
Ganga Ekatmata Yatra, 63
2G auction, 137
Ghosh, Acharya Deva Prasad, 23
Godhra train burning, 110
Godse, Nathuram, 5
Golden Temple, 47
Golwalkar, Madhavrao Sadashivrao, 4
    arrest, 5
    discussions with Mookerjee, 9
    education, 4
    in press statement 1948, 5
Goods and Services Tax (GST), 98,
    191
Govindacharya, K. N., 52, 76, 79, 164
Goyal, Piyush, 145
Gram Swaraj Abhiyan, 216, 235
green revolution, of 1960, 46

2G scam, 137
Gujarat assembly elections
    of 1995, 75
    of 2007, 133
    of 2012, 146
    of 2017, 214
Gujarat riots (2002), 132
Gujral, Inder Kumar
    as Prime Minister, 82
    resignation, 83
Gulbarg Society massacre, 147
Gulf crisis, 72
Guna Lok Sabha, 25
Gupta, Sadhan, 18

H
Hardikar, Narayan Subbarao, 4
Har Ghar Shauchalaya, 212
Har Har Modi, Ghar Ghar Modi, 158
Haryana Janhit Congress (HJC), 177
Haryana Vikas Party (HVP), 86
Hasan, Zoya, 55, 59, 179
'hawala' transaction, 73
Hazare, Anna
    indefinite hunger strike,
        148–149
    protest against UPA corruption,
        148
HDW submarine scandal, 54
Hedgewar, Keshav Baliram, 3, 64
    birth of, 3
    education, 3
    RSS founder and leader, 4
Hegde, Ramakrishna, 93
Heptulla, Najma, 127
'Hindavah Sahodara Sarve, Na
    Hindu Patiyo Bhave,' 101
Hind Swaraj, 2, 45